NOVA SCOTIA

ANDREW HEMPSTEAD

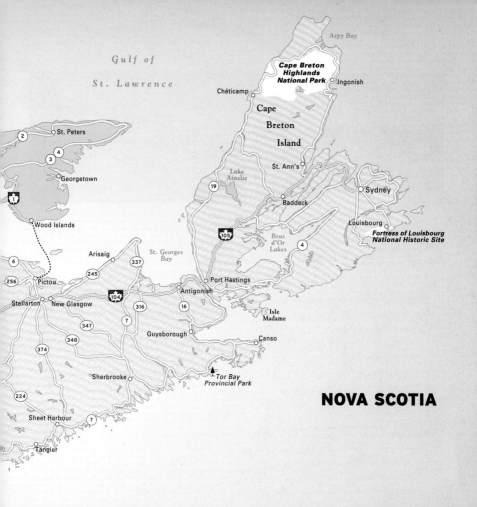

Gulf of St. Lawrence

Aspy Bay

Cape Breton Highlands National Park

Chéticamp

Ingonish

Cape Breton Island

Lake Ainslie

St. Ann's

19

Sydney

Baddeck

105

Louisbourg

Fortress of Louisbourg National Historic Site

Bras d'Or Lakes

4

St. Peters

2

4

3

Georgetown

1

Wood Islands

6

Arisaig

St. Georges Bay

245

337

256

Pictou

Port Hastings

Stellarton

New Glasgow

104

Antigonish

316

16

Isle Madame

347

7

Guysborough

Canso

348

374

Sherbrooke

Tor Bay Provincial Park

224

Sheet Harbour

7

Tangier

NOVA SCOTIA

ATLANTIC

OCEAN

Sable Island

0   30 mi

0   30 km

© AVALON TRAVEL

Contents

Discover Nova Scotia

Enticing Nova Scotia is a picture-book painting, a spacious canvas splashed with brightly colored fishing villages, richly historic towns, uncluttered parks, and a melting pot of cultures that create a destination like no other.

Situated on Canada's east coast, compact Nova Scotia is Canada's second-smallest province (55,490 square kilometers). It is almost an island, encircled completely by water except at its slender, 15-kilometer-long border with New Brunswick. The 7,400-kilometer-long coastline – even without the colorful villages – is beautiful and varied.

Despite its size, Nova Scotia offers visitors a wealth of adventures. The initial focus for many travelers is Halifax, the provincial capital and home of the region's main airport. Here, you can combine historic attractions such as imposing Citadel Hill with walks through coastal parks and feasts of seafood fresh from local waters. But Halifax is just the beginning of a Nova Scotia adventure. Beyond the city limits you can hike through national parks, bike along back roads, kayak the coast, and admire famously photogenic lighthouses, but the options don't end with the ordinary. It's also a place where you can feel the excitement of whitewater rafting on a tidal bore, get up close and personal with the world's rarest whales, or feel the fresh salt air on your face as you set sail aboard a famous racing schooner.

And then there are Nova Scotians themselves, the friendliest folk you're ever likely to meet. Like they have for centuries, the vast majority of Nova Scotians continue to live an unpretentious and resourceful lifestyle, yet they are welcoming to visitors and generous to a fault. Conversation comes easily and humor abounds, especially over a few drinks. As a visitor, you will be encouraged to immerse yourself in their culture – to join in the dancing at a *ceilidh* (Celtic dance), to taste rappie pie, to watch artisans at work, and to raise a glass in thanks to the local king of beer, Alexander Keith.

Nova Scotia does have its touristy areas, but for the most part the province is waiting to be discovered en masse. For you, the visitor, the province will reveal itself slowly. Sure, you'll snap a picture of the lighthouse at Peggy's Cove, tuck into boiled lobster, and take in a few museums, but your greatest memories will be beyond the ordinary – ones that go beyond the scope of what a guidebook can recommend and instead revolve around adventures of your own making.

Planning Your Trip

▶ WHERE TO GO

Halifax

Blending the old with the new, Halifax is an excellent city to explore on foot—and there's a lot to discover. Below the modern high-rises of downtown, the hilly streets are lined with historic stone buildings. Along the waterfront is the Maritime Museum of the Atlantic, as well as outdoor cafés serving fresh seafood, shops selling the work of Nova Scotian artisans, and pubs where traditional Celtic music is a constant.

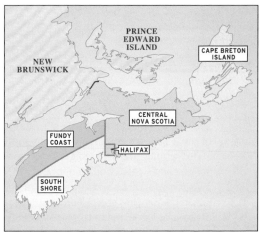

South Shore

Most visitors head to the South Shore once they've visited the capital. They take the requisite photograph at Peggy's Cove, they admire the trio of waterfront churches in Mahone Bay, and they wander through the

shops in Mahone Bay on the South Shore

Alexander Keith's Brewery in Halifax

Lunenburg Harbour

protected streets of Lunenburg, a UNESCO World Heritage Site. Further south are charmingly untouristy villages and towns, such as Shelburne, and deserted beaches.

Fundy Coast

Bordering the powerful Bay of Fundy is a stretch of dramatic coastline as naturally impressive as the scattered townships are culturally interesting. Twice a day, high tides sweep into the bay. Birdlife is prolific along the shoreline while whales find a food source in the plankton-rich moving water. Most important for seafood lovers, local fishermen bring ashore the world's plumpest scallops and sweet-tasting lobsters by the trap load.

Central Nova Scotia

Extending from the capital to Cape Breton Island, this region features the wonder of the world's highest tides, dinosaur footprints, and the warm waters of Northumberland Strait. Inland, wineries, restored grist mills, and charming villages make veering from the main highway an unpredictable joy. While the coastline along the Marine Drive is as rugged as the South Shore's, the landscape is more diverse, with long stretches of white-sand beach, windswept headlands topped by lighthouses, and fishing villages more practical than pretty.

Cape Breton Island

Attached to the rest of the province by a causeway, this island is a world unto its own. The 300-kilometer Cabot Trail is a driving route that hits all the highlights—the upscale historic lodgings of Baddeck, the Acadian restaurants of Chéticamp, the hiking trails of Cape Breton Highlands National Park, and the beaches of Ingonish. With moose common through the highlands, and whales frolicking offshore, the Cabot Trail also accesses some of the province's best wildlife-viewing opportunities.

Port Bickerton Lighthouse in Central Nova Scotia

La Côte Acadienne architecture

▶ WHEN TO GO

Summer revolves around outdoor activities such as hiking, biking, swimming, canoeing, fishing, and just about anything you can do outdoors. July and August are especially busy. This is the time of year when school is out and the parks come alive with campers, anglers, swimmers, and sunbathers. If you're traveling during this time you should book lodging as far in advance as possible.

Unless you're governed by a schedule, spring and fall are excellent times to visit Nova Scotia. While May-June is considered a shoulder season, in many ways the province is at its blooming best in spring. After the first weekend in September, there is a noticeable decrease in travelers across the province. But early fall (Sept.–Oct.) provides pleasant daytime temperatures, reduced room rates, and uncrowded attractions. By late September, fall colors are at their peak, creating a minisurge in visitors.

Officially winter extends from late December to March, but in reality most attractions and visitor information centers, as well as accommodations in resort towns, start closing in mid-October.

Public Gardens, Halifax

▶ BEFORE YOU GO

Passports and Visas

To enter Canada, a passport is required by citizens and permanent residents of the United States. At press time, the U.S. government was developing alternatives to the traditional passport. For further information, see the website http://travel.state.gov/travel. For current entry requirements to Canada, check the Citizenship and Immigration Canada website (www.cic.gc.ca).

mailbox painted as an Acadian flag

All other foreign visitors must have a valid passport and may need a visa or visitors permit, depending on their country of residence and the vagaries of international politics. At present, visas are not required for citizens of the United States, the British Commonwealth, or Western Europe. The standard entry permit is for six months, and you may be asked to show onward tickets or proof of sufficient funds to last you through your intended stay.

Transportation

Visitors to Nova Scotia have the option of arriving by road, rail, ferry, or air. The main gateway city for flights from North America and Europe is the capital, Halifax. Ferries cross to Yarmouth from Maine and to Digby from New Brunswick while the main rail line enters the region from New Brunswick and terminates at Halifax. Driving, whether it be your own vehicle or a rental car, is by far the best way to get around Nova Scotia, although some towns are served by bus. It is possible to visit Nova Scotia without your own vehicle (or a rental), but you'll be confining yourself to Halifax, and then relying on public transportation and guided tours to travel farther afield. Driving is more practical, especially if you plan to tour along the coastline and pursue outdoor endeavors.

driving the Cabot Trail on Cape Breton Island

Explore Nova Scotia

▶ THE BEST OF NOVA SCOTIA

Hitting all the highlights of Nova Scotia in one week is possible, but you're not going to see everything. In fact, you'll be covering so much ground it may not seem like a vacation at all. This itinerary balances a little bit of everything—Halifax, the prettiest coastal villages, the two national parks, and the main historic sites—with time out for enjoying a glass of Nova Scotian wine over a feast of local seafood. This itinerary, like those that follow, assumes you rent a vehicle or have your own.

Day 1

Check in for a two-night stay at a downtown Halifax accommodation such as the Halliburton, a historic lodging within walking distance of Halifax's harborfront. Rather than start ticking off attractions, settle into the city by walking along the waterfront and soaking up the sights and sounds of the busy harbor. You'll see all manner of vessels tied up at the docks, and plenty of places you may want to eat dinner at an outdoor table.

Day 2

Start at the top, literally, by visiting Halifax Citadel National Historic Site and then take a stroll through Halifax's formal Public Gardens. It's now lunchtime, and the Italian Gourmet is ideally situated en route to downtown. Take a tour of Alexander Keith's Brewery on your way to the *Titanic* exhibit at the Maritime Museum of the Atlantic. Dine at the Economy Shoe Shop.

Day 3

Rise early for the one-hour drive to Peggy's Cove, famous for its photogenic lighthouse. Continue south to Mahone Bay for an early lunch and a walk through the many shops lining the main street of this busy waterfront

Halifax Citadel National Historic Site

Peggy's Cove

town. Lunenburg is your overnight stop, and there's plenty of colorful seafaring history to soak up along the harbor of this town that UNESCO has dedicated as a World Heritage Site. Grand Banker Seafood Bar and Grill will be within walking distance of your room at the Spinnaker Inn (both have water views).

Day 4

Take Highway 8 to Kejimkujik National Park, which protects a large chunk of the forested interior. Rent a canoe for a paddle on the protected waterways. Continue to Annapolis Royal, where Port-Royal National Historic Site protects one of North America's oldest settlements. After dinner, watch the sun set across the Annapolis Basin from the grounds of Fort Anne National Historic Site. With reservations at the imposing Queen Anne Inn, you'll be within walking distance of everything.

Day 5

Drive through the apple orchards of the Annapolis Valley to Truro and take the TransCanada Highway across to Cape Breton Island and overnight lodgings at Baddeck's restored Telegraph House. The Alexander Graham Bell National Historic Site is the main attraction, but the town also has a picturesque lakefront area and a good choice of upscale eateries.

Day 6

Today's destination is Ingonish, along the Cabot Trail. You drive the long way around, but that's a good thing, because the rugged coastal scenery between Chéticamp and Ingonish is more beautiful than you could ever imagine. This also means that the 200-kilometer drive will take longer than you imagine. Plan on feasting on lobster at Seascapes Restaurant and staying the night at Glenghorm Beach Resort.

Day 7

It takes a little more than five hours to reach Halifax International Airport from Ingonish. If you're on an afternoon flight, there's enough time to spend an hour or two on Ingonish. To play the revered Highland Links golf course, you'll need to tee off early and fly out in the evening.

THE CURRENTS OF HISTORY

While Nova Scotia's history dates back literally millions of years, this tour focuses on the last 400 years, from the arrival of Samuel de Champlain in 1605 – which makes Annapolis Royal a sensible starting point for the tour.

BAY OF FUNDY

Make yourself comfortable at one of the many historic accommodations in **Annapolis Royal,** such as the Queen Anne Inn. From this lodging, you can walk down the oldest main street in North America to **Fort Anne National Historic Site,** which was the site of multiple turnovers between the British and French.

FUNDY COAST

Drive along **La Côte Acadienne,** admiring the old whitewashed churches and the resilience of the Acadian people who resettled here after the 1755 deportation from Nova Scotia. Allow a couple of hours for chatting about the importance of boatbuilding at the **Shelburne Historic District.**

SOUTH SHORE

Lunenburg will amaze you with its colorful nautical heritage, its downtown precinct protected as a UNESCO World Heritage Site. Plan ahead (reservations are essential), and you will find yourself with the wind at your back aboard the **Bluenose II,** a replica of the most famous schooner that ever sailed the waters of Nova Scotia.

HALIFAX

Plan on spending at least two days in the capital, resting your head at a historic accommodation like **The Halliburton.** Highlights include delving into Halifax's nautical history at the **Maritime Museum of the Atlantic,** wandering through **Citadel Hill National Historic Site,** and visiting the graves of *Titanic* victims at **Fairview Cemetery.** Make sure your itinerary includes a pint of Indian Pale Ale at **Alexander Keith's,** the oldest brewery in North America.

CENTRAL NOVA SCOTIA

With more than a week, you can incorporate Central Nova Scotia in your history-themed itinerary, which should include **Pictou** and a visit to the **Hector,** a replica of a splendid sailing ship.

CAPE BRETON ISLAND

Best known for its namesake national park, the island is also home to the dramatically located **Fortress of Louisbourg National Historic Site,** an ambitious re-creation of a French stronghold destroyed by the British in 1760. For true history lovers, this attraction – along with **Baddeck's Alexander Graham Bell National Historic Site** – make the longer drive to the island worthwhile.

Église de Sainte-Marie, La Côte Acadienne

► COASTAL CRUISING

Like the province itself, this tour is defined by the ocean. So pack your swimsuit, sunscreen, and sandals, and be prepared to get some sand between your toes as this tour circumnavigates the province without ever leaving sight of the sea. A word of warning—summer is short in Nova Scotia, so you'll want to schedule this itinerary for July through September.

Day 1

Don't worry: Even though you're flying into Halifax, you can see the city next time you're in town on business. Instead of heading downtown, make a beeline from the airport to the Bedford Institute of Oceanography to get a taste of the importance the ocean plays in everyday life for Nova Scotians. Then head along Marine Drive and wash away the jet lag by taking to the waves of Lawrencetown Beach on a rented surfboard (if the water seems a little chilly, consider a long walk along the beach's golden sands). Stay in Tangier at Paddlers Retreat Bed and Breakfast.

Day 2

Grab a kayak from Paddlers Retreat and go for an early morning paddle, then go for a walk along the deserted beaches protected by Taylor Head Provincial Park. Continue north and take a boat tour to Canso Islands National Historic Site, protecting a grassy island that was the site of an 18th-century fishing village. Continue up the west coast of Cape Breton Island. You can't see the ocean from the lodge rooms at Glenora Distillery at Glenora, but after a few sips of whiskey and some good food, it won't matter.

Day 3

Watch the crab boats being unloaded at Chéticamp. Drive north on the Cabot Trail along one of the most spectacular stretches of coastal road you could ever imagine. Don't look (unless you're driving) as the next section of road cuts across the interior, but you'll soon reach the water again. And this time, there are long stretches of sandy beach, perfect for sunbathing or swimming. Choose to stay at Ingonish's beachfront Glenghorm Beach Resort and dine on inexpensive seafood at the Chowder House.

Taylor Head Provincial Park

Lunenburg

Day 4

Take the morning off to relax at nearby Black Brook Cove, where a trail leads over a forested headland and tame waves break across the bay. Have lunch at the Muddy Rudder, where lobster and crab are cooked to order in huge pots of boiling water. Don't gorge yourself too much, as you have an afternoon tee time at Highland Links, where the ocean is never far from view. Soak up Old World luxury at the waterfront Duffus House Inn in Baddeck.

Day 5

Take a tour aboard Alexander Graham Bell's yacht at Baddeck and you'll pass by the inventor's waterfront estate (bald eagles are a bonus). The highway back to the mainland hugs expansive Bras d'Or Lakes, from where it's a two-hour drive to Pictou

and waterfront accommodations like the Consulate Inn.

Day 6

Rise early to drive along the Sunrise Trail, which follows Northumberland Strait to the isthmus of land linking Nova Scotia to the rest of Canada. There'll be opportunities at Seafoam and Northport Beach Provincial Park to swim or, for the not so brave, to walk through the shallow water that is warmed by the sun. Drive around the Minas Basin to Truro and watch the tidal bore rush up the Salmon River from your room at the Palliser Motel.

Day 7

Follow the Fundy Coast to Digby. Arrive in time for a lunchtime feast of Digby scallops. Drive out along the narrow Digby

Neck, where, after two short ferry trips, you reach Brier Island, in preparation for a whale-watching trip the next day. Brier Island Lodge has the best water views on the island.

Day 8

Join a whale-watching boat tour into the Bay of Fundy for the opportunity to see finback, minke, and humpback whales up close and personal. Return to the mainland and sample Acadian culture by driving through the coastal fishing villages of Meteghan and Mavillette on La Côte Acadienne. Overnight at Whispering Waves Cottages, near Shelburne (be sure to order the lobster dinner, delivered to your room).

ARTISTS AND ARTISANS

Arts and crafts shopping opportunities are numerous in Nova Scotia. Quilts, sweaters, hooked rugs, porcelains, and wooden carvings are deftly mixed among the watercolors, oils, and sculptures in many arts and crafts venues. About 60 major art galleries are scattered across the province. The farmers' markets are a source for local crafts; the major market is in Halifax, while other summer markets are held at major towns and seaports from Annapolis Royal to Tatamagouche.

For a distilled taste of the province's fine arts and crafts, plan a visit to Halifax's **Art Gallery of Nova Scotia** in Halifax. Quilts, porcelains, and wooden folk carvings are mixed among the watercolors, oils, and sculptures in the spacious galleries on Hollis Street, and the cream of provincial creativity is stocked at the museum's gift shop. The newest crafts developments are nurtured by the **Nova Scotia Centre for Craft and Design,** also in Halifax.

Beyond the ordinary, other homegrown products include delicate glassblowing from Halifax's **Nova Scotian Crystal;** furniture from **Bass River Chairs; pewter** products created in Mahone Bay and Pugwash; and **Grohmann Knives,** which sells its cutlery at its outlet in Pictou.

Nova Scotia is also the place for things Scottish. **Tartans** in innumerable clan variations are available by the yard in wool or blends; tartan apparel is stocked at shops in Halifax, Yarmouth, and Cape Breton's South Gut St. Ann's.

Studio Map is an excellent arts and crafts resource. The free paperback book divides crafts producers by regions and towns, and an index lists the producers by medium. It's available at information centers, listed outlets, and online at www.studiorally.ca.

Amos Pewter, Mahone Bay

Day 9

Wander through the shipbuilding precinct of Shelburne before starting the trip back up the South Shore to Halifax. This stretch of coastline is dotted with oceanfront parks—Rissers Beach, with sandy coves bookended by rocky headlands, is good for a leg stretcher. Continue to Lunenburg for an afternoon tour aboard a working lobster boat. Spend the night at nearby Mahone Bay at waterfront Fisherman's Daughter B&B.

Day 10

Spend the morning at your leisure in Mahone Bay. The main street, lined with fine boutiques, curves around the harbor to three photogenic waterfront churches. Drive along the old highway to charming Chester, where the natural harbor is filled with the curious combination of rusty fishing boats and million-dollar yachts. And yes, you will have time to stop for a picture of "the world's most photographed

Mahone Bay

lighthouse" at Peggy's Cove before catching your flight home.

quiet morning at Peggy's Cove

▶ FAMILY ROAD TRIP

Hector Heritage Quay

Trying to fit too much into your family travels will result in frustration for everyone. Because Nova Scotia is relatively compact, it is possible to spend at least two nights in each destination and still see the highlights of the province. It is especially important that accommodation reservations are made when traveling with children. Try to avoid bed-and-breakfasts and instead choose motels with lots of facilities or cottage complexes with outdoor activities.

Day 1

Halifax has no downtown accommodations that are super kid-friendly, but the Casino Nova Scotia Hotel is central and has amenities such as an indoor pool. Make reservations for two nights. Children will love walking along the harbor admiring tall ships and tugboats and exploring the alleyways of the Historic Properties. A two-minute walk from Casino Nova Scotia Hotel is Harbourside Market, an upscale waterfront food court where kids can order pizza and parents will enjoy seafood from Captain John's.

Day 2

Steps from the hotel is the Maritime Museum of the Atlantic, with interesting displays for all ages, while up the hill is the Museum of Natural History, where displays include a critter-filled nature center and a full-size whale skeleton. Drive around to Fisherman's Cove for lunch and catch the afternoon ferry to McNabs Island for easy hiking to a lookout over downtown.

Day 3

The Eastern Shore has lots of interesting coastal parks to explore, and none is better than Taylor Head Provincial Park, where rock pools come to life at low tide. Continue to Sherbrooke Village and poke around restored buildings that include a candy store and farm-animal-filled barn. Drive north to Antigonish and arrive at Pictou in time to climb aboard the *Hector* sailing ship at Hector Heritage Quay.

Day 4

From Pictou, head west along the Northumberland Strait to swim and sunbathe at Seafoam. If you can drag the kids from the beach, you'll want to make an inland detour to the bright red Balmoral Grist Mill, a restored mill reached along a delightful path through lush forest. Then it's on to a waterfront park such as Gulf Shore Picnic Park for lunch. Children will love the nautical decor at Murphy's in Truro, and thankfully the seafood is good and inexpensive also. By this time you're ready to call it a day, and the local Super 8 delivers, with an indoor pool and waterslide as a bonus.

Day 5

From Truro, head west. Older children will enjoy the outdoor attractions at Grand Pré National Historic Site, while all ages will want to try their hand at searching for semiprecious gems along the beaches of Blomidon Provincial Park. From either of these attractions, it's a short drive through the apple orchards of the Annapolis Valley to Annapolis Royal and Dunromin Campsite and Cabins, where lodging includes tepees and waterfront cabins. With a two-night booking you can relax while the children spend the remaining hours of sunlight on the private beach. In town, Cheri's Convenience is a popular spot for an after-dinner ice cream.

Day 6

Even though you may feel obliged to drag the children through Annapolis Royal's many historic attractions, you'll also feel guilty not telling them about Upper Clements Parks, Nova Scotia's largest theme park, which is on the outskirts of town. Between rides, they'll

the beach at Seafoam

get to glimpse animals such as black bears and moose at the adjacent wildlife park. Enquiring minds will have plenty to think about at the Annapolis Tidal Generating Station, which harnesses energy generated by the massive Fundy tides, making it a good spot to round out the day. Pick up fresh seafood at R. R. Shellfish, at Parker's Cove, and you can have an outdoor barbecue supper.

Day 7

The drive back to Halifax will take three or four hours. En route, plan on stopping for Shubenacadie Wildlife Park, or, for teenage children, riding the Tidal Bore along the Shubenacadie River. Those same children that enjoyed the wildlife park will fall in love with the less-than-wild farm animals at Cole Harbour Rural Heritage Farm, back in Halifax and the last stop of the day.

Day 8

It's your final day in Nova Scotia, and everyone is probably looking forward to getting home. But a tour aboard the Harbour Hopper, an amphibious craft that divides its time between the streets and the harbor, will delay the inevitable.

HALIFAX

Halifax (pop. 370,000), the 250-year-old provincial capital, presents Nova Scotia's strikingly modern face wrapped around a historic heart. It's one of the most vibrant cities in Canada, with an exuberant cultural life and cosmopolitan population. The tourist's Halifax is tidily compact, concentrated on the manageable, boot-shaped peninsula the city inhabits. Its prettiest parts are clustered between the bustling waterfront and the short, steep hillside that the early British developed two centuries ago. In these areas you'll find handsomely historic old districts meshed with stylishly chic new glass-sheathed buildings.

Halifax is more than a city, more than a seaport, and more than a provincial capital. Halifax is a harbor with a city attached, as the Haligonians say. Events in the harbor have shaped Nova Scotia's history. The savvy British military immediately grasped its potential when they first sailed in centuries ago. In fact, Halifax's founding as a settlement in 1749 was incidental to the harbor's development. From the first, the British used the 26-kilometer-long harbor as a watery warehouse of almost unlimited ship-holding capacity. The ships that defeated the French at Louisbourg in 1758—and ultimately conquered this part of Atlantic Canada—were launched from Halifax Harbour. A few years later, the Royal Navy sped from the harbor to harass the rebellious colonies on the Eastern Seaboard during the American Revolution. Ships from Halifax ran the blockades on the South's side during the American Civil War. And during World Wars I and II, the harbor bulged with troop convoys destined for Europe.

HALIFAX

HIGHLIGHTS

◖ Historic Properties: The oldest waterfront warehouses in Canada have been brought to life with an impressive restoration project and are now filled with bustling boutiques and restaurants (page 29).

◖ Maritime Museum of the Atlantic: If you visit just one museum in Nova Scotia, make it this one, which tells the many stories of the region's links to the ocean, from the *Titanic* tragedy to fishing the Grand Banks (page 29).

◖ Alexander Keith's Brewery: Tours of North America's oldest working brewery go beyond describing the beer-making process, delving deep into Halifax's history and its most colorful characters (page 31).

◖ Point Pleasant Park: On the southern tip of the Halifax Peninsula, this urban park is a favorite for walking and biking (page 31).

◖ Halifax Citadel National Historic Site: Canada's most visited historic site lies atop downtown Halifax's highest point. It provides a glimpse into the city's past as well as sweeping harbor views (page 32).

◖ Public Gardens: Strolling through these formal Victorian gardens is a morning rite of passage for many locals (page 33).

◖ Fairview Cemetery: Varying from three-digit numbers to moving family messages, the inscriptions on the headstones of more than 100 *Titanic* victims make this suburban cemetery a poignant place to visit (page 35).

◖ McNabs Island: Not a place to make a casual stop, spending the day exploring McNabs Island is a good way to get back to nature within city limits (page 36).

◖ Bedford Institute of Oceanography: Looking rather institutional from the outside, this government facility has provided an array of scientific and exploratory services that will awe anyone with an interest in the ocean (page 37).

◖ Fisherman's Cove: If you're not planning to travel beyond Halifax, a visit to this historic fishing village will give you a taste of what you'll be missing farther afield (page 38).

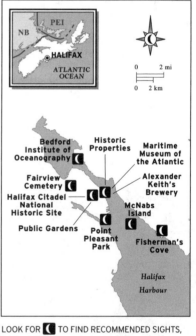

LOOK FOR ◖ TO FIND RECOMMENDED SIGHTS, ACTIVITIES, DINING, AND LODGING.

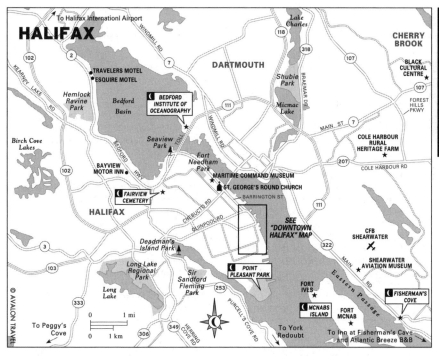

PLANNING YOUR TIME

Everyone will have his or her own idea as to how best to spend time in Halifax. History buffs will want to spend an entire week exploring the city's oldest corners, while outdoorsy types will want to hit the highlights before moving through to the rest of the province. Halifax has three attractions no one will want to miss, even if you have just one day. The first of these is the **Historic Properties,** a group of waterfront warehouses converted to restaurants and boutiques, while the nearby **Maritime Museum of the Atlantic** is the place to learn about the city's seafaring traditions. The third is **Halifax Citadel National Historic Site.** Any self-respecting beer drinker will want to join a tour of **Alexander Keith's Brewery,** but the brewery is also interesting for its history. These four attractions, along with time exploring the waterfront, would fill one day.

As it's both a gateway for air travelers and

the hub of three highways, chances are you'll be passing through Halifax more than once on your travels through Nova Scotia. This allows you to break up your sightseeing and to plan your schedule around the weather. If, for example, the sun is shining when you first arrive, plan to visit **Point Pleasant Park,** the **Public Gardens,** and **Fairview Cemetery.** These spots and historic downtown attractions should fill two full days. If you have a third day and the forecast is for fine weather, plan to spend time on **McNabs Island,** a delightful destination for hiking just a short ferry ride from the city.

Across the harbor from downtown is the city of Dartmouth, where the **Bedford Institute of Oceanography** overlooks the water. A guided tour of this government facility followed by lunch at the nearby fishing village of **Fisherman's Cove** makes a perfect half-day combination.

HALIFAX LINKS TO THE *TITANIC* TRAGEDY

"My God, the *Titanic* has struck a berg." With these fateful words, uttered on April 14, 1912, by wireless operator Jack Goodwin of Cape Race, Newfoundland, the outside world first heard about what would develop into the world's best-known maritime disaster – the sinking of the unsinkable ship on its maiden voyage between Southampton, England, and New York City. On board were 2,227 passengers and crew.

At the time of the wireless transmission, the vessel was 500 miles east of Halifax. Three Halifax ships were promptly chartered to search for the foundering vessel. By the time the first had arrived, the *Titanic* was lying on the bottom of the Atlantic Ocean. More than 1,500 passengers and crew perished while 702 lucky souls, mostly women and children, were rescued. Bodies were bought ashore at Karlsen's Wharf (2089 Upper Wharf St.) and **Coaling Wharf No. 4** (north of the MacDonald Bridge), both of which are not open to the public. They were then transported in coffins to a variety of locations, including a curling rink (now an army surplus store, at 2660 Agricola St.) and **Snow's Funeral Home** (1750 Argyle St.), which is now a seafood restaurant. Some bodies were claimed by families, but most were buried in three local cemeteries. The largest concentration is in a plot donated by the White Star Line within **Fairview Cemetery** (corner of Connaught and Chisholm Aves.). Most of the black headstones simply note the date of the tragedy and a number that relates to the order in which bodies were pulled from the ocean. Others have moving tributes to the bravery of loved ones. John Clarke, a band member famous for continuing to play as the ship was sinking, is buried at **Mount Olivet Cemetery** (Mumford Rd. off Joesph Howe Dr.).

The *Titanic*'s owners, the White Star Line, maintained an office in Halifax at 1682 Hollis Street that still stands. It became a hive of activity when the bodies began arriving, as staff members were an important link between the victims and their families from around the world.

Funerals and services were held at a number of downtown churches, including **St. George's Anglican Church** (222 Brunswick St.), **St. Paul's Anglican Church** (1749 Argyle St.), and **St. Mary's Catholic Church** (corner Spring Garden Rd. and Barrington St.).

The best place to learn about the tragedy is the **Maritime Museum of the Atlantic** (1675 Lower Water St., 902/424-7490; Mon.-Sat. 9:30 A.M.-5:30 P.M., Sun. 1-5:30 P.M.), which has a dedicated display area with artifacts such as the only deck chair recovered from the vessel. For archival records, including travel documents, photos, and correspondence related to *Titanic* passengers, visit the **Nova Scotia Archives** (6016 University Ave., 902/424-6060; Mon.-Fri. 8:30 A.M.-4:30 P.M., Sat. 9 A.M.-5 P.M.).

© ANDREW HEMPSTEAD

HISTORY

The French learned about the area in the early 1700s, when local Mi'Kmaq Indians escorted the French governor on a tour of what they called Chebuctook, the "Great Long Harbor," and adjacent waterways. But it was the British who saw the site's potential; in 1749 Colonel Edward Cornwallis arrived with about 2,500 settlers on 13 ships and founded Halifax along what is now Barrington Street. The settlement was named for Lord Halifax, then president of Britain's Board of Trade and Plantations.

Early Halifax was a stockaded settlement backed by the Grand Parade, the town green where the militia drilled. The first of four citadels was built on the hilltop. St. Paul's Church, the garrison church at Grand Parade's edge, opened in 1750, making it Canada's first Anglican sanctuary. It was a gift from King George III. More English settlers arrived in 1750 and founded Dartmouth across the harbor. By 1752 the two towns were linked by a ferry system, the oldest saltwater ferry system in North America. Nova Scotia was granted representative government in 1758.

The Royal Military

The completion of Her Majesty's Royal Dockyard in 1760 was the prelude to Louisbourg's absolute destruction the same year. The harbor's defensibility was ensured by a ring of batteries at McNabs Island, Northwest Arm, Point Pleasant with its Martello Tower, and the forts at George's Island and York Redoubt. In 1783 the settlement got another massive Anglo infusion with the arrival of thousands of Loyalists from the United States. Among them was John Wentworth, New Hampshire's former governor. He received a baronet title for his opposition to the revolution in the American colonies and was appointed Nova Scotia's lieutenant governor. Sir John and Lady Wentworth led the Halifax social scene, hobnobbing with Prince Edward (the Maritimes' military commander in chief, who would later sire Queen Victoria) and his French paramour Julie St. Laurent (to the chagrin of propriety-minded local society).

Prosperous Times

The seaport thrived in the 1800s. By 1807 the city's population topped 60,000. A proper government setting—the sandstone Colonial Building (now Province House)—opened in 1819, followed by a number of noteworthy academic institutions. The harbor front—which during the War of 1812 served as a black-market trade center for Halifax privateers—acquired commercial legitimacy when native Haligonian Samuel Cunard, rich from lumbering, whaling, and banking, turned his interests to shipping. By 1838 the Cunard Steamship Company handled the British and North American Royal Mail, and by 1840 Cunard's four ships provided the first regular transport between the two continents.

The seaport's incorporation in 1841 ushered in a prosperous mercantile era. Granville Street, with its stylish shops, became in its day Atlantic Canada's Fifth Avenue. Less stylish brothels and taverns lined Brunswick, Market, and Barrack Streets, and the military police swept through the area often, breaking up drunken fistfights and reestablishing order.

The Modern Era

By the 1960s, Halifax looked like a hoary victim of the centuries, somewhat the worse for wear. Massive federal, provincial, and private investment, however, restored the harbor to its early luster, with its warehouses groomed as the handsome Historic Properties.

The city continued to polish its image, as sandblasting renewed the exterior of architectural treasures such as Province House. The Art Gallery of Nova Scotia moved from cramped quarters near the Public Archives and settled within the stunningly renovated former Dominion Building. Municipal guidelines sought to control the city's growth. The unobstructed view on George Street between the harbor and the Citadel was secured with a municipal mandate, and the height of the hillside's high-rise buildings was also restricted to preserve the cityscape. During this time, the waterfront evolved into a bustling tourist precinct, but one that is also enjoyed by locals.

A LONG WEEKEND IN HALIFAX

Halifax is a major destination for conventioneers (modern facilities, well-priced accommodations, centrally located for delegates from both North America and Europe), and in this regard, you may find yourself wanting to hang around for a few days when the last meeting wraps up on Friday. Or, for leisure travelers, many flights to other parts of Atlantic Canada are routed through Halifax, so it will cost little or no extra to have a stopover, and then continue to Newfoundland, Prince Edward Island, or elsewhere. This itinerary covers both scenarios, and you don't have to worry about driving.

DAY 1

You've been staying at an upscale downtown Halifax hotel such as Four Points by Sheraton Halifax, and suddenly it's not business anymore. No worries; rates drop dramatically come the weekend, so you won't break the bank by staying another two nights. Join the after-work crowd at the **Seahorse Tavern**, and then plan on dining next door at the **Economy Shoe Shop.**

DAY 2

Visit **Halifax Citadel National Historic Site** to get a feel for the city's colorful history and then walk over to the **Public Gardens.** After lunch at the **Harbourside Market,** learn about the *Titanic* tragedy at the **Maritime Museum** **of the Atlantic** before visiting the graves of some of the victims at **Fairview Cemetery.** A two-minute walk from the Sheraton is **Bish,** one of the city's best restaurants, or if it's casual seafood you're after, continue along the waterfront to **Salty's.**

DAY 3

The local tour company Ambassatours operates an excellent full-day trip along the South Shore. It hits the highlights – scenic **Peggy's Cove** and the beautiful waterfront **churches of Mahone Bay** – while also allowing time to wander through the historic streets of downtown **Lunenburg,** where there's time for shopping and lunch. You'll be back in Halifax in time for dinner at **Chives Canadian Bistro,** which features lots of fresh seasonal produce.

DAY 4

Check the sailing schedule of the *Bluenose II* and make reservations for a morning cruise if this grand old lady is in port. Otherwise, you could start out with breakfast and checking your email at the **Paper Chase News Café,** followed by shopping at downtown stores as varied as **Nova Scotian Crystal** and **Rum Runners Rum Cake Factory.** Golfers may want to squeeze in a tee time at **Glen Arbour Golf Course,** which is on the way out to the airport.

Sights

Halifax is packed with attractions, all reasonably priced or absolutely free. The biggest concentration is within walking distance of the waterfront precinct and many accommodations. Beyond the downtown core are a number of interesting sights that are easy to miss but easy to reach by public transportation. Whatever your interests—searching out *Titanic*-related sights or exploring coastal parks—you will find plenty to do and see in the capital.

GETTING ORIENTED

The layout of Halifax is easy to grasp. **Downtown** lines the western side of **Halifax Harbour.** Lower and Upper Water Streets and Barrington Street run through downtown parallel to the water. This is the core of the city, chock-full of historic attractions, the city's finest accommodations, and a wonderful choice of restaurants. The waterfront itself bustles day and night. From Historic Properties' wharves at the waterfront,

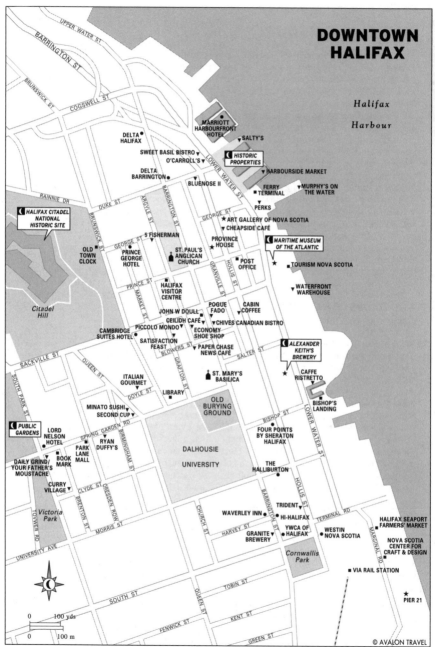

DOWNTOWN HALIFAX

Halifax

Harbour

UPPER WATER ST

BARRINGTON ST

BRUNSWICK ST

COGSWELL ST

MARRIOTT HARBOURFRONT HOTEL

DELTA HALIFAX

SALTY'S

SWEET BASIL BISTRO
O'CARROLL'S

HISTORIC PROPERTIES

DELTA BARRINGTON

HARBOURSIDE MARKET

BLUENOSE II

LOWER WATER ST

RAINNIE DR

FERRY TERMINAL

MURPHY'S ON THE WATER

DUKE ST

ARGYLE ST

BARRINGTON ST

PERKS

GEORGE ST

HALIFAX CITADEL NATIONAL HISTORIC SITE

BRUNSWICK ST

ART GALLERY OF NOVA SCOTIA
CHEAPSIDE CAFÉ

5 FISHERMAN

GEORGE ST

PROVINCE HOUSE

MARITIME MUSEUM OF THE ATLANTIC

OLD TOWN CLOCK

PRINCE GEORGE HOTEL

ST. PAUL'S ANGLICAN CHURCH

GRANVILLE ST

HOLLIS ST

POST OFFICE

TOURISM NOVA SCOTIA

PRINCE ST

MARKET ST

HALIFAX VISITOR CENTRE

WATERFRONT WAREHOUSE

Citadel Hill

JOHN W DOULL

POGUE FADO

CABIN COFFEE

CEILIDH CAFÉ
PICCOLO MONDO

CHIVES CANADIAN BISTRO

CAMBRIDGE SUITES HOTEL

SATISFACTION FEAST

ECONOMY SHOE SHOP

SACKVILLE ST

BLOWERS ST

PAPER CHASE NEWS CAFÉ

SALTER ST

ALEXANDER KEITH'S BREWERY

QUEEN ST

GRAFTON ST

SOUTH PARK ST

ITALIAN GOURMET

DOYLE ST

ST. MARY'S BASILICA

CAFFE RISTRETTO

LIBRARY

BISHOP'S LANDING

MINATO SUSHI
SECOND CUP

OLD BURYING GROUND

BISHOP ST

PUBLIC GARDENS

LORD NELSON HOTEL

SPRING GARDEN RD

RYAN DUFFY'S

BIRMINGHAM ST

FOUR POINTS BY SHERATON HALIFAX

LOWER WATER ST

PARK LANE MALL

BOOK MARK

DALHOUSIE UNIVERSITY

THE HALLIBURTON

DAILY GRIND/ YOUR FATHER'S MOUSTACHE

CLYDE ST

CRESDEN ROW

HOLLIS ST

CURRY VILLAGE

BRENTON ST

WAVERLEY INN

TRIDENT

TERMINAL RD

HALIFAX SEAPORT FARMERS' MARKET

Victoria Park

MORRIS ST

CHURCH ST

HI-HALIFAX

BARRINGTON ST

YWCA OF HALIFAX

NOVA SCOTIA CENTER FOR CRAFT & DESIGN

TOWER RD

UNIVERSITY AVE

HARVEY ST

GRANITE BREWERY

WESTIN NOVA SCOTIA

MARGINAL RD

Cornwallis Park

VIA RAIL STATION

SOUTH ST

QUEEN ST

TOBIN ST

PIER 21

0   100 yds
0   100 m

FENWICK ST

KENT ST

GREEN ST

© AVALON TRAVEL

HALIFAX HARBOUR

From a maritime standpoint, Halifax Harbour is a jewel, the world's second-largest natural harbor (after Sydney Harbour in Australia). High rocky bluffs notched with coves rim the wide entrance where the harbor meets the frothy Atlantic. **McNabs Island** is spread across the harbor's mouth and is so large that it almost clogs the entrance. Many an unwary ship has foundered on the island's shallow, treacherous Eastern Passage coastline.

On the western side of McNabs Island, the harbor is split in two by Halifax's peninsula. The Northwest Arm, a fjord-like sliver of sea, cuts off to one side and wraps around the city's back side. Along its banks are the long lawns of parks, estates, yacht clubs, and several university campuses. The main channel continues inland, shouldered by uptown Halifax on one side and its sister city of Dartmouth on the other.

THE TOURIST'S HARBOUR

The harbor puts on its best show directly in front of downtown. White-hulled cruise ships nose into port and dock alongside Halifax's **Point Pleasant Park** at the peninsula's southern tip. Freighters, tugs, tour boats, and sailboats skim the choppy waters, and ferries cut through the sea traffic, scurrying back and forth between the two cities with their loads of commuters and sightseers.

The scene has a transfixing quality about it. Tourist season unofficially starts and ends when the harborfront Halifax Sheraton hotel sets tables and chairs for alfresco dining on the waterfront promenade. Stiff summer breezes usually accompany lunch, but the view

is worth it. Less hardy diners jostle for tables with a harbor view at **Salty's**, the nearby restaurant with its enviable wide-windowed dining room overlooking the same scene.

Beyond the tourist's realm and the two cities' harbor-fronts, the spacious harbor compresses itself into **The Narrows**. Two high-flung steel expressways – the **MacDonald** and **MacKay Bridges** (toll $0.75) – cross the Narrows at either end. The MacDonald Bridge permits pedestrians and provides an aerial view of the **Maritime Command** and **Her Majesty's Canadian Dockyard** along the Halifax side.

The slender Narrows then opens into 40-square-kilometer **Bedford Basin,** 16 kilometers long and as capacious as a small inland sea. Sailboats cruise its waters now, but the expanse has seen a parade of ships cross its waters through the years – from the white-sailed British warships of centuries ago to the steel-hulled vessels of the Allies during both World Wars.

HALIFAX HARBOUR
FROM VARIED ANGLES

Halifax Harbour reveals itself in different views. Its pulse can be probed from one of the ferries or from the harborfront in either city. The approach from the Atlantic can be seen best from the historic fort at **York Redoubt** on Purcells Cove Road. And you get a good view of Northwest Arm's ritzy estate and university scene from Fleming Park's **Memorial Tower** on the same road. **Seaview Park** beneath the MacKay Bridge overlooks the Narrows where that slender strait meets Bedford Basin.

---

sightseeing boats explore the harbor. The splendid Maritime Museum and Art Gallery of Nova Scotia are close by.

A series of short streets rise like ramps from the waterfront, past the grassy Grand Parade and up **Citadel Hill.** Around the hill, a great swath of green space provides a welcome break from residential and commercial sprawl. Laid out by the city's original surveyor, **Central**

Common, on the west side of the hill, marks a meeting of roads. Major thoroughfares merge here (Robie Street running north to south, Bell Road running southeast, and Cogswell Street running east to west). Locals refer to everything south of the commons as the South End, everything to the north the North End, and to the west the West End.

In the South End is the city's **academic**

area, site of Dalhousie University, University of King's College, St. Mary's University, and the Atlantic School of Theology. At the southern tip of the downtown peninsula is **Point Pleasant Park,** an oasis of green surrounded by the grays of sprawling loading docks to the north and the sparkling blue waters of Halifax Harbour on all other sides.

The **Northwest Arm** of Halifax Harbour nearly cuts the downtown area off from the rest of the city. At the head of this waterway is the **Armdale Rotary,** from where Herring Cove Road spurs south to **Purcells Cove Road,** which passes yacht-filled marinas, Sir Sandford Fleming Park, and York Redoubt National Historic Site.

Across Halifax Harbour from downtown is the city of **Dartmouth.** Linked to downtown by ferry and bridge, this commercial and residential area has a smattering of sights and is also worth visiting for the views back across to Halifax. Beyond the two bridges spanning Halifax Harbour is Bedford Basin, a large body of water surrounded by development. At the head of the basin is the residential area of Bedford and suburbs, including Lower Sackville and Waverly. Traveling down Highway 102 from Truro and **Halifax International Airport** (38 kilometers north of downtown), you'll pass exits to these and other towns.

DOWNTOWN
The following sights are within walking distance of each other from the waterfront. You could easily spend a full day exploring this part of the city, taking time out to lunch at an outdoor harborfront restaurant.

◖ Historic Properties
Canada's oldest surviving group of waterfront warehouses is also one of the city's main tourist attractions, with excellent shopping and dining spread along a three-block expanse on Upper and Lower Water Streets. The wooden and stone warehouses, chandleries, and buildings once used by shipping interests and privateers have been restored to their early 1800s glory. They now house restaurants, shops, and other sites impressively styled with Victorian and Italianate facades. The history of the precinct is cataloged halfway along the Privateer Wharf building (on the inside) with interpretive panels.

◖ Maritime Museum of the Atlantic
The seaport's store of nautical memorabilia lies within this sleek, burnished-red waterfront museum (1675 Lower Water St., 902/424-7490; summer daily 9:30 A.M.–5:30 P.M., the rest of the year Tues.–Sat. 9:30 A.M.–5 P.M., Sun. 1–5 P.M.; adult $9, senior $8, child $5). The museum is one of the crowning achievements of the city's Waterfront Development Project. Most visitors find the *Titanic* display room most interesting. It contains the world's largest collection of artifacts from the floating palace deemed unsinkable by its owners; you will see the only deckchair recovered at the time of the sinking, a cribbage board, lounge paneling, and more. Also on display is a model of the *Titanic,* the wireless log taken as the vessel floundered, and a variety of information boards that tell the story of ship's construction. *Titanic 3D,* a National Geographic documentary created from footage taken from the wreck, shows continuously.

Outside, two historic vessels are tied up at the wharf. One of these, the **CSS *Acadia,*** spent its life as Canada's first hydrographic vessel, its crew surveying the east coast using sextants and graphing shoreline features. The other, **HMCS *Sackville,*** is the last remaining Canadian World War II convoy escort corvette. Admission is $1 to each, or free with proof of admission to the maritime museum.

Art Gallery of Nova Scotia
Atlantic Canada's largest and finest art collection is housed in two buildings separated by a cobbled courtyard just up from the harbor (1723 Hollis St., 902/424-7542; daily 10 A.M.–5 P.M.; adult $10, senior $8, child $4). The main entrance is within Gallery South (also home to an excellent little café).

© ANDREW HEMPSTEAD

Art Gallery of Nova Scotia

The vast majority of the collection is displayed in Gallery North, the sandstone Dominion Building. Some 2,000 works in oils, watercolors, stone, wood, and other media are exhibited throughout its four floors of spacious galleries. The permanent collections give priority to current and former Nova Scotia residents and include works by Mary Pratt, Arthur Lismer, Carol Fraser, and Alex Colville. The mezzanine-level regional folk-art collection is a particular delight. The ground-floor Gallery Shop trades in the cream of provincial arts and crafts and sells books, cards, and gifts.

Province House

The seat of the provincial government, Province House (1726 Hollis St., 902/424-4661; July–Aug. Mon.–Fri. 9 A.M.–5 P.M., Sat.–Sun. 10 A.M.–4 P.M., the rest of the year Mon.–Fri. 9 A.M.–4 P.M.; free) was completed in 1819. It's the smallest and oldest provincial legislature building in the country and features a fine Georgian exterior and splendid interior, resembling a rural English mansion more than an official residence. On his visit

to modest but dignified Province House in 1842, author Charles Dickens remarked, "It was like looking at Westminster through the wrong end of a telescope…a gem of Georgian architecture."

St. Paul's Anglican Church

This stately white wooden church (1749 Argyle St., 902/429-2240) was styled on the Palladian style of St. Peter's Church on Vere Street in London, England. Dating to 1749, it is the oldest surviving building in Halifax and was the first Anglican church in Canada. The interior is full of memorials to Halifax's early residents. Notice the bit of metal embedded above the door at the back of the north wall—it's a piece of shrapnel hurled from the *Mont Blanc*, two kilometers away, during the Halifax Explosion. The church is between Barrington and Argyle Streets at the edge of the Grand Parade; look for the square belfry topped by an octagonal cupola.

Old Burying Ground

Designated a national historic site in 1991, this cemetery (June–Sept. daily 9 A.M.–5 P.M.) sits opposite Government House at Barrington Street and Spring Garden Road. Its history goes back to the city's founding. The first customer, so to speak, was interred just one day after the arrival of the original convoy of English settlers in 1749. Also among the thicket of age-darkened, hand-carved, old-fashioned headstones is the 1754 grave of John Connor, the settlement's first ferry captain. The most recent burial took place more than 160 years ago, in 1844.

St. Mary's Basilica

Two popes and hundreds of thousands of parishioners have filed through the doors of this Gothic Revival church (1508 Barrington St., 902/423-4116), whose spires cast an afternoon shadow over the Old Burying Ground. It was built in 1860; the title "Basilica" was bestowed during a visit by Pope Pius XII in 1950. The stained-glass windows, replaced after the originals were destroyed by the 1917 Halifax Explosion, are particularly impressive.

▶ Alexander Keith's Brewery

Keith's, at the south end of downtown and one block back from the water (1496 Lower Water St., 902/455-1474) is North America's oldest operating brewery. Keith arrived in Halifax in 1795, bringing with him brewing techniques from his English homeland and finding a ready market among the soldiers and sailors living in the city. Although main brewing operations have been moved to the Oland Brewery, north of downtown, the original brewery, an impressive stone and granite edifice extending along an entire block, produces seasonal brews using traditional techniques. Tours led by costumed guides depart June–October Monday–Saturday 11 A.M.–8 P.M., Sunday noon–5 P.M., November–April Friday 5–8 P.M., Saturday noon–8 P.M., Sunday noon–5 P.M. Adults pay $16, seniors $14, and children $8, with the tour ending with a traditional toast to the "Father of Great Beer."

Pier 21

As you continue south along Lower Water Street from the brewery (take the Harbourwalk for the full effect), beyond the statue of Samuel Cunard, the waterfront is dominated by Halifax's massive cruise-ship terminal. This 3,900-square-meter structure has a long and colorful history of welcoming foreigners in its original capacity as an "immigration shed," where more than a million immigrants, refugees, and war brides first set foot on Canadian soil between 1928 and 1971. It was also the main departure point for 500,000 Canadians who fought in World War II. Upstairs within the building is the **Exhibition Hall** (1055 Marginal Rd., 902/425-7770; May–Nov. daily 9:30 A.M.–5:30 P.M., Dec.–Apr. Tues.–Sat. 10 A.M.–5 P.M.; adult $8.50, senior $7.50, child $5). This immigration museum does a wonderful job of bringing to life the stories of those who traveled across the ocean to make a new home in Canada. The firsthand accounts begin with the decision to leave home and go through the voyage and arrival to describe onward journeys by rail across Canada. Allow time to view *Oceans of Hope,* a 30-minute film narrated by a fictional immigration officer.

Beside the street-level reception area is the **Research Centre,** which can be used by individuals whose families arrived in Canada through Pier 21. It contains a wide variety of documents, passenger logs, and historic images of passenger vessels.

Nova Scotia Centre for Craft and Design

Provincial crafts development and innovation are nurtured at this workshop ensconced in the cruise-ship terminal (1061 Marginal Rd., 902/492-2522; Mon.–Sat. 9 A.M.–4 P.M.; free), geared to weaving, woodworking, metal, and multimedia production.

▶ Point Pleasant Park

Before dawn on September 29, 2003, Hurricane Juan hit Halifax like no other storm in living memory. Seventy-five–hectare Point Pleasant Park, at the southern tip of the Halifax peninsula, took the full brunt of the storm. By daybreak the next morning the full extent of the damage was first seen—more than 75,000 of the park's 100,000 trees had been destroyed, and the park's ecology had been changed forever. After the cleanup, a massive rejuvenation project that continues to this day began.

Although much of the forest may be gone, the park is still well worth visiting. To get to the main entrance, take South Park Street south from Sackville Street. South Park becomes Young Avenue, a tree-lined boulevard graced by magnificent mansions; turn left on Point Pleasant Drive. Marginal Road from downtown also terminates at the same waterside entrance. Views from the parking lot itself sweep across the harbor, with container terminals on one side and green space on the other. Forty kilometers of trails, many paved, allow for hiking, jogging, and cross-country skiing in winter. Bikes are allowed only Monday–Friday. Most of the main trails have reopened since the storm, allowing access to all corners of the spread, with terns, gulls, and ospreys

HALIFAX EXPLOSION

On the morning of Thursday, December 6, 1917, Halifax experienced a catastrophic explosion – at the time the largest man-made explosion in history, unrivaled until the detonation of the first atomic bomb. On that fateful morning, Halifax Harbour was busy with warships transporting troops, munitions, and other supplies bound for the war in Europe. A French ship, the *Mont Blanc*, filled to the gunwales with explosives – including 400,000 pounds of TNT – was heading through the narrows toward the harbor mouth when it was struck by a larger vessel, the *Imo*, which was steaming in the opposite direction, and caught fire. The terrified crew of the *Mont Blanc* took immediately to the lifeboats, as the burning ship drifted close to the Halifax shore.

A short time later, at 9:05 A.M., the *Mont Blanc* cargo blew up, instantly killing an estimated 2,000 people, wounding another 10,000, and obliterating about 130 hectares of the North End of downtown Halifax. So colossal was the explosion that windows were shattered 80 kilometers away, and the shock wave rocked Sydney on Cape Breton, 430 kilometers northeast. The barrel of one of the *Mont Blanc*'s cannons was hurled 5.5 kilometers, while its half-ton anchor shank landed more than three kilometers away in the opposite direction.

Serving as a memorial to the tragedy is **Fort Needham Memorial Park,** along Gottingen Street north from downtown. Here, a 14-bell carillon is on a high point of land from where the site of the original explosion can be seen. While the harborfront **Maritime Museum of the Atlantic** has an exhibit dedicated to the explosion, one of the most interesting reminders is up the hill at **St. Paul's Anglican Church** (1749 Argyle St.), where a chunk of metal from the doomed *Mont Blanc* is embedded in the north-facing wall.

winging overhead. A bit of real-estate trivia: The park is still rented from the British government, on a 999-year lease, for one shilling per year.

Point Pleasant's military significance is evidenced by the 1796 Prince of Wales Martello Tower (July–early Sept. daily 10 A.M.–6 P.M.) and Fort Ogilvie, built in 1862, both part of Halifax's defensive system. The former, a thick-walled round tower, based on those the British were building at the time to repel Napoleon's forces, was the first of its kind to be built in North America.

CITADEL HILL AND VICINITY

Walk up George Street from the harbor front to reach Citadel Hill. You'll know you're on the right street by the **Old Town Clock,** framed by the buildings of George Street at the base of Citadel Hill. Originally constructed as the official timekeeper for Halifax, the four-faced clock tower was completed in 1803 by order of the compulsively punctual Prince Edward. It

is not open to the public but instead stands as a city landmark.

⟨ Halifax Citadel National Historic Site

Halifax's premier landmark (Sackville St., 902/426-5080; May–Oct. daily 9 A.M.–5 P.M., until 6 P.M. in summer; adult $12, senior $10.50, child $6) is also the most visited National Historic Site in Canada. The Citadel crowns the hill at the top of George Street, commanding the strategic high ground above the city and harbor, with magnificent views of the entire area. This star-shaped, dressed-granite fortress, the fourth military works built on this site, was completed in 1856. In its heyday, the Citadel represented the pinnacle of defensive military technology, though its design was never tested by an attack.

In summer, students in period uniforms portray soldiers of the 78th Highlanders and the Royal Artillery, demonstrating military drills, powder magazine operation, changing of the sentries, and piping. At the stroke of noon each day, they load and fire a cannon with due military precision and ceremony, a shot heard round the city. Most of the fortress is open for exploration; exhibits include a museum, barrack rooms, a powder magazine, and a 50-minute audiovisual presentation on the fort's history. Guided tours are included in the admission price, while within the grounds are a gift shop and café.

The grounds are open year-round, but no services are offered November–April.

Museum of Natural History

This museum (1747 Summer St., 902/424-7353; June–mid-Oct. Mon.–Sat. 9 A.M.–5 P.M., Sun. noon–5 P.M., mid-Oct.–May Tues.–Sat. 9 A.M.–5 P.M., Sun. noon–5 P.M.; adult $5, senior $4.50, child $3) is a five-minute walk from Citadel Hill, but it also has plenty of its own parking. The rather plain exterior belies a treasure trove of exhibits that bring the province's natural world to life. Opposite the ticket desk is a kid-friendly nature center, with small critters in enclosures and tanks, and staff on hand to answer any questions. Beyond this point are exhibits that tell the story of Nova Scotia's first human inhabitants, Palaeo Indians, who moved into the region 11,000 years ago. The dinosaur displays are a major draw for young and old. You'll also learn about modern-day creatures in a room full of stuffed animals and a large hall dominated by a pilot whale skeleton. Other highlights include a gem and mineral display and artifacts from Acadian culture.

◖ Public Gardens

South across Sackville Street from the Citadel grounds, the Public Gardens (May–mid-Oct. daily 8 A.M.–dusk) are an irresistibly attractive oasis spread over seven hectares in the heart of the city. Bordered by Spring Garden Road, South Park Street, Summer Street, and Sackville Street, what started in 1753 as a private garden is now considered one of the loveliest formal

Halifax Citadel National Historic Site

© ANDREW HEMPSTEAD

gardens in North America and is reminiscent of the handsome parks of Europe.

Inside the wrought-iron fence (main entrance at the corner of South Park Street and Spring Garden Road), the setting revels in tulips that flower late May through early June, followed by rhododendrons and roses, and the roses and perennials through summer. Other highlights are the exotic and native trees, fountains, and lily ponds where ducks and geese make their home. The ornate bandstand dates from Queen Victoria's Golden Jubilee and is the site of free Sunday afternoon concerts in July and August. Also during the summer, vendors of arts and crafts hawk their wares outside the gardens along Spring Garden Road.

NORTH OF DOWNTOWN

The following sights are north of Cogswell Street. It's a two-kilometer walk from downtown to Fort Needham Memorial Park. Fairview Cemetery is not within walking distance.

St. George's Round Church

Architect William Hughes designed this unusual and charming timber-frame church, which at once accommodated the overflow of parishioners from the nearby Dutch Church on Brunswick Street and satisfied Prince Edward's penchant for round buildings. The cornerstone was laid in 1800, and the chancel and front porch were added later. A fire in 1994 destroyed the dome, but it has since been replaced. St. George's is a few blocks north of downtown at Brunswick and Cornwallis Streets.

Maritime Command Museum

On the grounds of Canadian Forces Base Halifax, this museum (Gottingen St. between North St. and Russell St., 902/721-8250; Mon.–Fri. 10 A.M.–3:30 P.M.; free) is ensconced in the 30-room Admiralty House, built in the 1840s as a residence for the base's admiral. Exhibits include presentation swords, memorabilia from the World War II Battle of the Atlantic, a military gun collection, uniforms, ship models, and other artifacts relating to the

© ANDREW HEMPSTEAD

St. George's Round Church

history of the Canadian Maritime Military Forces.

Fort Needham Memorial Park

Continue north along Gottingen Street from the maritime museum and veer right onto Dartmouth Street to reach this park, a high point of land with views across the head of Halifax Harbour. The park's most distinctive feature is a 14-bell carillon, a monument to the Halifax Explosion of 1917, at the time the largest man-made explosion the world had ever known. Stand in the break between the memorial's two halves and you get views through a clearing to the harbor and the actual site of the explosion.

Seaview Park

Halifax's peninsula is bookended by a pair of expansive green spaces. Seaview Park is at the north end, overlooking Bedford Basin from the foot of the A. Murray McKay Bridge. This was once the site of Africville, a community of black Haligonians established in the 1840s but since demolished. George Dixon, holder of three world boxing titles, was born here in 1870. As you head north from downtown along Barrington Street, access is along Service Road. A boat launch provides the only water access.

◖ Fairview Cemetery

Take Windsor Street north from Quinpool Road to reach Fairview Cemetery, final resting place of 121 *Titanic* victims. When the bodies were pulled from the Atlantic Ocean, they were given a number. These numbers, along with the date of the disaster, April 15, 1912 (it is assumed no one could have survived any longer than a day in the frigid ocean), adorn a majority of the simple black headstones paid for by the White Star Line, owners of the *Titanic*. Where identification was possible, a name accompanies the number, such as victim 227, J. Dawson, the origin of the character Jack Dawson played by Leonardo DiCaprio in the movie *Titanic*. Some headstones are engraved with moving tributes, such as that to Everett Edward Elliott, aged 24, which reads, "Each man stood at his port while all the weaker ones went by, and showed once more to all the world how Englishmen should die."

The turn into the cemetery is easy to miss; get in the left lane by Connaught Avenue and be prepared to turn against oncoming traffic to reach the cemetery's main entrance. The other option is to take Connaught Avenue off Windsor Street and park at the end of Chisholm Avenue. Once you're at the cemetery, the plot is well signposted, with an interpretive board describing events leading up to identifying victims long after they were buried. The cemetery is open from dawn to dusk.

Hemlock Ravine Park

This rugged tract of forest lies beside the western side of Bedford Basin between the busy Bedford and Bicentennial highways—but you'd never know urban civilization is so close as you walk along the five interconnecting walking trails. The park's namesake ravine, with its towering hemlocks, takes about 20 minutes to reach from the main parking lot, at the end of

Kent Avenue, which branches off the Bedford Highway (Highway 2) one kilometer north of the Kearney Lake Road intersection. Beside the parking lot is a heart-shaped pond designed by Prince Edward, who spent his summers here with his companion Julie St. Laurent.

Uniacke Estate Museum Park

This splendid 930-hectare estate (758 Main Rd., Mount Uniacke, 902/866-0032; June–mid-Oct. Mon.–Sat. 9:30 A.M.–5:30 P.M., Sun. 11 A.M.–5:30 P.M.; adult $3, child $2) is along Highway 1 beyond city limits 20 kilometers northwest from the intersection of Highway 102 (the easiest way to get there is to take Exit 3 from Highway 101). The home's interior features original furnishings, including four-poster beds and family portraits. The grounds offer seven hiking trails.

WEST SIDE OF NORTHWEST ARM

Carefully make your way onto the Armdale Rotary at the west end of Quinpool Road and take the Herring Cove Road exit. A short distance south along this road, Purcells Cove Road veers off to the left. This winding road hugs the Northwest Arm for nine kilometers to the fishing village of Herring Cove. Along the way are two yacht clubs filled with glistening white sailboats, and these two sights.

Sir Sandford Fleming Park

A 38-hectare grassy spread, this delightful piece of parkland is mostly forested, sloping to a seawall promenade fringing a quiet waterway. The land was donated by the Scottish-born Fleming, best known for establishing time zones. It is said a missed train led the enterprising Fleming to begin formulating a plan that would see the entire world operate on a 24-hour clock with time zones that related to longitude. Fleming, who also designed Canada's first postage stamp, lived in Halifax from the 1880s until his death in 1915.

On a slight rise above the bay is the 10-story **Dingle Tower** (June–Aug. daily 9 A.M.–5 P.M.). A stairway winds up the

© ANDREW HEMPSTEAD

The high point of Sir Sandford Fleming Park is the Dingle Tower.

interior of this stone edifice, presenting great views from the top.

The park is open daily 8 A.M.–dusk. The main entrance is off Purcells Cove Road; Dingle Road leads down through the wooded park to the waterfront.

York Redoubt National Historic Site

Set on a bluff high above the harbor entrance, York Redoubt National Historic Site (Purcells Cove Rd., 902/426-5080; grounds mid-May–Oct. daily 9 A.M.–6 P.M., buildings mid-June–Aug. daily 10 A.M.–6 P.M.; free) is six kilometers south of downtown. The setting draws visitors with walking paths that lead down the steep incline to picnic tables and protected coves. Up top are strategic fortifications dating to 1793, when Britain went to war with the French. Most of the fort is from later times, including massive muzzle-loading guns that were designed to fire nine-inch shells capable of piercing armored vessels.

◖ MCNABS ISLAND

Whatever your interests, this five-kilometer-long island at the entrance to Halifax Harbour is a wonderful place to spend a day. The island is mostly wooded, its forests filled with bird-life and its shoreline dotted with beaches and tidal pools. Archaeological evidence points to habitation by the Mi'Kmaq at least 1,600 years ago, but the most obvious signs of human development are more recent, including two forts and the remains of a number of residences (including the summer home of Frederick Perrin, of Lea & Perrins Worcestershire sauce fame). Although many of the early residences have disappeared, signs of their formal gardens remain; look for ash, oak, and apple trees.

Recreation

Most visitors come to the island to go hiking. Ferries land at Garrison Pier, from where trails radiate in all directions. The top of Jenkin's Hill, easily reached in 10 minutes, is a good place to get oriented while also enjoying sweeping harbor views. At the 1864 **Fort Ives,** an easy 30-minute walk from the pier, cannons are still in place. **Fort McNab,** a similar distance south of the pier, was built in 1889 and is protected as a National Historic Site. Sandy **Mauger's Beach,** just south of Garrison Pier, is the best and most accessible of many island beaches.

Getting There

Year-round access to the island is provided by **McNabs Island Ferry** (902/465-4563), which departs from Fisherman's Cove, on the Dartmouth side of the harbor. Round-trip fare is adult $14, senior and child $11.50. Ask at the Halifax Visitor Centre for ferries departing from downtown Halifax. No services are available on the island, so bring your own food and drink and be prepared for changeable weather by bringing a rain jacket.

DARTMOUTH

Dartmouth is a large residential, commercial, and industrial area across the harbor from Halifax. The two cities are joined by a bridge and Metro Transit's Halifax–Dartmouth ferry from the foot of downtown's George Street to the Alderney Gate Complex in Dartmouth. Ferries operate year-round Monday–Saturday 6:30 A.M.–midnight, and daily in summer. The fare is adult $2, senior and child $1.40 each way. The ferry arrives within walking distance of Dartmouth Heritage Museum properties and various shops and restaurants.

Dartmouth Heritage Museum

The Dartmouth Heritage Museum comprises two historic homes within walking distance of Alderney Gate. The 1867 **Evergreen House** (26 Newcastle St., 902/464-2300; summer Tues.–Sun. 10 A.M.–5 P.M., the rest of the year Tues.–Sat. 10 A.M.–5 P.M.; adult $2), filled with period antiques, is the grander of the two. Built by a cooper (barrel maker) in 1785, **Quaker House** (57 Ochterloney St., 902/464-5823; summer Tues.–Sun. 10 A.M.–5 P.M.) is one of Dartmouth's oldest residences. In addition to period furnishings, exhibits tell the story of the Quakers, who were drawn to Nova Scotia for the abundance of whales.

◖ Bedford Institute of Oceanography

This government-run facility (Baffin Blvd., 902/426-4306; Mon.–Fri. 9 A.M.–4 P.M.; free) has a mandate that includes everything from helping maintain Canada's sovereignty to federal fisheries, but is best known for its work on the sunken *Titanic*. On a guided tour (summer, by appointment only), you'll get to learn about all this work, as well as step aboard a simulated ship's bridge and get up close and personal at the Touch Tank. To get there from downtown Halifax, cross the Narrows and take the Shannon Park exit of the MacKay Bridge (immediately after the toll gates); turn right and then left onto Baffin Boulevard, which crosses under the bridge to the institute.

Shubie Park

In 1858, construction began on an ambitious canal system that linked Halifax Harbour with the Bay of Fundy via a string of lakes and the Shubenacadie River. The canal was abandoned just 12 years later. The canal between Lake Micmac and Lake Charles has been restored, complete with one of nine original locks. The park is laced with hiking and biking trails, but many visitors take to the water in canoes and kayaks, paddling from the main day-use area to Lake Charles. Access is signposted from Braemar Drive, which branches north from Exit 6 of Highway 111.

Cole Harbour Rural Heritage Farm

Surrounded by a residential subdivision, this outdoor attraction (471 Poplar Dr., 902/434-0222; mid-May–mid-Oct. Mon.–Sat. 10 A.M.–4 P.M., Sun. noon–4 P.M.; donation) is a great place for children. Buildings include a 200-year-old farmhouse, a blacksmith shop, various barns, and a tearoom, while garden plots represent early crops, with the produce used in the tearoom. Livestock is fenced, but rabbits, geese, and ducks roam free.

EASTERN PASSAGE

The Eastern Passage is a narrow waterway running between the Dartmouth side of Halifax Harbour and McNabs Island. From downtown Dartmouth take Pleasant Street south to Highway 322. This route passes oil refineries and Canadian Forces Base Shearwater before reaching the delightful Fisherman's Cove. Beyond this point, Highway 322 continues through an oceanfront residential area to Southeast Passage Provincial Park.

Shearwater Aviation Museum

At the entrance to Canadian Forces Base Shearwater, this museum (12 Wing, Pleasant St., 902/460-1083; June–Aug. Tues.–Fri. 10 A.M.–5 P.M., Sat.–Sun. noon–4 P.M., Apr.–May and Sept.–Nov. Tues.–Thurs. 10 A.M.–5 P.M., Sat. noon–4 P.M.; free) is home to 10 restored aircraft and an impressive collection of air force memorabilia. The museum is off Pleasant Street (Highway 322); turn left at the first set of lights beyond the Imperial oil refinery.

◖ Fisherman's Cove

Fisherman's Cove is no different from the hundreds of picturesque fishing villages that dot the Nova Scotia coastline, with one exception—it's within the city limits of the capital. Lying along the Eastern Passage two kilometers southeast of Dartmouth along Highway 322, the cove mixes the needs of working fishing vessels with a constant flow of curious visitors. You can drive along Government Wharf Road, which spurs right at the traffic lights in Eastern Passage, onto the main dock area, but it's much more enjoyable to explore the area on foot from the parking lot just beyond the cove's main entrance.

Opened in 2004, **Fisherman's Cove Marine Interpretative Centre** (Government Wharf Rd., 902/465-6093; Tues.–Sun. 11 A.M.–7 P.M.; $2) is the first building you come to after entering Fisherman's Cove. This museum tells the story of the village and its colorful history, and aquariums are filled with local underwater species. The interpretive center is the only official sight. Plan also to spend time browsing craft shops and soaking up the sights, sounds, and smells of this authentic fishing village.

Fisherman's Cove Visitor Information Centre (30 Government Wharf Rd., 902/465-8009; mid-May–mid-Oct. daily 9 A.M.–6 P.M.) is along the main street of touristy shops. Ask for the historic walking tour brochure.

NORTH OF DOWNTOWN
Atlantic Canada Aviation Museum

Across the highway from the airport (take Exit 6 from Hwy. 102), this museum (20 Sky Blvd., 902/873-3773; May–Oct. daily 9 A.M.–5 P.M.; adult $5) is a good place to visit on the way north to Truro or before your flight home. On display are around 30 aircraft—everything from fighter planes to a homemade helicopter—and a couple of simulators.

Recreation

WALKING AND HIKING

Even if you're not feeling overly energetic, plan to take a stroll along the downtown waterfront. A **seawall promenade** winds past docks filled with all manner of boats—tall ships, tugboats, and visiting yachts—harborfront restaurants, the Maritime Museum of the Atlantic, Historic Properties, and south to Pier 21. While it's possible to do all your downtown sightseeing on foot, an easier option is to catch a cab to Citadel Hill, from where it's downhill all the way back to the harbor. At Citadel Hill, take the time not only to visit the fort, but to walk around the perimeter, and then cross Sackville Street to the **Public Gardens,** a delightful place for a flower-filled stroll.

For information on **McNabs Island,** a popular destination for day-tripping hikers, see the *McNabs Island* section in this chapter.

Parks

Point Pleasant Park, 2.5 kilometers south of downtown off Young Avenue, is laced with hiking and biking trails. The obvious choice is to stick to the water, along a two-kilometer (each way) trail that hugs the shoreline, passing Point Pleasant itself before winding around to the Northwest Arm. Other trails lead inland to historic fortifications and through the remains of forests devastated by Hurricane Juan in 2003.

Across the Northwest Arm from downtown, **Sir Sandford Fleming Park** flanks the water in an upscale neighborhood. Again, it's the seawall walk that is most popular, but another pleasant trail leads up through the forest to Frog Lake.

Take the Bedford Highway north from downtown and then one kilometer north of the Kearney Lake Road junction and watch

Walking trails in Sir Sandford Fleming Park hug the water's edge.

for Kent Avenue (to the left), which leads into a dense old-growth forest protected as **Hemlock Ravine Park.** From the pond and picnic area, a world away from surrounding development, five trails branch off into the forest. Some are short and perfect for younger and older walkers, while others, including the trail to the hemlock-filled ravine, are steeper and can be slippery after rain.

BICYCLING

The local municipality, with its many lakes and harbor-side coves, has put considerable effort into making the city as bike-friendly as possible. The Halifax Regional Municipality website (www.halifax.ca) has a PDF file bike map, or pick one up at the information center. A centrally located source for rentals and advice is **Harbour Bike and Sea Rentals** (1781 Lower Water St., 902/423-1185). Standard bikes cost $10 per hour or $42 for a full day.

Freewheeling Adventures (902/857-3600 or 800/672-0775, www.freewheeling.ca) is a local

tour company that runs recommended guided bike trips along the South Shore, starting from Hubbards, just south of the city. Guests ride for up to six hours per day, stay in cottages or bed-and-breakfasts, and have all meals included in rates starting at $1,600 per person.

WATER SPORTS
Swimming and Sunbathing

Municipal swimming pools include **Northcliffe Pool** (111 Clayton Park Dr., 902/490-4690) and **Needham Pool** (3372 Devonshire Ave., 902/490-4633).

Crystal Crescent Beach Provincial Park lies a half hour south of Halifax off Highway 349 and is the locals' favorite Atlantic beach. Its sand is fine, and the sea is usually cold, but summer crowds heat up the action. Nature lovers will enjoy the 10-kilometer trail to remote Pennant Point while naturists will want to gravitate to the farthest of the park's three beaches—one of Canada's few official nude beaches.

If you're visiting Fisherman's Cove, head east for eight kilometers along Cow Bay Road to reach **Rainbow Haven Provincial Park.** The park protects wetlands at the mouth of Cole Harbour and an ocean-facing beach. The beach is often windy (it's not uncommon to see people sunbathing back in the dunes), but on calm days it's a delightful place to soak up some rays and maybe, if you're brave, take a dip in the water. At the end of the park access road are change rooms and a concession selling beachy food such as ice cream and hot dogs.

Canoeing and Kayaking

Based on the Northwest Arm, **Saint Mary's Boat Club** (1641 Fairfield Rd., 902/490-4688) rents canoes for $8 per hour on a limited basis through summer. Rentals are available June–Sept. Sat.–Sun. 11 A.M.–7 P.M.

GOLFING

Halifax and surrounding area is home to more than a dozen courses varying from nine-hole

© ANDREW HEMPSTEAD

public courses to exclusive 18-holers. The **Nova Scotia Golf Association** website (www.nsga .ns.ca) has links to all provincial courses.

The Courses

Host of a 2005 LPGA event, **Glen Arbour Golf Course** (Glen Arbour Way, off Hammonds Plains Rd., 1 km west of Bedford, 902/835-4653) is one of Canada's finest links. Choose from five sets of tees to a maximum of 6,800 yards. The course has abundant water hazards, 90 bunkers, and fairways lined by hardwood forests. Greens fees top out at $155 in midsummer, dropping as low as $75 for twilight golf in October.

Lost Creek Golf Club (902/865-4653) enjoys the same forested environment as Glen Arbour, but without the valet parking and high greens fees, which are just $42 at Lost Creek. To get there, take Exit 2 from Highway 101 and follow Beaverbank Road north for 10 kilometers; turn right on Kinsac Road and then left on William Nelson Drive.

One of the region's most enjoyable layouts is **Granite Springs** (25 km west of downtown off Hwy. 333 at 4441 Prospect Rd., Bayside, 902/852-4653). This challenging course winds through 120 hectares of mature forest, with distant ocean views. Greens fees are $55 ($38 twilight).

WINTER SPORTS

In winter, walking paths become **cross-country ski trails** at Point Pleasant Park, Sir Sandford Fleming Park, and Hemlock Ravine. Dartmouth maintains groomed surfaces at Lake Charles, and several lakes in Halifax are great for skating.

Skiing and Snowboarding

The closest downhill skiing and boarding is at **Ski Martock** (902/798-9501), an hour's drive northwest of Halifax off Highway 101 (signposted from Exit 5). It's a popular family hill, with mostly beginner runs accessible by two lifts rising 180 vertical meters. Snowmaking covers the entire resort while lights keep runs open nightly until 10 P.M. Day tickets are adult

Life in Halifax revolves around the water, and nowhere is this more apparent than the downtown harbor, where sailing ships like the famous *Bluenose II* are often tied up.

© ANDREW HEMPSTEAD

$35, child $25. Ski or snowboard rental packages are $22.

Hockey

Through the long winter, when outside activities are curtailed by the weather, there is much interest in ice hockey (known in Canada simply as "hockey"). When they're not watching the National Hockey League on television (the closest teams are in Boston, Montreal, and Toronto), local fans flock to the Halifax Metro Centre to cheer on their own **Halifax Mooseheads** (5284 Duke St., 902/429-3267, www.halifaxmooseheads.ca), who play mid-September to mid-March in the Quebec Major Junior Hockey League. Tickets start at $15.

HARBOR CRUISES AND LAND TOURS

If you don't have a lot of time to explore Halifax or just want an introduction to the city, consider one of the many tours available—they'll maximize your time and get you to the highlights with minimum stress.

Bluenose II

The harborfront's premier attraction, the magnificent schooner *Bluenose II,* divides her summertime between Halifax, her home port Lunenburg, and goodwill tours to other Canadian ports. The vessel is an exact replica of the famous *Bluenose.* It is operated by the Lunenburg Marine Museum Society on behalf of the Province of Nova Scotia. When in Halifax, two-hour harbor tours are available twice daily from the Maritime Museum's wharf. Check www.museum.gov.ns.ca/bluenose for a schedule. Departures are at 9:30 A.M. and 1 P.M. and the cost is adult $35, child $20. Each sailing has 75 spots—40 spots can be reserved by calling 902/634-4794 or 800/763-1963, with the remaining 35 going on sale 90 minutes before departure. Without a reservation, expect to line up for a spot.

Harbour Hopper Tours

This company (902/490-8687) picks up passengers from the north side of the maritime museum for a quick trip around the historic streets of Halifax, and then the fun really starts, as the company's distinctive green and yellow amphibious vehicles plunge into the water for a cruise around the harbor. The trip lasts around one hour, with up to 20 departures daily May–October between 9 A.M. and 9:30 P.M. The ticket kiosk is on Cable Wharf. Tickets are adult $25, senior $24, child $15.

Other Harbor Cruises

Many other sightseeing craft also offer harbor tours. **Murphy's on the Water** (Cable Wharf, 1751 Lower Water St., 902/420-1015) operates several vessels through a sailing season that runs mid-May–late October. The 23-meter wooden sailing ketch *Mar* departs up to six times daily on cruises that cost adult $23, senior $22, child $17. The *Harbour Queen I* is a 200-passenger paddle wheeler offering a narrated harbor cruise (adult $22, senior $21, child $17) and a variety of lunch and dinner cruises ($44 for dinner).

Bus Tours

Ambassatours (902/423-6242 or 800/565-7173) has the local Grayline franchise. The

© ANDREW HEMPSTEAD

Harbour Hopper Tours combine street touring with a harbor cruise.

three-hour Deluxe Historic Halifax City Tour includes stops at the Public Gardens, Halifax Citadel National Historic Site, and Fairview Cemetery. The tour also passes all major downtown attractions, working precincts of the harbor, and various university campuses. This tour departs June–mid-October daily at 9 A.M. and 1 P.M. and costs adult $36, child $18. Another option with Ambassatours is a downtown loop tour aboard an old English double-decker bus (mid-June–mid-Oct.; adult $44, child $31). You can get on and off as you please at any of the 11 stops on the one-hour loop and tickets are valid for two days (a good plan is to ride the entire loop once, and then plan your stops for the second go-round. This same company also has a three-hour trip to Peggy's Cove (departs June–mid-Oct. Tues., Thurs., and Sun. at 1 P.M.; adult $48, senior $44, child $34) and a full-day trip that combines a stop in Mahone Bay with time in Lunenburg (departs June–Oct. Mon., Wed., Fri., and Sat. at 9 A.M.; adult $98, senior $89, child $69).

Entertainment and Events

Halifax has a reputation as a party town, partly because of a large population of students. The city has dozens of pubs, many with local brews on tap and Celtic-inspired bands such as the Kilkenny Krew and the Navigators performing to small but raucous crowds. Most pubs close around midnight. The city also has a notable performing arts community. Although most seasons run through the cooler months, many companies put on events especially for summer crowds.

For complete listings of all that's happening around Halifax, pick up the free *Coast* (www .thecoast.ca). Friday and weekend editions of the *Halifax Herald* offer comprehensive entertainment listings. The website www.halifaxlocals.com is a user-driven vehicle for discussions on the local music scene.

NIGHTLIFE
Pubs
If you're going to have just one beer in Halifax, make it at the **Stag's Head Tavern,** part of the Keith's Brewery complex (Lower Water St., 902/455-1474). Best known as North America's oldest working brewery, Keith's still uses traditional British brewing techniques. Its famous India Pale Ale is widely available as draft and in bottles across the country, but it's best enjoyed in the Stag's Head, surrounded by the convivial atmosphere and with traditional Maritime music in the background.

In the vicinity of Keith's, the **Granite Brewery** (1662 Barrington St., 902/422-4954; daily from 11 A.M.) is ensconced in a historic stone building a couple of blocks back from Alexander Keith's Brewery. Its own excellent English-style ales are brewed on-site, using natural ingredients such as black malt imported from England. The pub itself attracts a slightly older crowd of well-dressed locals.

Live music at the **Lower Deck** (Upper Water St., 902/425-1501; daily from 11:30 A.M.) keeps the crowds humming nightly at this waterfront pub within the historic Privateers Warehouse.

Tug's Pub, in the Waterfront Warehouse complex (1549 Lower Water St., 902/425-7610; daily 11:30 A.M.–midnight), is a refined English-style pub with a tartan color scheme, lots of polished mahogany furnishings, and walls lined with historic photos.

As you move away from the harborfront, **Pogue Fado** (1581 Barrington St., 902/429-6222; daily from 11 A.M.) is one of the busiest Irish pubs in Halifax. The atmosphere is friendly and welcoming, there's live music on weekends, and the food is good—so it's easy to see why.

The Maxwell's Plum (1600 Grafton St., 902/423-5090) has an excellent selection of imported draft beers (notably Beamish Irish Stout, John Courage, and Newcastle Brown Ale) and single-malt scotches. That alone may be reason enough to visit there, but it's also a good venue for straight-ahead jazz, including Sunday afternoon jam sessions. **Your Father's Moustache** (5686 Spring Garden Rd., 902/423-6766) puts on excellent live, usually local, music most evenings. On Saturday afternoon it hosts its popular Blues Matinee.

Bars

Along the lively stretch of Argyle Street between Blowers and Sackville Streets is the **Seahorse Tavern** (1665 Argyle St., 902/423-7200), which has been around since 1948. Horsepower Beer, produced by the local Propeller Brewery, is available on tap only at the Seahorse, but most patrons are here for the music. Monday through Thursday are theme nights such as Mullet Mondays (retro rock and roll) and Indie Wednesdays while weekends are devoted to live music. Part of the same complex is the **Economy Shoe Shop** (1663 Argyle St., 902/423-8845; daily 11 A.M.–2 A.M.), a drinking and dining venue incorporating three restaurants and the Belgian Bar, with a gaudy but appealing tropical vibe. **Stayner's Bar and Grill** (5075 George St., 902/492-1800) is in the heart of the tourist district, but as it's away from the water, the casual visitor often misses this bar that remains quiet until local Celtic bands hit the stage.

Nightclubs

Around midnight, when the pubs start closing their doors, the crowds move on to nightclubs spread through downtown. The **Dome** (1741 Grafton St., 902/422-6907; Wed.–Sun. 10 P.M.–3:30 A.M.) is a mass of young heaving bodies who dance the night away in sync to one of Canada's most dynamic sound and light systems. It's also a bit of a pickup place (locals often refer to it as the Do-Me). Under the same roof is **Cheers** (902/421-1655), which attracts an older crowd. Another multivenue nightclub

is **Pacifico** (corner Barrington and Salter Streets, 902/422-3633), where **Crave** attracts serious dancers and the **Capitol** holds a stylish martini bar.

Starting out as a gay bar, **Reflections** (5184 Sackville St., 902/422-2957) now attracts an eclectic mix of locals of all sexual persuasions. Each night has a theme—Tuesday is house and techno, bands play Wednesday, Thursday is an anything-goes talent show—but the biggest crowds are on weekends, when the resident DJ spins his favorite tunes until 4 A.M.

The Palace (1721 Brunswick St., 902/420-0015) has a huge dance floor with a dynamic light and sound system. It's a bit rough around edges and busiest in the wee hours of morning when everywhere else is closing.

Jazz and Blues

The **Seahorse Tavern** (1665 Argyle St., 902/423-7200) hosts a blues jam every Thursday night. Next door, the Belgian Bar, within the **Economy Shoe Shop** (1663 Argyle St., 902/423-8845; daily 11 A.M.–2 A.M.) features no-charge Monday evening jazz.

The best blues bar in town is **Bearly's House of Blues and Ribs** (1269 Barrington St., 902/423-2526). As the name suggests, ribs ($16 for a full rack) are the dining specialty, but it is the music that draws the enthusiastic crowd. Weekends feature local talent while weekdays except Monday and Wednesday the stage is turned over to traveling talent. On Saturday afternoons through winter, bluegrass musicians strum their stuff.

PERFORMING ARTS

Haligonians have a sweet and sometimes bittersweet Canadian sense of humor (somewhat like the British), and local theater revels in their brand of fun. A $37 admission will get you into dinner-theater musical productions at **Grafton Street Dinner Theatre** (1741 Grafton St., 902/425-1961), which operates daily except Monday in summer and three times a week through the rest of the year. **Halifax Feast Dinner Theatre** (Maritime Centre, corner Barrington and Salter Sts., 902/420-1840) costs a few dollars more, but the production often has a historic Halifax angle. A lot of food is served very quickly at both venues, but the quality remains excellent.

At the **Neptune Theatre** (1593 Argyle St., 902/429-7070), private companies such as Legends of Broadway take to the boards during summer with musicals and Gilbert and Sullivan shows.

FESTIVALS AND EVENTS

Halifax hosts a number of well-known events that visitors plan their trips around, as well as many you probably haven't heard of but that are well worth attending if the dates correspond with your own travels. The most popular festivals are held outdoors and in summer, but the cooler months are the season of performing arts. For details and exact dates of the events listed, use the contacts given or check out the Tourism Nova Scotia website (www .novascotia.com).

Spring

The **Scotia Festival of Music** centers on the Music Room (6181 Lady Hammond Rd., 902/429-9467, www.scotiafestival.ns.ca) for two weeks in late May and early June. Chamber musicians present piano, cello, and violin recitals in a dignified yet casual atmosphere.

The **Nova Scotia Multicultural Festival** (Alderney Gate Complex, Dartmouth, 902/423-6534, www.multifest.ca) fills the Dartmouth waterfront precinct with the sounds, sights, and smells of various cultures the middle weekend of June. You can feast on barbecued Korean short ribs while watching Polish folk dancing or tap your feet to Celtic highland dancers while juggling a plate of German sausages. Ferries dock right at Alderney Gate, making this the best way to travel to the festival from downtown.

Summer

Nothing reflects Halifax's long military heritage better than the **Nova Scotia International Tattoo** (902/420-1114, www.nstattoo.ca), held annually for 10 days at the beginning of July

at the Halifax Metro Centre (5284 Duke St.). A "tattoo" is an outdoor military exercise presented as entertainment. Here it involves competitions, military bands, dancers, gymnasts, and choirs. The event has grown to be regarded as one of the world's greatest indoor events, bringing together thousands of performers from around the world. You can buy tickets (around $32–50) through the Halifax Metro Centre Box Office (902/451-1221).

In mid-July, jazz fans descend on Halifax for the **Atlantic Jazz Festival** (902/492-2225, www.jazzeast.com), the largest music festival east of Montréal. More than 400 musicians from around the world gather at venues as intimate as the Economy Shoe Shop and as character-filled as the old schoolhouse at Peggy's Cove to perform traditional and contemporary jazz.

Halifax and Dartmouth come together to celebrate their birthdays with a civic holiday known as **Natal Day** (902/490-6773, www .natalday.org) on the first Monday of every August. Events take place through the entire weekend, including a Saturday parade, talent shows, sporting events, and a grand finale fireworks presentation on the harbor Monday night.

Street performers fill five stages spread along the downtown waterfront for 11 days in early August during the **Halifax International Buskers Festival** (902/471-0550, www.buskers.ca).

Summer finishes with the **Atlantic Fringe Festival** (902/435-4837, www.atlanticfringe .ca), featuring 200 shows at various downtown venues through the first week of September.

Fall

The mid-September **Atlantic Film Festival** (902/422-3456, www.atlanticfilm.com) has been wowing moviegoers for more than a quarter of a century. It features the very best films from around the world, but the emphasis is on local and Canadian productions. Venues are mostly downtown theaters.

Celebrate **Alexander Keith's birthday** (902/455-1474, www.keiths.ca) on October 5 with hundreds of enthusiastic locals. Or pull up a bar stool at any local pub and raise a toast of India Pale Ale to "The Great Man of Beer," who began brewing beer in Halifax in 1820. The event (check the website for locations) is the epicenter of celebrations, with plenty of foot-stomping, beer-drinking East Coast music.

For 10 days from the first Friday in October, the country comes to the city for the **Maritime Fall Fair** (Exhibition Park, 200 Prospect Rd., 902/876-8221, www.maritimefallfair.com). It has everything a fall fair should—a craft marketplace, agricultural competitions, vegetable judging, a rodeo, and a midway. Exhibition Park is off Highway 333, the main road to Peggy's Cove.

Winter

The first full weekend of November, the **Christmas Craft Village** (902/463-2561, www.atlanticchristmasfair.com) fills Exhibition Park with hundreds of crafty booths selling everything from homemade preserves to self-published books to East Coast antiques.

Shopping

Shopaholics will love Halifax. Most shops and all major department stores are generally open Monday–Saturday 9:30 A.M.–5:30 P.M. Stores along the touristy harborfront usually have longer hours and also are open Sunday.

Arts and Crafts

The city's art galleries are superb. The newest fine arts trends are on exhibit at Nova Scotia College of Art and Design's **Anna Leonowens Gallery** (5163 Duke St., 902/494-8223; Tues.–Fri. 11 A.M.–5 P.M., Sat. noon–5 P.M.). The gallery displays and sells the work of Nova Scotia College of Art and Design students. This downtown university, one of North America's oldest cultural institutions, was founded by the gallery's namesake, Anna Leonowens, in 1887. Leonowens, a one-time English teacher who was governess to the King of Siam in the 1860s (the movie *Anna and the King,* starring Jodie Foster, tells her life story), spent 20 years in Halifax, during which time she established NSCAD.

Hundreds of clan fabrics and tartans in kilts, skirts, vests, ties, and other apparel are stocked at **Plaid Place** (1903 Barrington St., 902/429-6872). The capital's definitive crafts source is **Jennifer's of Nova Scotia** (5635 Spring Garden Rd., 902/425-3119), an outlet for 120 provincial producers of handicrafts such as patchwork quilts, pottery, and soaps. **Studio 21** (1223 Lower Water St., 902/420-1852) is a good source of contemporary paintings by local artists. For the unique combination of hand-built furniture and porcelain dog dishes, head to **Henhouse** (5533 Young St., 902/423-4499).

Crystal

Canada's only traditional glassworks is **Nova Scotian Crystal** (5080 George St., 902/492-0416), which is ensconced in a waterfront building that contains a showroom and workshop. You can watch master craftspeople at work every day, but Tuesday, Thursday, and Saturday are the days you won't want to miss—this is when the actual glassblowing takes place. Rather than taking a tour, interested folks crowd around open factory doors to watch the goings-on inside. The shop sells pieces such as Christmas ornaments, stemware, toasting flutes, candleholders, and bowls, many with Nova Scotian–inspired designs.

Markets

Halifax Seaport Farmers' Market happens every Saturday 7 A.M.–1 P.M. at Pier 20 (Marginal Rd., 902/492-4043). North America's oldest such market, its stands are filled with local crafts and produce that make the perfect memento of your time in Nova Scotia.

In the same vicinity, **Pavilion 22** (May–Oct.) is designed as a market-style shopping experience for cruise-ship visitors, but it is also worth stopping by if you are at this end of town.

Local Delicacies

You'll no doubt eat a lot of seafood while in Nova Scotia, but it can also make a great souvenir to take home for friends and family. Or plan a get-together upon your return and impress everyone with a Nova Scotian feast.

Clearwater (757 Bedford Hwy., 902/443-0550) is a high-profile supplier with a huge shop front along the Bedford Highway waterfront. The outlet is anchored by a massive lobster tank divided into sections that make choosing the right-size lobster easy (from $8 per pound). You can also pick up cooked crab legs to go, attend cooking demonstrations, and buy all manner of seafood cookbooks. Better still for those departing Halifax International Airport, Clearwater has an airport location (902/873-4509) with a lobster tank. For an additional fee, live lobsters can be packaged for air travel. Clearwater also sells crabs, scallops, clams, and shrimp.

The days of Prohibition, when smuggling rum into the United States was a way to make a living for seafaring Nova Scotians, may be a distant memory, but at the **Rum Runners Rum Cake Factory** (facing the harbor at 1479 Lower Water St., 902/421-6079) you can buy rum cakes whose recipe was passed down from a rum-running family. The cakes are deliciously rich and sweet, and travel well.

Outdoor and Camping Gear

Halifax's largest outdoor equipment store is **Mountain Equipment Co-op** (1550 Granville St., 902/421-2667; Mon.–Wed. 10 A.M.–7 P.M., Thurs.–Fri. 10 A.M.–9 P.M., Sat. 10 A.M.–6 P.M.). Like the American REI stores, it is a cooperative owned by its members; to make a purchase, you must be a member (a once-only charge of $5). The store holds a massive selection of clothing, climbing and mountaineering equipment, tents, backpacks, sleeping bags, books, and other accessories. To order a copy of the mail-order catalog, call 800/663-2667 or go online to www.mec.ca.

Accommodations and Camping

Accommodations in Halifax vary from a hostel and budget-priced roadside motels to luxurious bed-and-breakfasts. Downtown is home to a number of full-service hotels catering to top-end travelers and business conventions. In general, these properties offer drastically reduced rates on weekends—Friday and Saturday nights might be half the regular room rate. No matter when you plan to visit, arriving in Halifax without a reservation is unwise, but especially in the summer, when gaggles of tourists compete for a relative paucity of rooms. If you do arrive without a confirmed reservation, staff at the **Halifax Visitor Centre** (1598 Argyle St., 902/490-5946; daily 9 A.M.–6 P.M.) will try their best to find you somewhere to stay.

All rates quoted below are for a double room in summer.

DOWNTOWN
Under $50

Also known as the Halifax Heritage House Hostel, **HI-Halifax** (1253 Barrington St., 902/422-3863, www.hihostels.ca) has 75 beds two blocks from the harbor and a 15-minute walk to attractions such as the maritime museum and Citadel Hill. Facilities include a communal kitchen, laundry room, television in the common room, and a storeroom for bikes. Beds in four- to eight-bed dorms are $25 per night ($30 for nonmembers) while those in private rooms are $57 s or d.

$100-150

Oscar Wilde and P. T. Barnum both slept (not together) at the **Waverley Inn** (1266 Barrington St., 902/423-9346 or 800/565-9346, www.waverleyinn.com), which, at its completion in 1866, was one of the city's grandest residences. Rates for the 34 rooms ($125–229 s, $165–229 d) include breakfast; tea, coffee, and snacks are offered all day and evening in the hospitality suite. Rooms are furnished with Victorian-era antiques, and deluxe rooms contain whirlpool tubs and feather beds. The least expensive single rooms are very small while the deluxe twins are spacious and extravagantly luxurious.

$150-200

(Cambridge Suites Hotel (1583 Brunswick St., 902/425-4076 or 800/565-1263, www.cambridgesuiteshalifax.com; $155–205 s or d) is a modern, centrally located, all-suite hotel with 200 rooms. Even the smallest have separate bedrooms, and continental breakfast is included in the rates. Rooms are packed with amenities, including high-speed Internet, beautiful bathrooms, lounge and work areas, and basic cooking facilities. The rooftop patio, a fitness center, and a bistro-style restaurant are pluses. Ask about rates that include free parking, full breakfast, and extras for traveling families.

(The Halliburton (5184 Morris St., 902/420-0658 or 888/512-3344, www.thehalliburton.com; from $185 s or d) is a beautiful heritage property transformed into a boutique hotel. The 29 rooms come with super-comfortable beds topped with goose-down duvets and luxurious en suite bathrooms. Rates include continental breakfast, and wireless Internet is available throughout the building. The acclaimed in-house dining room, Stories, is open nightly for dinner.

Halifax is home to two Delta properties. In both cases, click on the "Packages and Specials" link at www.deltahotels.com for the best rates. **Delta Barrington** (1875 Barrington St., 902/429-7410 or 888/890-3222, www.deltahotels.com; from $190 s or d) shares space with Barrington Place Mall in the historic area

and has 200 comfortable rooms. Amenities include a fitness room, indoor pool, business center, a street-side café (with a summer seafood menu), and a lounge bar. Rack rates are around $190 s or d midweek and $160 on weekends. Nearby, the **Delta Halifax** (1990 Barrington St., 902/425-6700 or 877/814-7706, www.deltahotels.com; $190 s or d) was one of the city's first grande dame hotels, and the old girl's still a handsome dowager. A highlight is the lavish indoor pool complex, complete with whirlpools and a sauna, as well as an adjacent fitness room.

$200-250

In any other Canadian capital, you'd pay a lot more for a room of similar standard as those at the full-service **Prince George Hotel** (1725 Market St., 902/425-1986 or 800/565-1567, www.princegeorgehotel.com; from $205 s or d), one block below the Halifax Citadel and seven blocks uphill from the harbor. The rooms feature contemporary furnishings, and amenities include a midsize indoor pool, a business center with Internet access, a restaurant, a lounge, and quiet public areas off the main lobby. Although rack rates start at just over $200, check the website for weekend specials or upgrade to the Crown Floor for an extra $30.

Part of the Casino Nova Scotia complex, **Marriott Harbourfront Hotel** (1919 Upper Water St., 902/421-1700 or 800/943-6760, www.marriott.com; $220 s or d) is a modern edifice designed to resemble the garrison that once occupied the waterfront. Although many guests are from Atlantic Canada and are staying especially to play the tables, it is also a convenient choice for leisure travelers. In addition to the casino, there are multiple restaurants, a stylish English-style pub, and live entertainment. Almost no one pays rack rates. Instead, check the website for a world of options starting at $149 s or d. For information on the casino, go to www.casinonovascotia.com.

Over $250

If you're after modern accommodations,

consider **Four Points by Sheraton Halifax** (1496 Hollis St., 902/423-4444, www.starwoodhotels.com; from $255 s or d), one block back from the harbor. Guest rooms are filled with modern conveniences (free high-speed Internet, 27-inch TVs, multiple phones, and well-designed work areas) while other facilities include an indoor pool and fitness room. Disregard the rack rates, book online, and you'll pay as little as $150 s or d, even in midsummer.

Opened in 1930 to coincide with the arrival of the first passenger trains to Halifax, the station's adjacent **Westin Nova Scotian** (1181 Hollis St., 902/421-1000 or 877/993-7846, www.westin.ns.ca; from $275 s or d) was extensively renovated in 2008. Linked to the railway station—many guests are still rail passengers—it oozes Old World charm throughout public areas (poke your head into the Atlantic Ballroom) and the 300 guest rooms. Amenities include a fine-dining restaurant featuring contemporary cooking, a hip lounge, café, fitness room, indoor pool, spa services, and a shuttle to the central business district (one kilometer away).

CITADEL HILL AND VICINITY

The following accommodations are in the vicinity of Citadel Hill, from where it's downhill all the way to the harbor. Even the fittest visitors may not feel like tramping back up to the Citadel Hill area after a full day sightseeing or a big meal at a downtown restaurant—no worries; a cab will cost around $6.

$50-100

A rambling old house directly opposite North Common has been renovated as **Fountain View Guest House** (2138 Robie St. between Williams St. and Compton Ave., 902/422-4169 or 800/565-4877; $25 s, $50 d). The seven rooms share bathrooms, there is no kitchen or laundry, and parking is limited to what you can find on the street.

$100-150

Across North Common from Citadel Hill is

the **Commons Inn** (5780 West St., 902/484-3466 or 877/797-7999, www.commonsinn.ca; $110–150 s or d), an older three-story building with basic 40 guest rooms. The rooms are on the small side, but are well-decorated with comfortable beds, en suite bathrooms, free local calls, and cable TV. The spacious suite, complete with a separate sitting area and jetted tub, is excellent value. Other pluses are free parking, a rooftop patio, and a continental breakfast.

$150-200

The grandiose **Lord Nelson Hotel** (1515 S. Park St., 902/423-6331 or 800/565-2020, www.lordnelsonhotel.com; from $199 s or d) presides over a busy Spring Garden Road intersection and overlooks the famous Public Gardens. Originally opened in 1928, the Lord Nelson underwent a transformation in the late 1990s, reopening as one of the city's finest hotels. It is probably a little too far for some to walk from downtown, but location aside, it is one of Halifax's best and best-value accommodations. Beyond the extravagant marble-floored lobby are 260 elegantly furnished rooms, each with large bathrooms, high-speed Internet access, coffeemakers, and irons. Other amenities include a fitness room, restaurant, English-style pub, and room service. Parking is $14 per night. Check the website for specials under $140 year-round.

BEDFORD HIGHWAY

Running along the western edge of the Bedford Basin, the Bedford Highway (Highway 2) is the original route north from downtown to the airport and beyond. A few motels from prebypass days exist, providing inexpensive accommodations a 10-minute or quicker drive from the city center. If you make this part of the city your base, you'll need a vehicle, or be prepared to ride transit buses. To get there from the north, take Exit 3 from Highway 102 and follow the signs toward downtown.

$50-100

Nestled in treed grounds on the harbor side

of the Bedford Highway is the **Travelers Motel** (773 Bedford Hwy., 902/835-3394 or 800/565-3394, www.travelersmotel.ca). It is a classic 1950s park-at-the-door roadside motel where rates start at $82 for smallish rooms with dated decor, cable TVs, and phones. Summer-only cabins with TV but no phones are $58–90 s or d. This place is surprisingly busy, so you'll need reservations in summer.

Over the rise toward the city from the Travelers and opposite a busy diner of the same name is the **Esquire Motel** (771 Bedford Hwy., 902/835-3367 or 800/565-3367, www.esquiremotel.ca; $85–145 s or d). Amenities are similar to its neighbor's, with the only real difference a small outdoor pool and free local calls. Outside of summer, rates start at $65.

NEAR THE AIRPORT

No accommodations are right at the airport, but it's only 40 minutes to downtown on the Airporter, which operates daily 5 A.M.–1 A.M. Here are a few options just in case you *must* stay in the vicinity.

$100-150

Across the highway from the airport and linked by free shuttle is the **Airport Hotel Halifax** (60 Sky Blvd., 902/873-3000 or 800/667-3333, ww.airporthotelhalifax.com; $130 s or d), which has regularly revamped rooms, an indoor and outdoor pool, a fitness room, a restaurant, and a desk for Discount car rentals.

$150-200

Four kilometers south of the airport, **Hilton Garden Inn** (200 Pratt & Whitney Dr., Enfield, 902/873-1400, www.hilton.com; from $179 s or d) offers 24-hour shuttle service for guests. It's a newer property with a high standard of guest rooms, as well as a restaurant and fitness room.

Around halfway between the airport and downtown is **Inn on the Lake** (3009 Hwy. 2, Fall River, 902/861-3480 or 800/463-6465, www.innonthelake.com; from $169 s or d), which has expanded from a 1970s roadside motel into a full-blown resort, complete with

multiple dining rooms, recreational opportunities spread over two hectares of landscaped lakefront, and even a white sandy beach.

FISHERMAN'S COVE

If you don't need to be right downtown, consider the following oceanfront accommodation—which is both excellent value and a world away from the bustle of the city.

Under $100

Overlooking the historic fishing village, ◖ **Inn at Fisherman's Cove** (1531 Shore Rd., Eastern Passage, 902/465-3455 or 866/725-3455, www.theinnatfishermanscove.com; $75–125 s or d) is a modern three-story building with its own private dock on the "crick" that has been chock-full of fishing boats for more than 200 years. Each room has an en suite bathroom and TV while downstairs is a breakfast room that opens to the dock. Four of the eight guest rooms face the water and have private balconies. Rates include a light breakfast.

© ANDREW HEMPSTEAD

Inn at Fisherman's Cove

CAMPGROUNDS

You won't find any campgrounds in the city center area, but a few commercial campgrounds lie within a 30-minute drive of downtown. Farther out are two provincial parks that offer camping without hookups.

Dartmouth

The closest camping to downtown is at ◖ **Shubie Park Campground** (Jaybee Dr., Dartmouth, 902/435-8328, www.shubiecampground.com; mid-May–mid-Oct.). Facilities such as the washrooms have been recently renovated, while public Internet access and landscaping have been added. The adjacent beach on Lake Charles comes with supervised swimming, and the campground is linked to walking trails along the Shubenacadie Canal. On the downside, sites offer little privacy. Unserviced sites are $27, hookups $32–40. To get there, take Exit 6 from Highway 111 and follow Braemer Drive north for 2.5 kilometers to Jaybee Drive. Coming from the north, take Exit 5 from Highway 102 and follow Highway 118 to Highway 111; from this point, it's a short way east to the Braemer Drive exit.

West

Woodhaven RV Park (1757 Hammonds Plains Rd., 902/835-2271, www.woodhavenrvpark.com; May–mid-Oct.; $28–36) is 18 kilometers from downtown and handy for an early-morning start out to the South Shore. To get there, take Exit 3 from Highway 102 and follow Hammonds Plains Road west for eight kilometers. From the South Shore, you bypass the city by taking Exit 5 from Highway 103. Facilities include coin-operated showers, two launderettes, a swimming pool, a playground, a games room, and wireless Internet access.

Halifax West KOA (3070 Hwy. 1, Upper Sackville, 902/865-4342, www.koa.com; mid-May–mid-Oct.; $31–49, cabins with shared bathrooms $60) is northwest of the city, farther out than Woodhaven and a 45-minute drive from downtown. To get there, take Exit 4B from Highway 102 and follow Highway 1 (Sackville Road) for 15 kilometers. If you're traveling toward Halifax from Windsor along Highway 101, take Exit 3 and follow the signs.

North

Take Exit 5 from Highway 102 and head north beyond Fall River for 10 kilometers to reach **Laurie Provincial Park** (coming from the north, take Exit 7 south to Highway 2), which lies on the southern shore of Grand Lake. Here, 71 sites are spread around a treed loop. Each site has a picnic table and fire pit, while park amenities include toilets, a short walking trail, and a day-use area, but no showers or hookups. The campground is open mid-June to early September and sites are $18 per night.

Dollar Lake Provincial Park (mid-May–early Sept.; $24) is farther from the city than Laurie Provincial Park, but it has showers and a concession, as well as a nicer beach, with swimming, boating, walking trails, and a playground. Sites are spread around three loops, with Loop A closest to the water.

Food

Halifax may not have a reputation as a gastronomical wonderland, but the dining scene has improved greatly during the last decade. Not only is the standard of food high in many of the better restaurants, but prices are generally reasonable, with mains in even the very best restaurants rarely more than $30. The many pubs are a good place to start looking for an inexpensive meal, but you can also find old-style diners, cheap ethnic meals, and the usual choice of city-style coffeehouses.

Naturally, **seafood** dominates many menus—especially lobster, crab, mussels, scallops, shrimp, halibut, and salmon, all of which are harvested in Nova Scotia. Some of the best seafood is, surprisingly, found along the touristy waterfront precinct. You can also buy it fresh from trawlers at Fisherman's Cove and even pick up live lobsters packed for flying out at the airport.

DOWNTOWN
Cafés

You can get a caffeine hit at outlets of Second Cup and Tim Hortons spread throughout the city (for fancily named Starbucks brews, your choices are limited to two mall locations, both well outside downtown), but the absence of coffeehouse chains in downtown Halifax is refreshing.

Perks (1781 Lower Water St., 902/429-9386; daily 6:30 A.M.–11:30 P.M.) is always busy. Sure, the coffee is good, food such as chicken Caesar salad is well priced ($6), there's wireless Internet, and the service efficient, but it's the location—at a busy waterfront intersection where ferries from Dartmouth unload—that ensures a constant lineup.

Serious coffee-lovers gravitate to **Just Us!** (1678 Barrington St., 902/422-5651; Mon.–Fri. 7:30 A.M.–5:30 P.M., Sat. 9 A.M.–5:30 P.M.,

dining along the downtown waterfront

© ANDREW HEMPSTEAD

BOOTHS AND BURGERS

Beyond the white linens and perfectly presented seafood of Halifax's finer restaurants are a smattering of old-style diners. The following are my favorites – one downtown, another overlooking the city's most notorious intersection, and another handy for those traveling into downtown from the north.

In the heart of the central business district, the venerable **Bluenose II** (1824 Hollis St., 902/425-5092; daily from 7 A.M.) is named for the famous schooner that calls Halifax home on a part-time basis. The booths fill with an eclectic crowd of locals for breakfast, but the space is bright and welcoming, meaning many regulars are families. Eggs Benedict is $7.50, steak and eggs $8.50, while the rest of the day choices vary from a lobster sandwich ($10) to Greek specialties ($9-14).

Overlooking the confusing-even-for-the-locals Armdale Rotary is **Armview Restaurant** (7156 Chebucto Rd., 902/455-4395; Mon.-Sat. from 7 A.M., Sun. from 9 A.M.), an old-style breakfast and lunch spot where everything is less than $10. Cooked breakfasts are from $6.50 and burgers from $2.80.

On Monday, Tuesday, and Wednesday, coupon-clipping retirees fill **Esquire Restaurant** (772 Bedford Hwy., 902/835-9033; daily 7 A.M.-9 P.M.) for specials such as home-style pork dinners for $6. It's across from the Bedford Basin, and there's plenty of parking, or, if you're staying across the road at the Esquire Motel, you need only to negotiate traffic zooming along the busy Bedford Highway.

and comfortable couches inside, but it's the coffee that shines—as good as it gets in Halifax.

At ◖ **Paper Chase News Café** (5228 Blowers St., 902/423-0750; Mon.–Thurs. 8 A.M.–8 P.M., Fri.–Sat. 8 A.M.–9 P.M., Sun. 9 A.M.–8 P.M.), a narrow stairway leads upstairs to a funky space where windows roll up garage door–style and seating spreads from one side of the building to the other, with a split level and slightly arty decor in between. The food is remarkably inexpensive; scrambled eggs and toast is $5, a Swiss melt is $4.75, and vegetarian lasagna is $4.50. The café also has Internet access.

Off to one side of the reception area for the Art Gallery of Nova Scotia, ◖ **Cheapside Café** (1723 Hollis St., 902/425-4494; Tues.–Sat. 10 A.M.–5 P.M.) is not named for the prices, but rather for a historic designation for the cobbled area out front where vendors once peddled their wares. Fittingly, the room itself is a work of art, decorated with colorful paintings that hang on bright orange walls. Lunches such as warm Thai chicken salad and seared salmon on coconut-drizzled spinach range $10–14, or stop by for just a coffee and a generous slab of raspberry mousse torte ($7).

On the south side of downtown, **Trident** (1256 Hollis St., 902/423-7100; Mon.–Fri. 8 A.M.–5 P.M., Sat. 8:30 A.M.–5 P.M., Sun. 11 A.M.–5 P.M.) is a secondhand bookstore on one side and an old-fashioned café with leather-backed chairs on the other—the perfect place to relax with a newly bought literary treasure.

Harbourside Market

Multiple dining choices and food-court seating that spreads outside onto the adjacent wharf make Harbourside Market, at the waterfront end of the Privateers Warehouse along Lower Water Street, the perfect place for lunch on the run or a casual dinner. At the ◖ **Captain John's** (902/420-9255, daily lunch and dinner) outlet, order fish-and-chips (from $10), a huge plate of steamed mussels to share ($10), or the grilled fish special of the day (around $13).

Brisket Boardwalk Deli (902/423-7625) and **Loaf, Leaf N Ladle** (902/422-1137) both

Sun. 10 A.M.–5 P.M.), which does an admirable job of sourcing fair-trade coffee from Mexico.

If you take a walk south along the harborfront, ◖ **Caffe Ristretto** (1475 Lower Water St., 902/425-3087; daily 7 A.M.–10 P.M.), tucked into the back of Bishop's Landing, is a good turnaround point. It has a few outdoor tables, make sandwiches and wraps to order, with the latter open daily at 8 A.M. for breakfast.

Tucked into a corner of the market is **John Shippey Brewing Company** (902/423-7386), a microbrewery (look up in the rafters to see the brew tanks) pouring traditional English ales.

Seafood Along the Waterfront

While **Captain John's** in the Harbourside Market is a good choice for inexpensive seafood in a food-court setting, the following places are excellent choices for a sit-down meal with water views. Whereas other downtown restaurants have spotty weekend openings, you'll find each of the following open every day for lunch and dinner.

In the Historic Properties, **Salty's** (1869 Lower Water St., 902/423-6818) mixes seafood with succulent meat dishes in a sublime setting. But first, kick back with a margarita and watch the boats sail in and out of the harbor. Then sit indoors or out to enjoy some of the city's best food in a casual atmosphere. And don't miss the scrumptious desserts.

Just north of Salty's, diners at **Murphy's on the Water** (1751 Lower Water St., 902/420-1015) also enjoy panoramic harbor views. This restaurant fills a converted warehouse, with outside tables at the end of the pier. Naturally, the emphasis is on seafood, with lunches starting at around $12 and rising to $17 for a lobster sandwich. Dinner mains range $18–32, or share the impressive Taste of Nova Scotia platter for $70.

Continue south along the harborfront to **Waterfront Warehouse** (1549 Lower Water St., 902/425-7610; May–Oct. daily for lunch and dinner), which is exactly that—a converted waterfront warehouse where tugboats were once repaired. The setting is more upscale than you might imagine from the outside, with white linens, nautical-themed furnishings, and an oversized fireplace. The seafood chowder ($12) is a hearty starter while seafood-oriented mains ($22–32) include bouillabaisse served in an iron pot and the signature dish—maple-glazed salmon grilled on a cedar plank.

Other Seafood Restaurants

(5 Fishermen (1740 Argyle St., 902/422-4421, daily lunch and dinner) occupies one of Halifax's oldest buildings—it was built in 1816 and once used by famed governess Anna Leonowens (of *Anna and the King* fame) for her Victorian School of Art and Design. The restaurant is popular with seafood-loving Haligonians for its 68-dish menu, which includes swordfish, Louisiana shrimp, Malpeque oysters, and Digby scallops, as well as chicken and Alberta steaks. All entrées ($35–50) come with all-you-can-eat mussels, steamed clams, and salad bar at no extra charge.

Pub Dining

Pogue Fado (1581 Barrington St., 902/429-6222; daily from 11 A.M.) is Irish in more than name only. The long and narrow room with a couple of sidewalk tables out front offers a menu that includes traditional treats such as Tipperary chicken caudle (chicken stew served

© ANDREW HEMPSTEAD

5 Fishermen is one of Halifax's better seafood restaurants.

on a bed of mashed potato), Guinness steak pie, and cottage pie. Almost everything except the steak is under $10.

Tug's Pub (Waterfront Warehouse, 1549 Lower Water St., 902/425-7610; daily 11:30 A.M.–midnight) is a comfortable place for a pint of ale before heading to the adjacent restaurant, but the food in the pub itself is excellent, including warm crab dip ($9) and maple-glazed salmon cooked on a cedar plank ($19).

It's a little away from the tourist precinct, but the (**Granite Brewery** (1662 Barrington St., 902/422-4954; daily from 11 A.M.) offers some excellent food. Melt-in-your-mouth baby back ribs ($21 with Caesar salad) are a house specialty, or choose healthy options such as a salmon baked in crushed cashews ($20). On Sunday 11 A.M.–3 P.M. you can indulge in an all-you-can-eat brunch for $12 or tasty treats such as a smoked salmon and goat cheese omelet for $10.

Bistros

Affiliated with the excellent Cheapside Café, **Sweet Basil Bistro** (1866 Upper Water St., 902/425-2133; daily 11:30 A.M.–9 P.M.) serves fresh and flavorful cooking in a casual and cheerful room—basically everything that a bistro should be. You could start with seared Digby scallops on an avocado salad, move on to walnut-crusted chicken breast stuffed with gorgonzola and pear and basil cream, and then finish with blueberry cheesecake. Dinner starters are mostly under $12, mains range $16–28, and all desserts are $8. Unusually, the lunch menu is not simply a recycled version of dinner, with dishes such as shrimp pad thai for $9–16.50.

(**Chives Canadian Bistro** (1537 Barrington St., 902/420-9626; daily 5–9:30 P.M.) is well worth searching out, and even though it's away from the touristy waterfront, you'll need a reservation. The menu revolves around seasonal ingredients and produce sourced from throughout Nova Scotia. Add immaculate presentation to fresh and healthy cooking styles, and you have a meal

to remember. Mains such as lamb shepherd's pie range $19–26 and desserts such as buttered rhubarb cake are under $10.

A Halifax Original

The stretch of Argyle Street between Sackville and Blowers Streets has emerged as a dining hotspot, with the utterly original (**Economy Shoe Shop** (1663 Argyle St., 902/423-8845; daily 11 A.M.–2 A.M.) anchoring the strip. The unusual name originated when one of the owners was starting out in the restaurant business; with little cash to spare, he found an old neon sign bearing the name and hung it out front. The original space has grown to encompass three very different restaurants and a bar—one a bohemian-themed space, another a glass-roofed room enclosing a jungle of rainforest that adds a tropical vibe even in the dead of winter. On offer is everything from run-of-the-mill hamburgers ($6) to baked halibut and scallop mornay ($18). Throw entertaining servers into the mix and you get a unique dining experience without spending a fortune.

Steakhouse

For carnivorous cravings, prepare to splurge at **Ryan Duffy's** (1650 Bedford Row, 902/421-1116; Mon.–Sat. lunch, daily dinner). Some cuts, such as the signature strip loin, are wheeled to your table by a waitperson wielding a carving knife who asks how much of the loin you'd like before carving the cut and telling you the price (around $30 for an average-size serving). Back in the kitchen it is cooked exactly the way you ordered it over charcoal coals. American visitors will be pleased to know that the better cuts come from corn-fed steers raised south of the Canadian border, with prices topping out at $75 for the tomahawk steak. As in many upscale steakhouses, you'll be charged extra for accompanying vegetables.

Italian

Pasta is a ubiquitous and usually bland choice

on menus throughout North America, but to taste the real thing, you need to find a truly traditional Italian restaurant. Downtown Halifax has two such choices.

Da Maurizio (1496 Lower Water St., 902/423-0859; Mon.–Sat. 5–10 P.M.) is the most upscale of the two. In the historic brewery building, the character-filled room is decorated in mellow hues, its walls lined with Italian art, the wine rack filled with thoughtfully selected bottles from around the world, and the linen-draped tables highlighted by vases of fresh flowers. The menu represents the best of northern Italian cooking, with mains such as veal delicately sautéed with lobster in a tomato and sherry base topping out at $33.

Among a strip of restaurants with outdoor tables, **Piccolo Mondo** (1580 Argyle St., 902/429-0080; daily for lunch and dinner) is casual Italian dining at its best. Pasta is made in-house every morning and, when combined with local seafood such as calamari or shrimp, is divine. Expect to pay up to $15 for a lunchtime main and $24–31 in the evening.

Asian

Halifax doesn't have a concentration of Asian restaurants, but throughout downtown you'll find a smattering of good choices. One of the best is **Cheelin** (1496 Lower Water St., 902/422-2252; Mon.–Sat. 11:30 A.M.–2:30 P.M. and Tues.–Sun. 5:30–10 P.M.), within the Alexander Keith's Brewery complex. The atmosphere is informal, with chefs in an open kitchen churning out flavorful Chinese favorites in the $12–18 range. The seafood-stuffed eggplant is a unique treat.

Hamachi Steakhouse (Bishop's Landing, 1477 Lower Water St., 902/422-1600; daily lunch and dinner) is a contemporary Japanese restaurant specializing in *teppan* cooking. In the center of communal tables are grills where chefs slice, dice, and then grill your choice of beef, chicken, or seafood main ($24–38) as you sample starters such as *niku balu*

(tenderloin meatballs with pineapple chili dipping sauce). For dessert, the Mount Fuji (a combination of brownie, ice cream, cream, and chocolate sauce) is an easy choice.

SPRING GARDEN ROAD

This restaurant-lined thoroughfare begins at Barrington Street and heads uphill past the main library and the Sexton Campus of Dalhousie University to the Public Gardens. Downstairs in **Spring Garden Place** is one of the city's better food courts.

Cafés

The Canadian coffeehouse chain **Second Cup** has a popular location here (5425 Spring Garden Rd., 902/429-0883; daily 6:30 A.M.–11 P.M.) with comfortable couches and wireless Internet access.

At the other end of the food-filled strip, opposite the Lord Nelson Hotel, is **Daily Grind** (5686 Spring Garden Rd., 902/429-6397; Mon.–Fri. 7 A.M.–10 P.M., Sat.–Sun. 8 A.M.–10 P.M.), tucked away in the back corner of a newsagent. Cooked breakfasts are small, but sandwiches, hot dishes such as lasagna, and muffins are all delicious and inexpensive.

Delis

One block off Spring Garden Road at its downtown end, **Italian Gourmet** (5431 Doyle St., 902/423-7880; Mon.–Sat. 9 A.M.–7 P.M., Sun. 10 A.M.–5 P.M.) is an absolute delight. Along one side is a deli counter with premade dishes while another side is home to the desserts and drinks. In between, the shelves are lined with goodies imported from around the world. But back to the counters, where you choose from cabbage rolls, quiche, meatloaf meatballs, sun-dried tomato–crusted chicken breasts, smoked salmon pâté, and more. Prices are reasonable (less than $10 for lunch) and there are tables inside and out.

Restaurants

Your Father's Moustache (5686 Spring Garden Rd., 902/423-6766) is a casual favorite with a reasonably priced menu of seafood, steaks, and pasta. It's open year-round daily for lunch and dinner, and a popular brunch is served Sunday 11 A.M.–3 P.M.

My favorite Indian restaurant in Halifax is **Curry Village** (5677 Brenton Pl., 902/429-5010; Mon.–Sat. lunch, daily dinner), which prepares chicken tandoori, *biryanis,* lamb *vindaloo,* and other Indian dishes to order for around $15. It's just off Spring Garden Road at the Public Gardens end.

For no-frills Japanese and Korean cooking at reasonable prices, consider a meal at **Minato Sushi** (1520 Queen St., 902/420-0331; Mon.–Sat. 11:30 A.M.–9:30 P.M.). Dishes such as sautéed scallops and mushrooms in a butter sauce are all under $15 and *bulkokee* (a sweet beef teriyaki), the unofficial national dish of Korea, is $16.

DARTMOUTH AND VICINITY
From **MacAskill's** (88 Alderney Dr., 902/466-3100; Mon.–Fri. 11:30 A.M.–2 P.M., Mon.–Sat. 5–10 P.M.), views extend back across Halifax Harbour to downtown, a real treat when the night lights of downtown are sparkling across the water. The menu is dominated by simple yet stylish seafood dishes, all reasonably priced (some under $20) and well presented. The seafood Cajun sampler is a good starter to share while the pan-fried haddock ($17) is a tasty yet inexpensive main. MacAskill's is on the upper floor of the Alderney Gate complex, where ferries from Halifax terminate. With ferries running until midnight, there's plenty of time to enjoy a meal before returning to your downtown accommodation.

Fisherman's Cove
At this historic fishing village, two kilometers southeast of Dartmouth alongside the Eastern Passage, it's no surprise that seafood dominates local menus. The most obvious place to eat is **Boondocks** (200 Government Wharf Rd., 902/465-3474; daily lunch and dinner), a big red-roofed building with a pleasant oceanfront patio. The menu offers the usual collection of seafood, including pan-seared halibut and chips for $18 and a rich lobster stew for $16. For a more authentic atmosphere, continue to smaller places such as **Fish Basket** (100 Government Wharf Rd., 902/465-5902), which is primarily in business selling fresh seafood, but which also sells lobster sandwiches for $8.50. **Wayne's World Lobster** (Government Wharf Rd., 902/465-6686) is a larger seafood shop, with fresh lobster, crab, scallops, clams, mussels, halibut, and salmon—perfect if you have cooking facilities at your accommodation. **Sea Gulps** (18 Government Wharf Rd., 902/461-8007; May daily 10 A.M.–5 P.M., June–Sept. daily 10 A.M.–8 P.M.) is a friendly little coffee shop set among the fishing shacks.

Information and Services

As always when traveling, do as much research as you can before leaving home. **Tourism Nova Scotia** (902/425-5781 or 800/565-0000, www.novascotia.com) is a wealth of information, and it sends out free information packs and maps on request. For information specific to Halifax, contact **Destination Halifax** (902/422-9334 or 877/422-9334, www.destinationhalifax.com). The **Halifax Regional Municipality** website (www.halifaxinfo.com) has general information about the city, such as festivals and events, transportation, and park programs.

INFORMATION CENTERS
Downtown
Make your first stop the **Halifax Visitor Centre** (1598 Argyle St., 902/490-5946; daily 9 A.M.–6 P.M., the rest of the year daily, but shorter hours), a few blocks up from the waterfront but still central to many attractions.

Tourism Nova Scotia operates an information center along the downtown waterfront at Sackville Landing (1655 Lower Water St., 902/424-4248; daily 8:30 A.M.–6 P.M.). Its shelves are filled with provincewide information, so this is the place to get help planning your travels beyond the capital.

Fisherman's Cove
Along the Eastern Passage, two kilometers southeast of downtown Dartmouth, **Fisherman's Cove Visitor Information Centre** (30 Government Wharf Rd., 902/465-8009, www.fishermanscove.ns.ca; mid-May–mid-Oct. daily 9 A.M.–6 P.M.) has information on the historic fishing village, as well as general Halifax information.

Airport
After retrieving your bags from the luggage carousels, you'll pass right by the **Airport**

Visitor Information Centre (902/873-1223; daily 9 A.M.–9 P.M.), which is a provincially operated facility. Most questions thrown its way relate to Halifax, but the center represents the entire province.

BOOKS AND BOOKSTORES
Libraries
Halifax Public Libraries (www.halifaxpubliclibraries.ca) has 14 branches across the city. The largest and most central is **Spring Garden Road Memorial Public Library** (5381 Spring Garden Rd., 902/490-5700; Tues.–Thurs. 10 A.M.–9 P.M., Fri.–Sat. 10 A.M.–5 P.M., and outside of summer Sun. 2–5 P.M.), which has a pleasant tree-shaded park out front. Inside, you'll find more than 280,000 volumes, historical documents, newspapers from around the world, magazines from around North America, and free Internet access.

General Bookstores and Maps
In the Historic Properties, **Maps and Ducks** (1869 Upper Water St., 902/422-7106; daily 10 A.M.–9 P.M.) has a wide range of antique maps, globes, nautical charts, road atlases, guidebooks, and specialty travel guides. As the name suggests, it also has ducks, as in duck decoys.

Upstairs in the Park Lane Mall, **Frog Hollow Books** (5640 Spring Garden Rd., 902/429-3318) is a comfortable store that occasionally hosts visiting literati. A few doors farther from downtown is **Bookmark** (5686 Spring Garden Rd., 902/423-0419), a small independent with a solid collection of Nova Scotian reading.

The **Trail Shop** (6210 Quinpool Rd., 902/423-8736, Mon.–Wed. 9 A.M.–6 P.M., Thurs.–Fri. to 9 P.M.) is an outdoor sports shop with a wide selection of maps. **Binnacle** (15 Purcell's Cove Rd., 902/423-6464) specializes in nautical charts.

Secondhand Bookstores

John W. Doull (1684 Barrington St., 902/429-1652, www.doullbooks.com; Mon.–Tues. 9:30 A.M.–6 P.M., Wed.–Fri. 9:30 A.M.–9 P.M., Sat. 10 A.M.–5 P.M.) is the most centrally located of Halifax's secondhand bookstores. Its shelves are literally stocked to the ceiling, making finding specific titles difficult.

Schooner Books (5378 Inglis St., 902/423-8419, www.schoonerbooks.com; Mon.–Thurs. 9:30 A.M.–6 P.M., Fri. 9:30 A.M.–9 P.M., Sat. 9:30 A.M.–5 P.M.) fills two stories of a converted Victorian-era home off Barrington Street. Specialties include Atlantic Canada history and literature, early Canadiana, and Canadian art.

At the south end of downtown, **Trident** (1256 Hollis St., 902/423-7100; Mon.–Fri. 8 A.M.–5 P.M., Sat. 8:30 A.M.–5 P.M., Sun. 11 A.M.–5 P.M.) is stacked from floor to ceiling with everything from 1970s best-selling romances to titles that will have political historians salivating.

Media

The daily *Halifax Herald* circulates throughout the province and *Coast* is a free arts and entertainment weekly.

EMERGENCY SERVICES

The city's hospital services are coordinated under the auspices of the **Queen Elizabeth II Hospital** (1796 Summer St., 902/473-3383).

Municipal **police** are assigned to Halifax and Dartmouth; in emergencies, dial 911, and for nonemergency business call 902/490-5026. The **RCMP** can be reached by calling 911 or 902/426-1323.

ACCESS FOR TRAVELERS WITH DISABILITIES

The good news about Halifax specifically is that the major attractions as well as a small percentage of rooms in most major hotels are wheelchair-accessible. Theaters and performing arts venues are also usually wheelchair-accessible. Halifax's public transit system, Metro Transit, has low-floor buses along all major routes as well as the **Access-A-Bus** program, providing wheelchair-accessible transportation on a door-to-door basis. Register at 902/490-6681.

MONEY AND COMMUNICATIONS

Banks

As Nova Scotia's capital, Halifax has banks by the dozens. **Scotiabank** has nine city branches and does not charge to convert foreign currency to Canadian dollars. The fee for cashing traveler's checks is $2, so it pays to convert several checks at one time. Branches are open Monday–Wednesday and Saturday 10 A.M.–3 P.M., Thursday–Friday until 5 P.M.

Hotel desks also exchange currency, but rates are more favorable at the banks.

Postal Services

The city has three post offices open Monday–Friday 8 A.M.–5 P.M., including the General Post Office (1680 Bedford Row, 902/494-4734); branches are at 6175 Almon Street and 1969 Upper Water Street.

Public Internet Access

Internet access is free at the **Spring Garden Road Memorial Public Library** (5381 Spring Garden Rd., 902/490-5700; Tues.–Thurs. 10 A.M.–9 P.M., Fri.–Sat. 10 A.M.–5 P.M., and outside of summer Sun. 2–5 P.M.), as well as at other city libraries, but you may have to wait for a terminal. Right downtown, **Ceilidh Connection** (1672 Barrington St., 902/422-9800; Mon.–Fri. 10 A.M.–10 P.M., Sat.–Sun. noon–8 P.M.) charges around $10 per hour for access. **Paper Chase** (5228 Blowers St., 902/423-0750; Mon.–Thurs. 8 A.M.–8 P.M., Fri.–Sat. 8 A.M.–9 P.M., Sun. 9 A.M.–8 P.M.) combines public Internet access with good-value healthy food.

The **Community Access Program (CAP)**

provides free Internet access to members of the public across Nova Scotia. To find out addresses and hours of the 30-odd locations within Halifax call 866/569-8428 or go to www.hrca.ns.ca.

PHOTOGRAPHY

General photography shops are plentiful throughout downtown and are all up on digital technology, allowing you to print from memory cards or transfer your images to compact disc. Reliable equipment and hard-to-find films are stocked at **Carsand-Mosher Photographic** (1559 Barrington St., 902/421-

1980). **Camera Repair Centre** (2342 Hunter St., 902/423-6450; Mon.–Fri. 9 A.M.–5 P.M.) handles repairs.

LAUNDRIES

You'll find coin-operated laundries around the fringes of downtown. These include **Murphy's Laundromat** (corner North and Robie Sts., 902/454-6294) and **Spin and Tumble** (1022 Barrington St., 902/422-8099).

Bluenose Laundromat (2198 Windsor St., 902/422-7098; Mon.–Sat. 7:30 A.M.–7:30 P.M.) will wash, dry, and fold your clothes with same-day service.

Getting There

AIR

Halifax International Airport (YHZ) is beside Highway 102, 38 kilometers north of Halifax. It is Atlantic Canada's busiest airport, handling more than 3.4 million passengers annually.

The airport is easy to navigate on foot. Beside the baggage carousels is the **Nova Scotia Visitor Information Centre** (902/873-1223; daily 9 A.M.–9 P.M.), which helps out with all the usual tourist information and maps. Beyond this point are the car-rental desks and an information counter specifically for helping out with airport transportation. The arrivals area is linked to the rest of the terminal by a short concourse. In between is the main concentration of food and retail shops, including a currency exchange (daily 7 A.M.–9 P.M.); **Clearwater Seafood,** which plucks live lobsters from a tank and packs them for air travel; a bookstore; and a variety of souvenir shops. There are also a play area and wireless Internet hotspots.

The Halifax International Airport Authority operates two websites: www.hiaa.ca has lots of information about the airport itself, while www.flyhalifax.com has general travel-planning information, as well as a nifty virtual

flight map that tracks flights in real time as they arrive and depart from Halifax.

Airport Transportation

The **Airporter** (902/873-2091) runs between the airport and major downtown hotels ($18 one-way) 1–2 times every hour between 5 A.M. and 1 A.M. You need reservations only when returning to the airport from your hotel.

Taxi and limousine services are available curbside in the Domestic Arrivals area for all arriving flights. A one-way trip to Halifax city center is $53 by taxi or limousine.

Airport Car Rental

Once you've picked up your bags from the baggage carousels, you'll find a row of check-in desks for major car-rental companies immediately behind you. Airport phone numbers are: **Avis** (902/429-0963), **Budget** (902/492-7551), **Enterprise** (902/873-4700), **Hertz** (902/873-2273), **National/Alamo** (902/873-3505), and **Thrifty** (902/873-3527). **Discount** (902/468-7171) operates out of a nearby motel; call for a pickup upon arrival.

Along the airport access road is **Petro Canada,** perfect for ensuring that you are not hit with outrageous charges for not returning the vehicle with a full tank of gas.

Parking

Short-term airport parking within walking distance of the terminal costs $3 per hour to a maximum of $12 per day and $70 per week. For long-term parking, nearby **Park'N Fly** (668 Barnes Dr., 902/873-4574, www .parknfly.ca) charges $9 per day and $43 per week, inclusive of a free ride to and from the airport. (Check the Park'N Fly website for a discount coupon.)

RAIL

Halifax is served by **VIA Rail** (416/366-8411 or 888/842-7245, www.viarail.ca) passenger trains from Montréal.

The **VIA Rail Station** is one kilometer south of downtown at the corner of Barrington and Cornwallis Streets. It's a classic old terminal, with a colonnaded facade, high ceiling, and tiled floors, but it is only ever busy when a train rolls in. **Hertz** has a desk at the terminal, and a concourse links the terminal to the grand Westin hotel.

BUS

Long-distance bus services arrive and depart from the **VIA Rail Station** (corner of Barrington and Cornwallis Sts.), one kilometer south of downtown and within walking distance of HI–Halifax. The main carrier is **Acadian Lines** (902/454-9321 or 800/567-5151, www.smtbus.com), which has departures from Halifax to points throughout the province and beyond. Acadian Lines services run as far as Montréal, Toronto, and Bangor, Maine, from where connections can be made to Greyhound buses.

Getting Around

PUBLIC TRANSPORTATION

Metro Transit (902/490-4000, www.halifax .ca/metrotransit) buses saturate city streets, charge adult $2, senior and child $1.40 (exact change only) with free transfers, and operate daily 6 A.M.–midnight. Main bus stops are on Water, Barrington, Cornwallis, Cogswell, and Duke Streets, Spring Garden Road, and Gottingen Street, with service to Quinpool Road and Bayers Street. If you're at a stop waiting for a bus, dial 465 followed by the four-digit route number (marked in red at every stop) for real-time information on when the next bus will be arriving.

FRED (an acronym for "Free Rides Everywhere Downtown") is a free July–late October bus service that makes 18 stops on a circuit that begins northbound along Lower Water Street and then heads along Barrington Street and Spring Garden Road before returning to Water Street on South Street.

Ferries

Metro Transit runs the **Halifax-Dartmouth ferry** from the foot of George Street (beside Historic Properties) to Alderney Drive in Dartmouth. It is the oldest saltwater passenger service in North America, having transported its first passengers by rowboat more than 200 years ago. Today, three modern vessels ply the route in just 12 minutes. The service runs year-round, Monday–Saturday 6:30 A.M.–midnight, and June–September on Sunday, same hours. The one-way fare is the same as by bus—adult $2, senior and child $1.40.

Taxi

Cabs are easiest to flag outside major hotels

and Dartmouth, the A. Murray MacKay and the Angus L. MacDonald; the toll is $0.75 one-way for vehicles, free for bicyclists and pedestrians.

Downtown Parking

Metered parking costs $1 per 30 minutes but is difficult to find during business hours. Most major hotels have underground public parking, and a few multistory parking lots are scattered throughout the city core. The most convenient parking lots are along Lower Water Street, at the foot of Prince and Salter Streets, but these are also the most costly ($5 per hour). If you're staying at a downtown hotel, expect to pay up to $24 per day for parking (ask about free parking for weekend reservations).

The ferry trip between downtown and Dartmouth makes for an inexpensive harbor cruise.

© ANDREW HEMPSTEAD

or transportation hubs, such as the VIA Rail Station. All rides start at $2.75, with an additional $2.25 charged for each mile plus $0.50 for each additional person. Taxi fares within downtown usually run under $8 while the trip between the airport and downtown is set at $53. Major companies include: **Airport Taxi** (902/455-2232), **Co-op Taxi** (902/444-0001), **Halifax Taxi** (902/877-0404), and **Yellow Cab** (902/420-0000).

DRIVING

Getting into the city is made easy by a number of major arteries that spill right into downtown. Once in the commercial core, Haligonians are painstakingly careful and slow drivers—a wise way to go as hillside streets are steep, and many roads are posted for one-way traffic. Pedestrians have the right-of-way on crosswalks. Two **bridges** link Halifax

DRIVING IN HALIFAX

The compactness of downtown Halifax means driving is not essential. If you're planning to spend a few days in the capital before heading out to explore the rest of the province, delay renting a vehicle and plan to explore the city on foot.

If you do plan to drive, the good news is that locals are remarkably accommodating to other drivers – allowing others to merge, stopping for pedestrians even where no crosswalk exists, and generally keeping to the speed limits. The most confusing meeting of roads is the **Armdale Rotary,** a large traffic circle west of downtown along Quinpool Road. Officially now a roundabout (meaning that vehicles on the circle have right of way over those joining the flow), locals continue to alternate and ignore the traffic lights, creating an intimidating intersection that is remarkably simple to use – although it may not seem so at first glance.

Car Rental

Each of the major car-rental companies is represented at the airport and downtown. As always, book as far in advance as possible, and use the Internet to find the best deals. Vehicles rented from downtown are generally the same price as out at the airport, but the final bill comes with fewer taxes.

SOUTH SHORE

Nova Scotians must have had this region in mind when they coined the province's motto, "So Much to Sea." The crashing Atlantic lays itself out in foaming breakers along the deeply scored Atlantic coastline that extends from Lunenburg to Yarmouth. It's a three-hour drive between these two towns, but you'll want at least two days and preferably more to explore the hidden corners of this quintessential corner of Nova Scotia. The seaports and towns follow one another, like a series of glossy, life-size picture postcards. There are those that outsiders will know by name—Peggy's Cove, Mahone Bay, and Lunenburg—but one of the joys of touring the South Shore is discovering your own Peggy's Cove (and I give you some ideas throughout this chapter).

The South Shore ends at Yarmouth, where the Atlantic meets the Bay of Fundy. Locals say the Vikings came ashore a thousand years ago and inscribed the boulder that now sits at the Yarmouth County Museum's front door. Yarmouth's ragged coastline impressed early explorer Samuel de Champlain, who named the seaport's outermost peninsula Cap Forchu ("Forked Cape"). Like the Vikings, Champlain arrived and departed, as do thousands of visitors who arrive on the ferries and quickly disperse on routes to distant provincial destinations. Their loss is the gain of the tourist who stays. Cyclists like to bike the Yarmouth area's backcountry coastal roads. At Chebogue Point south of the seaport, pink, purple, and white lupines bloom in June, and

HIGHLIGHTS

◖ Peggy's Cove: Nova Scotia's most famous village is a photogenic gem that you won't want to miss (page 66).

◖ The Churches of Mahone Bay: Lining up along the waterfront, three historic churches reflect across the waters of charming Mahone Bay (page 72).

◖ Classic Boat Festival: In early August, Mahone Bay fills with wooden boats and the interesting characters who build and sail them (page 73).

◖ Historic Downtown Lunenburg: Designated a World Heritage Site by UNESCO, Lunenburg is as interesting as it is charming (page 76).

◖ Blue Rocks: A world away from the crowds of Peggy's Cove, this picture-perfect fishing village clings to the shore of a rocky harbor (page 78).

◖ *Bluenose II:* Lunenburg is a wooden-ships kind of town, and what better way to tour the harbor than aboard one (page 78)?

◖ LaHave Islands: Just a short detour from the busy South Shore highway, these small islands are dotted with a colorful collection of cottages and cabins (page 84).

◖ Shelburne Historic District: A wonderful collection of 200-year-old wooden buildings brings the shipbuilding era to life (page 87).

LOOK FOR ◖ TO FIND RECOMMENDED SIGHTS, ACTIVITIES, DINING, AND LODGING.

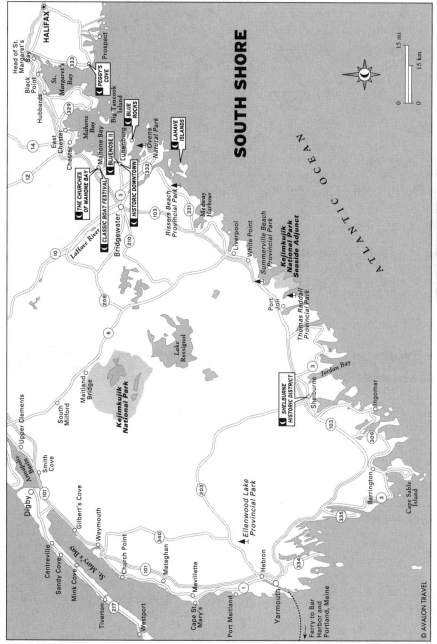

SOUTH SHORE

SOUTH SHORE

HALIFAX

Head of St. Margaret's Bay

Black Point

Prospect

Hubbards

St. Margaret's Bay

PEGGY'S COVE

East Chester

Mahone Bay

Big Tancook Island

BLUE ROCKS

Chester

Mahone Bay

THE CHURCHES OF MAHONE BAY

CLASSIC BOAT FESTIVAL

BLUENOSE II

Lunenburg

Ovens Natural Park

LAHAVE ISLANDS

HISTORIC DOWNTOWN

LaHave River

Bridgewater

Rissers Beach Provincial Park

Medway Harbour

ATLANTIC OCEAN

Liverpool

White Point

Summerville Beach Provincial Park

Kejimkujik National Park Seaside Adjunct

Port Joli

Thomas Raddall Provincial Park

Lake Rossignol

Maitland Bridge

Kejimkujik National Park

South Milford

Upper Clements

Smith Cove

Annapolis Basin

Digby

Shelburne

SHELBURNE HISTORIC DISTRICT

Jordan Bay

Ingomar

Gilbert's Cove

Weymouth

Centreville

Sandy Cove

Mink Cove

St. Mary's Bay

Tiverton

Westport

Church Point

Meteghan

Mavillette

Cape St. Mary's

Port Maitland

Yarmouth

Hebron

Barrington

Cape Sable Island

Ellenwood Lake Provincial Park

Ferry to Bar Harbor and Portland, Maine

15 mi

15 km

© AVALON TRAVEL

in summertime white-winged willets roam the marshes.

PLANNING YOUR TIME

It is possible to visit the best-known towns along this stretch of coast in a day and return to Halifax. But don't. More realistically, plan a day in each place that interests you. As elsewhere in Nova Scotia, dining at its best is superb, and the region's specialty is its abundance of top-notch country inns with public dining rooms. Many lodgings are in historic houses and mansions converted to country inns and in categories best described as better, best, and beautiful. But it is the towns themselves that are this region's highlight. Even with just one week to explore the entire province, plan to spend at least one night in **Mahone Bay** or **Lunenburg,** the former recognized for its three waterfront churches and the latter as a UNESCO World Heritage Site. While the detour to **Peggy's Cove** is almost de rigueur, you should work into your itinerary less publicized villages such as **Blue Rocks,** near Lunenburg. Taking part in two highlights of the South Shore involves some planning—Mahone Bay's **Classic Boat Festival** requires a visit in early August, while a sailing trip on the *Bluenose II* calls for reservations.

Travelers on a tight schedule make Lunenburg a turnaround point, but the rest of the South Shore is well worth exploring and sets you up for exploring the Fundy Coast. This stretch of coast is dotted with coastal provincial parks and hideaways such as the **LaHave Islands,** which a few hundred souls call home. The major historic attraction between Lunenburg and Yarmouth is **Shelburne Historic District.** If you are planning to circumnavigate southwestern Nova Scotia, or if you're arriving by ferry at Yarmouth from Maine, Shelburne is an ideal location for an overnight stay. Coupled with a night in Lunenburg or Mahone Bay, give yourself three days for the South Shore—not enough time to see everything, but a chance to spend quality time visiting each of the highlights.

Halifax to Mahone Bay

From downtown Halifax, it's 105 kilometers along Highway 103 to Lunenburg, but for the most scenic views and interesting insights, forget the expressway and drive the secondary coastal routes. The best-known village in all of Nova Scotia is Peggy's Cove, a 40-minute drive south from downtown Halifax along Highway 333. Meanwhile, Highway 103 takes a direct route across to St. Margaret's Bay, from where secondary Highway 3 passes the charming towns set around Mahone Bay and its islands. One of these, Oak Island, looms large in the world of treasure-hunting legends—pirates are believed to have buried incalculable booty on it in the 1500s.

◖ PEGGY'S COVE

Atlantic Canada's most photographed site is a 40-minute drive along Highway 333 southwest from Halifax, and the place is everything its fans say it is. With the houses of the tiny fishing village clinging like mussels to weathered granite boulders at the edge of St. Margaret's Bay, the Atlantic lathering against the boulder-bound coast, the fishing boats moored in the small cove, and the white octagonal lighthouse overlooking it all, the scene is the quintessence of the Nova Scotia coast.

Sightseers clog the village during the daytime (to miss the worst of the crowds, get there before 9 A.M. or after 5 P.M.), wandering along the wharves and around the weathered granite boulders surrounding the photogenic lighthouse. Peggy's Cove has a population of just 60 souls, so don't come expecting the services of a tourist town. The village has just one bed-and-breakfast, a restaurant, and the **deGarthe Gallery** (902/823-2256; mid-May–mid-Oct.

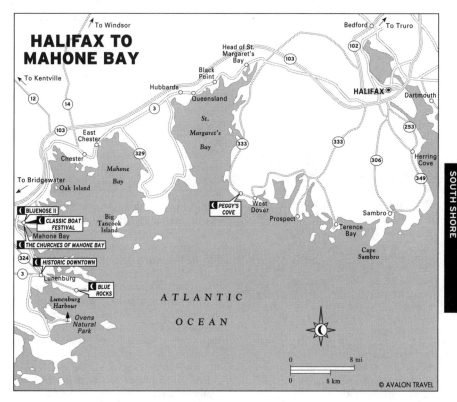

HALIFAX TO
MAHONE BAY

To Windsor
Bedford   To Truro
To Kentville
Head of St.
Margaret's
Bay
Black
Point
Hubbards
HALIFAX
Dartmouth
Queensland
St.
Margaret's
Bay
East
Chester
Chester
Mahone
Bay
Herring
Cove
To Bridgewater
Oak Island
PEGGY'S
COVE
West
Dover
Sambro
BLUENOSE II
Prospect
Terence
Bay
CLASSIC BOAT
FESTIVAL
Big
Tancook
Island
Mahone Bay
Cape
Sambro
THE CHURCHES OF MAHONE BAY
HISTORIC DOWNTOWN
Lunenburg
ATLANTIC
BLUE
ROCKS
Lunenburg
Harbour
OCEAN
Ovens
Natural
Park
0   8 mi
0   8 km
© AVALON TRAVEL

SOUTH SHORE

daily 9 A.M.–5 P.M.). The latter, along the main road through town, displays the work of well-known artist William deGarthe, whose stunning nautically themed oil paintings grace galleries the world over. Behind the gallery, deGarthe sculpted a 30-meter-long frieze on a granite outcropping. It depicts 32 of the seaside village's fishermen and families.

On a sad note, the town received worldwide attention in September 1998, when a Swissair MD-11 jetliner bound from New York City to Geneva crashed in shallow waters off the coast here, killing all 229 people aboard. A small memorial overlooks the ocean along Highway 333, two kilometers west of the village.

Accommodations

The only accommodation has just five guest rooms, so book well ahead if you'd like to stay overnight in this delightful village. At the head of the actual cove, **◖ Peggy's Cove Bed and Breakfast** (17 Church Rd., 902/823-2265 or 877/725-8732, www.peggyscovebb.com; $125–145 s or d including breakfast) has five well-furnished guest rooms with Wi-Fi Internet, a living area, a dining room, and a deck with magnificent views across the cove. It's open year-round; rates are discounted to $95–115 in winter.

Food

The road through the village ends at the **Sou'wester Restaurant** (178 Peggy's Point Rd., 902/823-2561; June–Sept. daily 8 A.M.–9 P.M., Oct.–May daily 9 A.M.–8 P.M.), a cavernous room with a menu designed to appeal to the tourist crowd. And as the only place in town to eat, attract them it does—try to

Peggy's Cove, just a short drive from Halifax, is the most famous of all Nova Scotian fishing villages.

plan your meal before 10 A.M. or after 5 P.M. The menu does have a distinct maritime flavor, with dishes such as fish cakes, pickled beets, and eggs offered in the morning.

Tours

If you are in Halifax without transportation, there are two options for visiting Peggy's Cove. **Peggy's Cove Express** (902/422-4200; June–Sept.) is a boat service that departs Halifax's Cable Wharf daily at 10 A.M. for the 2.5-hour run down the coast to Peggy's Cove and returns at 4:15 P.M. The fare is adult $70, senior $63, child $50, which includes a walking tour of the village. **Ambassatours** (902/423-6242 or 800/565-7173) offers a three-hour trip to Peggy's Cove (departs Halifax June–mid-Oct. daily at 12:30 P.M.) for adult $48, child $34.

PEGGY'S COVE TO CHESTER

Highway 333 beyond Peggy's Cove winds north past a string of small fishing villages before reaching Highway 3 (Highway 103, the divided highway along the South Shore, takes an inland route, so turn at the older Highway 3). Rather than places that you simply must stop, this route that lazily rounds St. Margaret's Bay is simply an enjoyable drive.

Grand View Motel and Cottages (Hwy. 3, Black Point, 902/857-9776 or 888/591-5122, www.grandviewmotelandcottages.com; May–mid-Nov.) occupies a prime waterfront location about eight kilometers from the Highway 333 intersection. The row of 10 motel rooms ($80–100 s or d) is well maintained and has windows looking out on the water. Three two-bedroom cottages ($165 s or d) are more spacious and have kitchens and decks. Outdoor furniture is set along the waterfront.

Continue west to **Hubbards,** where the **Trellis Café** (22 Main St., 902/857-1188; Mon.–Thurs. 9 A.M.–4 P.M., Fri.–Sun. 10 A.M.–9 P.M.) is a casual restaurant with colorful decor and occasional live entertainment on weekends. The namesake trellised deck is a good spot for lunch on warmer days. Most mains are less than $20, but you can spend less by ordering a combination of starters, such as fish chowder ($9) with fish cakes ($8).

Beyond Hubbards, **Queensland Beach** is a popular stretch of sand with safe but chilly swimming and a freshwater lagoon that attracts lots of birdlife.

CHESTER AND VICINITY

The bayside town of Chester, first settled by New Englanders in 1759, lies at the northern head of Mahone Bay, just off Highway 103 (take Exit 8). Its first hotel was built in 1827, and the town, with its ideal sailing conditions and many vacation homes, has been a popular summer retreat ever since. Getting oriented beyond the downtown core can be confusing, so start your visit at the **Tourist Information Centre** (Hwy. 3, 902/275-4616; May–early Oct. daily 10 A.M.–5 P.M.), which is on the Mahone Bay side of town (coming into town from Halifax, continue up the hill to the right of the downtown turnoff).

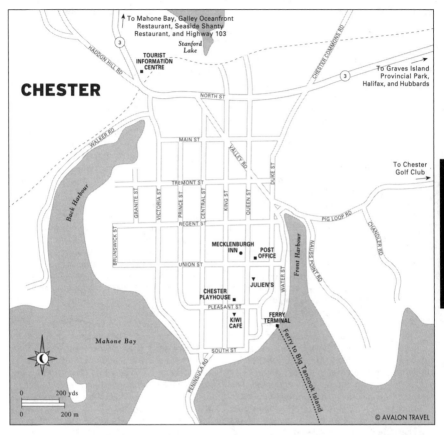

SOUTH SHORE

Sights and Recreation

Most visitors to Chester are content to browse through downtown shops and wander lazily along the Front Harbour waterfront.

An easy excursion is to **Big Tancook Island** (adult $5, vehicle $21 round-trip) via ferries departing regularly from Front Harbour. The islands are mostly residential, but it's a pleasant trip across and walking parks lace the island.

Dating to 1914, **Chester Golf Club** (Golf Course Rd., Prescott Point, 902/275-4543) is an old-style golf course that opens up along the oceanfront to give sweeping views on holes lapped by the water. Greens fees are a good value at $50.

Chester Playhouse (22 Pleasant St., 902/275-3933 or 800/363-7529, www.chesterplayhouse.ca) hosts some form of live entertainment weekly between March and December. Its Summer Theatre Festival draws professional talents in July and August. Past seasons have included musicals, Broadway-style revues, comedy improv, puppet shows, and children's programs.

Accommodations and Camping

The most noteworthy of Chester's inns is **C** **Mecklenburgh Inn** (78 Queen St., 902/275-4638, www.mecklenburghinn.ca; May–Dec.; $95–155 s or d), a 100-year-old sea captain's home that has been given a bohemian-chic look. Guests tend to gather on the wide veranda to watch the world of Chester go

THE MYSTERY OF OAK ISLAND

In 1795, on Oak Island, a small island in Mahone Bay, a young man came upon an area where the forest had been cut away. Besides the stumps, he found a large forked limb with an old tackle block and a "treenail," and the ground nearby was sunken in a pit. His first thought would have been buried treasure, as the bay was a known haunt for pirates such as "Captain" William Kidd, Sir Henry Morgan, and Edward "Blackbeard" Teach 100 years previously. After hours of digging, McGinnis and two farmer friends reached a depth of 10 feet and hit wood. It turned out, however, to be not the rotted lid of a treasure chest but rather a platform of logs. So the men pressed on, convinced that the treasure lay just below. At the depth of 25 feet, digging became difficult, and they halted.

The first organized dig occurred in 1804, when a boat loaded with equipment arrived. Along with McGinnis and his friends, another log platform was uncovered at the 30-foot level, others at 40 and then 50 feet from the surface. At 60 feet the men uncovered a layer of coconut fiber, which hinted at cargo from warmer climes. At the 90-foot level, a large slab of granite that was later verified as being from Europe was uncovered. The next morning, the men returned to the pit to find it had filled with water. Having no success pumping the water out, the search was abandoned until the following spring. In 1805 a second shaft was dug, and at the 100-foot mark a horizontal tunnel was dug in the hope of reaching the treasure, but the search was abandoned. It would be another 40 years before the next serious attempt was made to retrieve whatever lay deep below Oak Island. While the secondary shafts filled with water only when linked to the original pit, it had been noted that the level of water in all three shafts rose and fell with that of the tide. This deepened the mystery even further, but what the men found next amazed everyone present. Along the adjacent bay, just below the low-tide mark, were five drains that, it was later found, converged on a single tunnel. While it was understood that this simple manmade flooding system had been put in place after the treasure pit had been dug, this didn't help solve the mystery. Nor did it help the next round of investors, who spent the summer of 1863 in a futile attempt to reach below the 100-foot level, or the numerous other treasure seekers who attempted to get to the bottom of the pit during the next 140 years.

The saga has cost six lives, sent many investors broke, and created numerous feuds between island property owners. Two treasure hunters, Dan Blankenship and Fred Nolan, spent a combined 100 years trying to outsmart those who designed the "Money Pit" many centuries ago. In 2005, Blankenship, who had sole road access to the island via a causeway, sold his share of the island to the government of Nova Scotia in the hopes that it would be opened to tourism. Incredibly, one of the world's great mysteries and longest treasure hunts continues to this day.

by, and then after dinner at a local restaurant gravitate to the comfortable couches set around two fireplaces in the living room. Three of the four rooms have en suite bathrooms with clawfoot tubs while a fourth has a private bathroom down the hall. A big breakfast of pancakes or smoked salmon eggs Benedict will set you up for a day of sightseeing.

Signposted from Highway 3 three kilometers northeast of Chester, **Graves Island Provincial Park** (mid-May–mid-Sept.; $24)

covers a small island connected to the mainland by a causeway. An open area at a high point of the island allows for pull-through RVs while tent sites are scattered around the surrounding forest. If you're just visiting for the day, plan on a picnic at the waterfront day-use area just across the causeway.

Food

In downtown Chester, the **Kiwi Café** (19 Pleasant St., 902/275-1492) opens daily at

© ANDREW HEMPSTEAD

charming Chester

8:30 A.M. for simple healthy breakfasts and lunches along with a wide range of hot drinks, including chai tea and creamy hot chocolate. It's painted a cheery blue and kiwifruit green, with outside tables down one side. Around the corner and up the hill, **Julien's** (43 Queen St., 902/275-2324; Tues.–Sun. daily 8 A.M.–5 P.M.) serves delectable fresh breads, pastries, desserts, as well as more substantial healthy cooking.

Mahone Bay

The town of Mahone Bay (pop. 1,200), on the island-speckled bay of the same name, is one of the most charming in all of Nova Scotia. The town's prosperous past is mirrored in its architecture, with Gothic Revival, Classic Revival, and Italianate styles in evidence. Many of these buildings have been converted to restaurants specializing in seafood and shops selling the work of local artisans. The distinctive bayside trio of 19th-century churches reflected in the still water has become one of the most photographed scenes in Nova Scotia.

SIGHTS AND EVENTS

Most visitors to Mahone Bay are quite happy to spend their time admiring the architecture, browsing through the shops, and enjoying lunch at one of the many cafés. If you are interested in the town's architectural highlights, ask for the three walking-tour brochures at the museum.

Mahone Bay Settler's Museum

Inside a 150-year-old wooden house, this museum (578 Main St., 902/624-6263; June–early Sept. Tues.–Sat. 10 A.M.–5 P.M., Sun. 1–5 P.M.; donation) describes the town's 250-year history. One room is dedicated to settlement of the area in the mid-1700s by German, French, and Swiss Protestants and the story of how they were enticed by the British government's offer of free land, farm equipment, and a year's "victuals." You also learn about the importance of shipbuilding, which thrived in a dozen shipyards from the 1850s to the early part of last century, and you can admire historic arts and crafts.

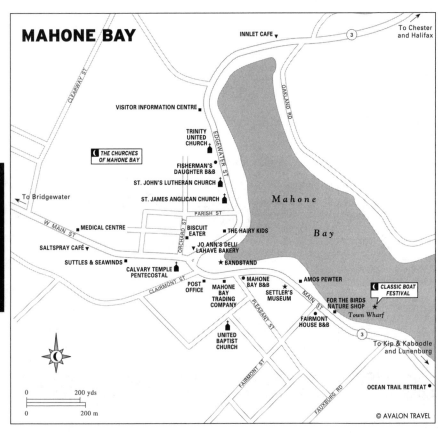

◖ The Churches of Mahone Bay

From the flower-bedecked bandstand on Main Street, three churches can be seen shoulder to shoulder across the water. The oldest (and farthest from this viewpoint) is the **Trinity United Church** (Edgewater St., 902/624-9287), which dates to 1861 and was dragged by oxen to its current site in 1885. **St. John's Lutheran** (Edgewater St., 902/624-9660) is a symmetrical wooden structure standing in the middle of the three. Right on the corner is the Gothic Revival **St. James Anglican Church** (Edgewater St., 902/624-8614). This is the only one of the three open for tours (July–Aug. Thurs.–Sat. 11 A.M.–3 P.M.).

Music at the Three Churches is a series of classical music concerts hosted by the churches on select Friday nights through summer. The cost is adult $15, child free. Visit www.threechurches.com or check with the information center for a schedule and pay at the door.

If you walk along the waterfront beyond the information center, you'll see a different angle on the churches, as well as two others. Completed in 1875, the white spire you see rising above the trees is the **United Baptist Church** (56 Maple St., 902/624-9124), open for services Sunday at 11 A.M. The **Calvary Temple Pentecostal** (at the traffic circle where Main and Edgewater Sts. meet, 902/624-8420) opens its doors Sunday at 7 P.M. for hymn singing.

© ANDREW HEMPSTEAD

Mahone Bay is famous for its photogenic churches.

〖 Classic Boat Festival

Mahone Bay's annual Classic Boat Festival (902/624-0348, www.mahonebayclassicboatfestival.org) centers on the Town Wharf the weekend closest to August 1. This annual event draws thousands of spectators, who gather to take part in workshops, marvel over boatbuilding demonstrations, listen to tales from the sea, and cheer on competitors in boat-race series that vary from classic old yachts to floating contraptions constructed in less than four hours. A parade of sail, live entertainment, and the re-creation of a boat-launching using oxen are other highlights. Best of all, everything is free.

SHOPPING

Many artists are attracted to Mahone Bay for its scenic setting, and the main street has developed into a hub for shoppers. Most shops are open from late spring to Christmas.

At **Amos Pewter** (589 Main St., 902/624-9547), you can watch artists at work as they cast, spin, and finish pewter pieces. **Mahone Bay Trading Company** (544 Main St.,

© ANDREW HEMPSTEAD

Plan on spending time browsing through the many shops along Mahone Bay's Main Street.

902/624-8425) is a large old-fashioned general store, but in keeping with the town's nautical feel, the sales clerks work from behind a boat-shaped counter. Tea connoisseurs will be in their element at the **Tea Brewery** (525 Main St., 902/624-0566) while birders are attracted to the **For the Birds Nature Shop** (647 Main St., 902/624-0784; closed Tues.), which sells binoculars, field guides, and related arts and crafts. Up the hill from the Tea Brewery, **Suttles and Seawinds** (466 Main St., 902/624-8375) sells stylish but colorful clothing. Even our four-legged friends aren't forgotten; **The Hairy Kids** (21 Edgewater St., 902/624-9097) is stocked with doggy fashions and treats.

ACCOMMODATIONS

Through summer, and especially on weekends, demand is high for a limited number of rooms, so plan accordingly and book as far in advance as possible.

Under $50

Mahone Bay is home to one of Nova Scotia's only privately operated backpacker lodges, ◖ **Kip and Kaboodle** (9466 Hwy. 3, Mader's Cove, 902/531-5494 or 866/549-4522, www .kiwikaboodle.com; $25 per person), which is three kilometers from the center of town toward Lunenburg. It's small, with facilities to match, but everything is well maintained, including a communal kitchen, living area, and outdoor pool. Other amenities include a barbecue and Wi-Fi Internet access. Rates include linen and a light breakfast.

$50-100

Opposite the Town Wharf, you can sit on the veranda of **Fairmont House B&B** (654 Main St., 902/624-8089, www.fairmonthouse .com; $85–150 s or d) and watch the world of Mahone Bay go by. A local shipbuilder built this Gothic Revival home in 1857, and it was converted to a bed-and-breakfast in 1991. In the ensuing years its exterior has been given a coat of stately blue paint, and three guest rooms have been outfitted in stylish colored

themes. All rooms have en suite bathrooms, air-conditioning, and niceties such as hair dryers and irons. Downstairs is a library with board games and a TV. Rates include a continental breakfast.

Set right in the shopping heart of town, **Mahone Bay B&B** (558 Main St., 902/624-6388; $75–120 s or d) is a bright-yellow two-story home with a wraparound veranda bedecked in gingerbread trim—in other words, impossible to miss. The building, dating to 1860, is filled with antiques. The four guest rooms have a distinct grandmotherly look, and a full breakfast is served in the grand dining room.

$100-150

Nestled amid the famous three churches is ◖ **Fisherman's Daughter B&B** (97 Edgewater St., 902/624-0483, www.fishermans-daughter.com; $100–125 s or d). Built in 1840 by a local shipbuilder, the home is understated but shows a restrained Gothic Revival style. A couple of the four guest rooms have funky layouts (such as beds nestled under the eaves), but this adds to the charm. Throw in a host of modern amenities and a full breakfast to make this place an excellent choice.

Two kilometers southeast of town toward Lunenburg, **Ocean Trail Retreat** (Hwy. 3, Mader's Cove, 902/624-8824 or 888/624-8824, www.oceantrailretreat.com; Apr.–Nov.) is set on a large grassed chunk of land that slopes down to the highway and Mahone Harbour. Two modern wings contain 17 motel-style rooms ($110–130 s or d) with big windows that take full advantage of the water views. Closer to the road are three two-bedroom chalets with full kitchens, living areas with propane fireplaces, and decks along the ocean-facing sides ($1,200 per week, but ask for nightly rates outside of summer). The outdoor heated pool is always a hit for families.

FOOD

Mahone Bay's main street is lined with cafés, but most close in the late afternoon.

Cafés

With a bag of carrots serving as a counter-weight on the front door, **[** **Jo Ann's Deli** (9 Edgewater St., 902/624-6305; late May–Oct. daily 9 A.M.–7 P.M.) is a welcoming food shop filled with goodies. Locals come for organic produce, but everyone comes out with something—gourmet sandwiches, filled bagels, oatmeal cakes, brownies, homemade jams and preserves, and more. If you're planning a picnic, this is the place to get everything together.

Of the many places to eat in the village, the **[** **Saltspray Café** (436 Main St., 902/624-9902; daily 7:30 A.M.–6 P.M.), uphill from the waterfront, stands out for value and quality. The café offers cooked breakfasts for less than $7, *including* bottomless cups of coffee. Chowder is a lunchtime mainstay, but also check the blackboard for daily specials. As you'd imagine, the Saltspray is perpetually busy.

Restaurant

More of a restaurant than a café, **[** **Innlet Cafe** (249 Edgewater St., 902/624-6363; daily 11:30 A.M.–9 P.M.) sits at the head of the bay, a 10-minute waterfront walk from downtown and with a classic view of all five Mahone Bay churches and tables on a stone patio perfect for warmer weather. Most mains are under $20, including Irish-inspired seafood stews and a wide range of fettuccini. Leave room for a slice of the delicious mud cake.

INFORMATION AND SERVICES

The **Visitor Information Centre** (Edgewater St., 902/624-6151; summer Mon.–Sat. 9 A.M.–5 P.M., Sun. 11 A.M.–5 P.M.) is in a small building just before you reach the first church.

The **post office** is at the corner of Main and Clairmont Streets. Also along Main Street is a grocery store, pharmacy, and bank, while up West Main Street is a small medical center and launderette. Opposite the gazebo is the town's lone gas station.

Check your email over a coffee, and then browse the collection of used books at **Biscuit Eater** (16 Orchard St., 902/624-2665; 8:30 A.M.–5:30 P.M., Sun. 11 A.M.–5 P.M.).

Lunenburg

Lunenburg (pop. 2,400) lies about equidistant between Halifax and Shelburne off Highway 103. Sited on a hilly peninsula between two harbors, this is one of the most attractive towns in Nova Scotia, with a wealth of beautiful homes painted in a crayon box of bold primary colors. In 1991 Lunenburg's Old Town was designated a national historic district, and in December 1995 the town received the ultimate honor when UNESCO designated it a World Heritage Site—one of only two cities in North America to enjoy that status (the other is Quebec City). More recently, in 2005, the provincial government stepped in and bought a chunk of waterfront buildings and wharves, saving them from development that would take away from the town's well-preserved history.

History

To understand what the fuss is all about, you have to go back in time a couple of centuries. Protestant German, Swiss, and French immigrants, recruited by the British to help stabilize their new dominion, settled the town in 1753; their influence is still apparent in the town's architectural details. With its excellent harbor—a protected inner arm of the Atlantic embraced by two long, curving peninsulas—Lunenburg became one of Nova Scotia's premier fishing ports and shipbuilding centers in the 19th century. In 1921 the famous schooner *Bluenose* was built here. The 49-meter fishing vessel won the International Fisherman's Trophy race that same year, and for the next 18 years it remained the undefeated champion

SOUTH SHORE

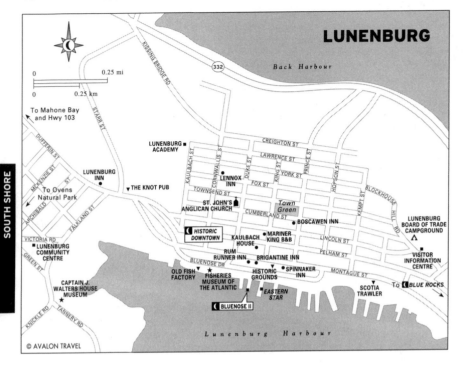

LUNENBURG

of the Atlantic fleets. The ship has become the proud symbol of the province, and its image is embossed on the back of the Canadian dime.

Today, the fishing industry that fostered the town's growth and boatbuilding reputation is comatose, and the Atlantic fisheries are mere shadows of their former selves. But here in Lunenburg, the townspeople carry on the shipbuilding and shipfitting skills of their ancestors. The port is still known as a tall ship mecca, and big multimasted sailing ships, old and new alike from around the world, continue to put in here for repairs, shipfitting, or provisions—whatever excuse the owners can come up with. Underneath the tourist glitz, the community pride in this tradition runs strong and deep, and the town's international reputation among mariners remains formidable. Strike up a conversation with a local about sailing ships and see what happens.

◖ HISTORIC DOWNTOWN

The port's oldest part is set on the hillside overlooking the harbor. The nine blocks of Old Town, designated a World Heritage Site by UNESCO, rise steeply from the water, and the village green spreads across the center. Bluenose Drive, the narrow lane along the harbor, and Montague Street, a block uphill, define the main sightseeing area. A mesh of one-way streets connects Old Town with the newer area built with shipbuilding profits. One of the pleasures of Lunenburg is strolling the residential and commercial streets, admiring the town's many meticulously preserved architectural gems. At the northern end of the harbor is the **Scotia Trawler Shipyard,** where the *Bluenose* was built. This shipyard and 16 other properties and most of the wharves are off-limits, but in 2005 the provincial government bought

Life in Lunenburg revolves around the colorful harborfront.

this entire precinct from a private company, and as the years go by they will be opened to the public.

Fisheries Museum of the Atlantic

This spacious bright-red museum (68 Bluenose Dr., 902/634-4794; early May–mid-Oct. daily 9:30 A.M.–5:30 P.M., adult $10, senior $7, child $3; mid-Oct.–early May Mon.–Fri. 9:30 A.M.–4 P.M.; free) boasts a trove of artifacts and exhibits on shipbuilding, seafaring, rum-running, and marine biology. This thoroughly fascinating museum engages the visitor with demonstrations on fish filleting, lobster-trap construction, dory building, net mending, and other maritime arts. Inside are aquariums, tanks with touchable marine life, a gallery of ship models, full-size fishing vessels from around Atlantic Canada, a theater, a restaurant, and a gift shop. Tied up at the wharf outside are the fishing schooner *Theresa E. Connor,* built in Lunenburg in 1938; the steel-hulled trawler *Cape Sable,* an example of the sort of vessel

that made the former obsolete; the *Royal Wave,* a Digby scallop dragger; and, when it's in its home port, the *Bluenose II.* All the vessels may be boarded and explored.

St. John's Anglican Church

This church (Cumberland and Cornwallis Sts., 902/634-4994; May–Oct. Mon.–Sat. 10 A.M.–5 P.M., Sun. noon–7 P.M.) stood for almost 250 years. In 2001, at the time the second-oldest church in Canada, it was destroyed by fire. It has now been rebuilt and can be visited on volunteer-led tours.

Lunenburg Academy

High above the port and surrounded by parkland, the imposing Lunenburg Academy (97 Kaulbach St.) is easily spotted from afar. Dating to 1885, this black and white wooden building, with its mansard roof and worn wooden stairways, was originally a prestigious high school. Today, it is the local elementary school, but it remains as one of the oldest academy schools in Canada.

Captain J. Walters House Museum

Captain Walters was the captain of the *Bluenose* during its racing days and was alive to sail aboard the *Bluenose II*. On the edge of the historic precinct, his modest home (37 Tannery Rd., 902/634-4410; July–Aug. Mon.–Sat. 10 A.M.–4 P.M.; $2.50) was donated to the town by his son and is now a museum. Displays center on the captain and his famous ship, but others describe the importance of shipbuilding to the local economy and the early fishing industry in general.

OTHER SIGHTS
(Blue Rocks

Follow any of Lunenburg's downtown streets eastbound to link with a road that leads eight kilometers to Blue Rocks, toward the end of the peninsula. This tiny fishing village is set along a jagged coastline wrapped with blue-gray slate and sandstone, and the combination of color and texture will inspire photographers. Blue Rocks has no official attractions or services. Instead, drive to the end of the road, from where you need to explore on foot to get the full effect of a part of Nova Scotia far removed from touristy Lunenburg and Peggy's Cove. The shoreline is littered with boats and fishing gear such as nets and traps in various states of repair while simple but colorful homes cling to the rocky foreshore.

Ovens Natural Park

A 15-minute drive south of Lunenburg on Highway 332, spectacular sea caves have been scooped out of the coastal cliffs. Early prospectors discovered veins of gold embedded in the slate and white quartz cliffs, sparking a small gold rush in 1861. During the following several decades, the cliffs surrendered 15,500 grams of the precious metal, while the Cunard family, of shipping fame, had the beach sand transported to England to retrieve the gold. Today, the site is privately owned, combining camping, cabins, hiking trails, and a restaurant on a 75-hectare site. Below the main parking lot, visitors can try their hand at panning for gold

along Cunard's Beach. A trail leads along the sea cliffs and into one of the "ovens," and you can jump aboard an inflatable boat to get a sea-level view of the caves. The day-use fee is adult $8, senior and child $4. Call 902/766-4621 for information.

RECREATION
(Bluenose II

Without a doubt, to immerse yourself fully in the Lunenburg experience you should set sail aboard the *Bluenose II,* an exact replica of the famous sailing ship.

When not in Halifax or visiting other Canadian ports, the *Bluenose II* (902/634-4794 or 866/579-4909, www.museum.gov.ns.ca/bluenose) can be found here at her home berth, outside the Fisheries Museum. Rather than separating you from the maritime experience with cushy reclining seats, acrylic plastic windows, and a cocktail lounge, the *Bluenose II* takes you to sea as a sailor. Cruising out of the harbor under a fresh breeze—the sails snapping taut and the hull slicing through the chilly waters—you'll begin to understand, to actually feel the history and lifeblood of Lunenburg.

When in Lunenburg she departs twice daily (9:30 A.M. and 1 P.M.; adult $35, child $20) for a two-hour harbor cruise. A total of 75 spots are offered on each sailing. Of these, 40 can be reserved through the phone numbers or website. The remaining 35 are offered on a first-come, first-served basis from the booth at the entrance to the Fisheries Museum 90 minutes before departure. (Tickets are always in high demand, so making a reservation well in advance is essential). Check the website for a sailing schedule.

Other Boat Tours

The *Bluenose II* isn't always in port, and when she is, tickets sell fast. An excellent alternative is the *Eastern Star,* a character-imbued 48-foot wooden ketch lovingly tended by an amiable and knowledgeable crew passionately intent on perpetuating the seafaring tradition that put Lunenburg on the map. The *Eastern Star* makes four 90-minute cruises a

THE FAMOUS *BLUENOSE*

Featured on Nova Scotian license plates and the back of the Canadian dime, the original *Bluenose* was launched from Lunenburg in 1921. Built as a fishing schooner, she was designed specifically for competing in the International Fishermen's Trophy, a racing series that pitted working ships from Canada and the United States against each other. Much to the joy of Canadians, the *Bluenose* won every racing competition she entered, while also serving as a working fishing boat. In 1942 the era of the sail-powered fishing industry was giving way to that of modern steel-hulled trawlers. The great *Bluenose* was sold to carry freight in the West Indies. Four years later, she foundered and was lost on a Haitian reef.

The ship herself was black. The name is thought to have originated from local fishermen, who, when conditions were cold and wet, would wipe their noses with their blue mittens, and the dye would consequently run.

In July 1963, the *Bluenose II* was recreated from the plans of the original and launched at Lunenburg. Some of the same craftspeople who had built the first *Bluenose* even participated in her construction.

day June–October, with a two-hour sunset cruise added in July and August. These tours cost adult $24–27, child $11–14, and the boat is operated by **Star Charters** (902/634-3535), which has a ticket booth down at the east end of the Fisheries Museum.

For a chance to see a lobster boat at work, sign up with **Lobstermen Tours** (902/634-3434 or 866/708-3434) for a two-hour trip that allows the chance to see local fishermen at work as they set traps and then bring them to the surface (preferably filled with lobsters). Departures are through summer daily at 11 A.M. and 1:30 P.M., and the cost is

reasonable (adult $34, child $14). Even though it's a working boat, conditions are comfortable, with indoor seating and a washroom.

Lunenburg Whale Watching Tours (902/527-7175) depart Government Wharf May–October four times daily. While whales are definitely the highlight, regular sightings are also made of sunfish, turtles, dolphins, seals, and puffins. The cost is adult $45, child $30.

ENTERTAINMENT AND EVENTS
Nightlife

The seaport is usually quiet evenings and Sundays. Locals frequent **The Knot Pub** (4 Dufferin St.; daily noon–11 P.M.), a comfortable and lively place where you can get "knotwurst" and kraut with your draft beer. Up from the harbor, the **Lunenburg Arms** (94 Pelham St., 902/640-4040) has a lounge bar with tables that spill out onto a quiet patio.

Performing Arts

Drama, dance, puppet shows, children's theater, and music performances regularly take place at **Pearl Theatre** (37 Hall St., 902/634-8716). **Lunenburg Opera House** (290 Lincoln St., 902/640-6500) hosts gigs by musicians from throughout Atlantic Canada. Cover charges are up to $20.

Lunenburg Folk Harbour Festival

For four days from the first Thursday in August, a roster of traditional, roots, and contemporary folk musicians come together for the Lunenburg Folk Harbour Festival (902/634-3180, www.folkharbour.com). They perform under a tent atop Blockhouse Hill, at the Opera House, in the downtown bandstand, and out on the wharf. Many performances are free, with big-name acts under the big tent costing $20.

SHOPPING

The **farmers' market** at Lunenburg Community Centre (corner Victoria Rd. and Green St.; July–Oct. Thurs. 8 A.M.–noon) lures crowds for fresh produce, smoked meats, and crafts at the former railroad depot grounds; wares are high quality and priced accordingly.

Houston North Gallery (110 Montague St., 902/634-8869) specializes in folk art, Inuit crafts and sculptures, and imported sculpture. Nautical gifts are available at the **Yacht Shop** (280 Montague St., 902/634-4331), which is also a full-service marine-supply center, and at the nonprofit **Bluenose II Company Store** (121 Bluenose Dr., 902/634-1963), which sells all manner of *Bluenose* clothing, gifts, and art to support preservation of the vessel.

ACCOMMODATIONS AND CAMPING

Whatever Mahone Bay may lack in accommodation is more than made up for in Lunenburg, where more than 60 bed-and-breakfasts—more than Halifax, which has more than 100 times the population—clog the historic streets. Still, you should try to make reservations ahead of time in summer, but be prepared for an answering machine in winter, when many lodgings are closed.

$50–100

Many of the bed-and-breakfasts in the $100–150 range have rooms under $100 outside of summer, but in July and August, your choices are limited. One of the best is the **⊂ Lennox Inn** (69 Fox St., 902/521-0214 or 888/379-7605, www.lennoxinn.com; May–Oct.; $95–120 s or d), which dates to 1791, making it Canada's oldest inn. The present owners breathed life into the building through a meticulous restoration using the original plans. Two guest rooms share a single bathroom, and the other two have en suites. Breakfast in what was originally the tavern is included in the rates.

Right downtown, above Grand Banker Restaurant, the tidy **Brigantine Inn and Suites** (82 Montague St., 902/634-3300 or 800/360-1181, www.brigantineinn.com; $75–160 s or d) provides excellent value. It offers seven nautically themed rooms, each with a private bathroom and named for a famous sailing ship. The smallest of the rooms is the brightly decorated Cutty Sark room, while

the much larger Brigantine Romance room features a jetted tub on a glass-enclosed balcony overlooking the harbor. Part of the inn is a complex of seven suites one block from the main inn. These have separate bedrooms, as well as sitting areas, coffeemakers, microwaves, and fridges.

Incorporating two (circa 1888 and 1905) buildings, the **Boscawen Inn and McLachlan House** (150 Cumberland St., 902/634-3325 or 800/354-5009, www.boscawen.ca; $95–205 s or d) also has a couple of rooms under $100, but most are more. This European-style hotel occupies a scenic perch above the harbor and is surrounded by gardens. The five guest rooms in McLachlan House are less expensive than those across the road at what was originally known as the Boscawen Manor, but all guests enjoy a light breakfast included in the rates. Other amenities include a formal dining room and sun-soaked terrace, both open to the public for meals.

$100–150

Kaulbach House (75 Pelham St., 902/634-8818 or 800/568-8818, www.kaulbachhouse.com; mid-Mar.–Oct.; $112–169 s or d) is one of Lunenburg's many historic treasures (circa 1880) converted to an inn, complete with the unique "Lunenburg bump" architectural feature. Two blocks up from the harbor but with partial water views, the six antiques-filled rooms have en suite or private bathrooms and wireless Internet. A full breakfast is included in the rates.

The ornately detailed **Mariner King B&B** (15 King St., 902/634-8509 or 800/565-8509, www.marinerking.com; $110–220 s or d) is also right downtown. Its cheaper rooms are a little more threadbare than those at Kaulbach House, but the character-filled Attic Suite is a gem. It even has its own rooftop patio. Public areas include two sitting rooms and a small stone patio.

Rum Runner Inn (66 Montague St., 902/634-9200 or 888/778-6786, www.rumrunnerinn.com; $109–169 s or d) is right along the busy restaurant strip opposite the waterfront. It's a historic building, but the 13

© ANDREW HEMPSTEAD

Lunenburg Inn

rooms are thoroughly modernized and look no different from a regular motel. Each has a coffeemaker, fridge, air-conditioning, and Internet connections. The most expensive rooms have a king bed and glassed-in veranda. A light breakfast is included.

If you're looking to stay in a historic building with a modern feel, consider the centrally situated **Spinnaker Inn** (126 Montague St., 902/634-4543 or 888/777-8606, www .spinnakerinn.com; $125–175 s or d). Overlooking the harbor, all four guest rooms have polished hardwood floors and antique-style beds. Two are split-level with jetted tubs in the en suite bathrooms and harbor views.

The **Lunenburg Inn** (26 Dufferin St., 902/634-3963 or 800/565-3963, www.lunenburginn.com; Apr.–Oct.; $155–195 s or d) is an elaborate Victorian home that has been taking in guests since 1924. It underwent serious renovations in the mid-1990s and now provides some of the nicest rooms in town. If I had a choice, I'd stay in the Hillside Suite, which has a sitting area with a TV, a jetted tub in the en suite bathroom, and a private entrance

from the veranda. Guests enjoy a sitting room with a fireplace, a private bar, and high-speed Internet access.

Campgrounds

The **Lunenburg Board of Trade Campground** (Blockhouse Hill Rd., 902/634-8100; May–Oct.; $22–28) sits on Blockhouse Hill, high above downtown and beside the information center. It's on the small side (55 sites) but facilities are adequate (showers, views, Internet access).

A lot more than a campground, **Ovens Natural Park** (off Hwy. 332, 902/766-4621, www.ovenspark.com; mid-May–mid-Oct.) has campsites (tents $25, hookups $38–55) and cabins varying from those with shared bathrooms ($60 s or d) to self-contained two-bedroom chalets ($180). Amenities include lawn games, a playground, evening bonfires, a restaurant, and a gift shop. Relations of Harry Chapin (of *Cat's in the Cradle* fame) own and operate the property, making the evening sing-alongs a real treat. On the middle weekend of August, the entire Chapin family comes together as a tribute to the singer, with everyone welcome to join in the fun.

FOOD

Lunenburg has a great number of restaurants, nearly all serving seafood in a casual setting. Local specialties appearing on some menus include Solomon Gundy (pickled herring, usually served with sour cream), Lunenburg pudding (pork sausage), and fish cakes topped with rhubarb relish. Beyond the tourist precinct, **Scotia Trawler** (266 Montague St., 902/634-4914) is where fishermen come for their supplies. Beyond the rows of dry goods and canned food are salted cod, Solomon Gundy and Lunenburg pudding, as well as many other "treats" you won't find in your local grocery store.

Café and Pub Dining

(**Historic Grounds** (100 Montague St., 902/634-9995; June–mid-Sept. Mon.–Fri. 7:30 A.M.–10 P.M., Sat.–Sun. 8 A.M.–10 P.M., the rest of the year daily 7:30 A.M.–5:30 P.M.) is Lunenburg's best place for a coffee concoction (especially if you nab one of two tables on the balcony overlooking the harbor). But this café is a lot more than a coffeehouse. It also serves sandwiches made to order, chowder, and salads.

Away from the waterfront, **Knot Pub** (4 Dufferin St., 902/634-3334; daily noon–9:30 P.M.) is a small space with decent pub grub, including battered fish-and-chips for $10.

Restaurants

In the big red building down on the water, the **Old Fish Factory** (68 Bluenose Dr., 902/634-3333; May–Oct. 11 A.M.–10 P.M.) is a large restaurant in a converted fish storehouse. Specialties include creamy seafood chowder, beer-battered haddock, and fish baked on a cedar plank. After Solomon Gundy (pickled herring), a sour-tasting local specialty, you'll be ready for Blueberry Grunt, sweet dumplings floating in a blueberry compote and topped with whipped cream. Nonseafood dishes with a Canadian twist are also offered, such as maple-

glazed chicken for $18.50. All other dinner entrées are similarly priced, while lunches run $8–15.

One block back from the harbor, several restaurants line Montague Street. All have decks or floor-to-ceiling windows facing the water. **Big Red's Family Restaurant** (80 Montague St., 902/634-3554; daily 9 A.M.–10 P.M., until 11 P.M. on weekends) is exactly that—a cavernous family-friendly restaurant with a standard seafood menu. Portions are generous and prices reasonable.

The **(** **Grand Banker Seafood Bar & Grill** (82 Montague St., 902/634-3300; daily 8:30 A.M.–9 P.M.) offers similarly great views from an enclosed dining room and serves a wide-ranging menu of seafood, salads, pastas, and sandwiches. The food is well prepared and the atmosphere pleasant—it feels a little more relaxed and a little less tourist-driven than some of its neighbors. Mains ranging $10–20 include crab cakes, Acadian seafood stew, and maple-pecan glazed salmon. A half dozen good beers and a couple of Nova Scotia wines are available. The Grand Banker puts on a fine brunch (weekends 11 A.M.–2:30 P.M.) that includes lobster eggs Benedict ($12).

INFORMATION AND SERVICES

Lunenburg Visitor Information Centre (Blockhouse Hill Rd., 902/634-8100; May–Oct. daily 9 A.M.–8 P.M.) stocks locally written, informative literature about the port's historic architecture. *Understanding Lunenburg's Architecture* describes the design elements, and *An Inventory of Historic Buildings* provides details on almost every seaport building, organized street by street. Staff will help those without reservations find accommodation. For the uninitiated, the office can be a little hard to find; as you enter town, stay on Lincoln Street as it passes the signs for the waterfront and you'll soon find yourself on Blockhouse Hill.

Fishermen's Memorial Hospital (14 High St., 902/634-8801) is between Dufferin and Green Streets. For the **RCMP,** call 902/634-8674.

Banks dot King Street, while the **post office** is on the corner of King and Lincoln Streets. **Soap Bubble Cleanette** (39 Lincoln St., 902/634-4601; Mon.–Sat. 8 A.M.–8 P.M., Sun. 10 A.M.–8 P.M.) is the local launderette.

GETTING THERE AND AROUND

Along divided Highway 103, it takes a little more than one hour to reach Lunenburg from Halifax, taking Exit 10 via Mahone Bay for the final stretch. Most visitors arrive this way, as part of a tour, or in their own or a rental car. If you're in Halifax without a vehicle, consider a six-hour tour with **Ambassatours** (902/423-6242 or 800/565-7173). These depart June–October Wednesday, Friday, and Saturday at 8:30 A.M. for adult $98, senior $88.20, child $69.

Bridgewater-based **Try Town Transit** (902/521-0855) operates an on-demand shuttle between Halifax and Lunenburg for about $120 for up to eight passengers.

Lunenburg to Shelburne

Beyond Lunenburg, the divided highway continues south to Bridgewater, but the crowds thin out quickly. This is one of the best reasons to continue south—the coastline is dotted with Peggy's Cove–like villages steeped in history but unaffected by tourism and a rugged coastline where parks with designated hiking trails and sandy beaches beckon.

The 140-kilometer drive between Lunenburg and Shelburne takes less than two hours nonstop. As accommodations are limited along this stretch of coast, a sensible schedule is to plan to leave Lunenburg after breakfast, spend the day exploring the following parks and towns, and have a room booked in Shelburne for that night.

BRIDGEWATER

Situated on the LaHave River, west of Lunenburg, Bridgewater (pop. 7,000) is the main service town of the South Shore. Industry revolves around a Michelin tire plant, and if you're traveling south, this is the last place to fill up on fast food (if you must) and do your mall shopping.

Sights

The 1860 **Wile Carding Mill** (242 Victoria Rd., 902/543-8233; June–Sept. Mon.–Sat. 9:30 A.M.–5:30 P.M., Sun. 1–5:30 P.M.; adult $4, child $2) was once a wool-processing mill. The wool was carded for spinning and weaving or made into batts for quilts. The original machinery is still in operation, powered by a waterwheel, and now demonstrates old carding methods. It's on the south side of the river (take Exit 13 from Highway 103).

Surrounded by parkland on the east side of downtown, **DesBrisay Museum** (130 Jubilee Rd., 902/543-4033; July–Sept. Mon.–Sat. 9 A.M.–5 P.M., Sun. 1–5:30 P.M., the rest of the year Wed.–Sun. 1–5 P.M.; adult $3:50, senior $2.25, child $2) tells the story of Bridgewater's first European settlers and the importance of local industries. Highlights include Mi'Kmaq quilting and a wooden plough dating to 1800.

Accommodations and Food

Nova Scotia's oldest accommodation is Bridgewater's **Fairview Inn** (25 Queen St., 902/543-2233 or 800/725-8732, www .thefairviewinn.ca; $95–145 s or d), a gracious three-story wooden building that dates to 1863. It has been beautifully restored, now with 24 stylish guest rooms that vary from simple but comfortable to a nautically themed suite. In-room niceties include plush linens, bathrobes, and room service, while other amenities include an outdoor pool and hot tub, a restaurant, a lounge, and even room service. To get there from Highway 103, take Exit 13 and follow Victoria Road to Queen Street.

About six kilometers east of town along

Highway 331 is the **Lighthouse Motel** (1101 Hwy. 331, Pleasantville, 902/543-8151, www .lighthousemotel.ca; May–Oct.; $75–100 s or d). It occupies a prime riverside location, and guests have access to a private beach, a picnic area, and a playground.

Cranberry's (Fairview Inn, 25 Queen St., 902/543-2233; daily 7 A.M.–9 P.M.) is an inviting space with a creative menu to match. It's very popular in the morning ($6 for a full cooked breakfast with coffee or $9 for eggs Benedict with smoked salmon), but it is lunch and dinner that set this restaurant apart. You could start with Solomon Gundy (a local delicacy of pickled herring), and then choose a main as simple as curried shrimp or as rich as baked haddock stuffed with asparagus and smoked salmon. Just make sure to save room for the divinely rich chocolate mousse.

HIGHWAY 331 TO LIVERPOOL

Highway 331, which begins in downtown Bridgewater as King Street, follows the LaHave River to its mouth and then winds along the coast to Exit 17 of Highway 103. It adds just 30 minutes to the trip between Bridgewater and Liverpool, but you'll want to allow longer— it's a beautiful introduction to the untouristy South Shore beyond Lunenburg.

◖ LaHave Islands

A causeway from **Crescent Beach** crosses to Bush Island, from where quirky old iron bridges provide access to Bell Island and LaHave Island. Just three of dozens of islands in the group, they are dotted with old fishing cottages inhabited by those who have escaped the rat race. On Bell Island, a museum filled with local history is in the church, while Bush Island Provincial Park is little more than a boat launch, but for the rugged scenery and funky fishing cottages the drive to the end of the road makes a delightful detour from the main South Shore tourist route.

Just one of many parks along this stretch of coast, **Rissers Beach Provincial Park** boasts a beach of finely ground quartz sand and an area of pristine salt marsh laced with

boardwalks. The park campground (902/688-2034; mid-May–mid-Oct.; $24) fills every weekend through summer, but midweek even sites close to the sandy beach remain empty. The park is right by the causeway leading across to the islands.

LIVERPOOL

This historic town, at the mouth of the Mersey River 50 kilometers south of Bridgewater, doesn't get as much attention as it deserves. Throughout the compact downtown core are a number of interesting attractions, while Privateer Days (early July) provide a lively glimpse of the town's colorful past.

Sights and Events
THE PORT OF PRIVATEERS
Privateers were government-sanctioned pirates who had permission to capture enemy vessels. American privateers found their way to Nova Scotia during the American Revolution, but the British responded by attacking American boats. Privateers were required by law to take captured vessels to Halifax's Privateers Wharf, where the boats and cargo were auctioned off, a portion of which was handed back to the privateer and his crew. Liverpool local Simeon Perkins had a share in a privateering boat, along with dozens of others who used Liverpool as their home port. The most prolific of the privateer vessels was the *Liverpool Packet* captained by Joseph Barss, which captured an estimated 200 vessels during its lifetime. With plundered goods from a single vessel selling for up to $1 million at auction, Liverpool became a wealthy town, and many of the grand homes still standing were financed from privateering.

SHERMAN HINES MUSEUM OF PHOTOGRAPHY
Renowned landscape and portrait photographer Sherman Hines developed this photography museum (219 Main St., 902/354-2667; mid-May–mid-Oct. Mon.–Sat. 10 A.M.–5:30 P.M. and July–Aug. also Sun. noon–5:30 P.M.; adult $4, child $3) to display the work of prominent Nova Scotian photographers, including the

museum's namesake. The wooden building, a 1901 National Historic Site in itself, also holds the re-creation of a Victorian-era photography studio, a gallery of changing exhibits, a research library, and a gift shop. In the foyer is an impressive mounted tuna—at 400 kilograms, the largest of its species ever caught on rod and reel.

OTHER SIGHTS

In addition to his photography museum, Sherman Hines has injected his own resources into developing the **Rossignol Cultural Centre** (205 Church St., 902/354-3067; mid-May–mid-Oct. Mon.–Sat. 10 A.M.–5:30 P.M. and July–Aug. also Sun. noon–5:30 P.M.; adult $4, child $3) in a school building once slated for demolition. One block south of Main Street along Old Bridge Street, it encompasses multiple small museums, including one devoted to outhouses (Hines is well known for his outhouse photography), and others to folk art, the Mi'Kmaq, and wildlife.

Built by an infamous privateer, **Perkins House** (105 Main St., 902/354-4058; mid-May–mid-Oct. Mon.–Sat. 9:30 A.M.–5:30 P.M., Sun. 1–5:30 P.M.; free) is a classic example of a New England planter's adaptation to Nova Scotia. Built in 1766, it is furnished with antiques and displays that tell the story of Perkins's colorful life on the high seas.

Country music legend Hank Snow, who sold 70 million records, was born in nearby Brooklyn. Across the river from downtown, a railway station has been converted to the **Hank Snow Country Music Centre** (148 Bristol St., 902/354-4675; mid-May–mid-Oct. Mon.–Sat. 9 A.M.–5 P.M., and July–Aug. also Sun. noon–5:30 P.M.; $3) in his memory. Displays catalog his life, from the earliest performances in Halifax through details of his seven number 1 hits from 120 albums, to his Grand Ole Opry performances, his role in introducing Elvis Presley to the entertainment world, and, finally, the huge collection of awards accumulated through six decades of performing. To get there from Highway 103, take Exit 19; from downtown, cross the Mersey River via Bristol Street.

PRIVATEER DAYS

There's no better place to immerse yourself in the colorful history of Nova Scotia's privateers than **Privateer Days** (902/354-4500, www.privateerdays.com), a Liverpool tradition held the first weekend in July. Walking tours led by locals in period dress and a re-creation of when two American privateer boats invaded the town are highlights, but events go on all week, culminating with a bang during final night's fireworks.

Accommodations and Food

Once home to a privateer, **Lane's Privateer Inn** (27 Bristol Ave., 902/354-3456 or 800/794-3332, www.lanesprivateerinn.com; $90–120 s, $105–135 d) has everything you need for an overnight stay under one roof. The 27 rooms all have en suite bathrooms and air-conditioning while some have king beds and balconies overlooking the Mersey River. Downstairs is an excellent restaurant. Breakfast includes all the usual options, with Nova Scotian specialties such as smoked salmon sausage as a substitute for bacon. The lunch and dinner includes haddock topped with fruit salsa for $16 and lamb chops doused in blueberry-brandy sauce for $20.

Information and Services

The **Visitor Information Centre** (28 Henry Hensey Dr., 902/354-5421, www.queens.ca; mid-May–Sept. daily 9:30 A.M.–5:30 P.M.) is on the riverfront right downtown. **Snug Harbour Books** (Lane's Privateer Inn, 27 Bristol Ave., 902/354-3456) is a welcoming spot at street level of the town's best accommodation. This is the place to pick up books on privateering, but you will find the many Nova Scotian cookbooks also make great souvenirs. The bookstore is part café, sharing the same menu as the affiliated restaurant.

LIVERPOOL TO PORT JOLI

If you've left Highway 103 to explore Liverpool, continue south through town along the older Highway 3 to reach White Point before rejoining the main route south at Summerville.

White Point

Activities at **White Point Beach Resort** (White Point Beach, 902/354-2711 or 800/565-5068, www.whitepoint.com) make this lodging a destination in itself. Stretching along a wide stretch of white sand, it has indoor and outdoor pools, swimming in a freshwater lake, surfboard and kayak rentals, tennis courts, a nine-hole golf course, a games room, two restaurants, and nightly entertainment in the lounge. Most guests are families, many returning annually for summer vacation. Comfortable motel-like rooms are $140–165 s or d depending on the view, and cottages are $265–310.

Continue along Highway 3 from White Point to Hunts Point is **Hunts Point Beach Cottages** (Hwy. 3, 902/683-2077, www.huntspointbeach.com; mid-May–mid-Oct.), a much quieter spot, where guests laze their time away on the grassed grounds, which extend to the beach. The cottages have one or two bedrooms ($135 and $145 s or d respectively), kitchens, covered decks, and living rooms with TVs.

Summerville Beach Provincial Park

Just before Highway 3 rejoins Highway 103, a turnoff leads to this small provincial park, which protects a spit of sand jutting across Port Mouton. It's a day-use park with picnic tables and plenty of room to spread your towel on the beach.

Kejimkujik National Park Seaside Adjunct

About 25 kilometers southwest of Liverpool is one of the largest remaining undisturbed areas of Nova Scotian coastline. Affiliated with the inland Kejimkujik National Park (along Highway 8 between Liverpool and Annapolis Royal), this section of the park encompasses unspoiled beaches and offshore isles. The park is accessible only on foot. The main access is along an easy three-kilometer trail beginning at the parking lot on St. Catherine's Road (turn off in Port Joli) and ending at the southwest end of St. Catherine's River Beach.

Some sections of this beach close late April–late July to protect piping plover nesting sites. The Seaside Adjunct has no visitor facilities, and camping is not permitted.

PORT JOLI

It's another picturesque coastal village with another seaside park that gets busy only on the hottest of summer weekends.

Thomas Raddall Provincial Park

This gem of a park protects rock formations suggesting it was the point where the Gondwana and North American continents collided many millions of years ago. But for most, the beaches are the main draw. Left behind by the retreating ice cap at the end of the last ice age, banks of sand have washed ashore, forming beautiful stretches of beach now protected by the park.

The park has an 11-kilometer trail system, half of which is paved and set aside for both cyclists and walkers. The most popular destination is Sandy Bay, a short beach bookended by rocky headlands. If you can pull yourself away from the beach, follow the **Sandy Bay Trail** over the northern headland to the **Herring Rock Trail,** where the remains of a 1700s fishing station can be seen. Take both these trails and you'll be back on your beach towel within an hour. In the north of the park, beaches are lapped by the protected waters of Port Joli Harbour. Starting from the top end of the campground, the **Port Joli Trail** (one kilometer each way) winds south past interpretive panels to Scotch Point Beach. To the north, a string of beaches spread out well beyond the park boundary.

The park campground (902/683-2664; mid-May–mid-Oct.; $24) has 82 large sites, including a few designated for tents. Each site has a picnic table and fire pit, while other amenities include washrooms with showers, a playground, and firewood sales.

To get to the park continue along Highway 103 south from Port Joli and turn south on East Port L'Herbert Road; it's three kilometers from the highway.

Shelburne and Vicinity

Like Lunenburg, 140 kilometers to the northeast, Shelburne (pop. 2,300) sits at the innermost end of a long harbor formed between two peninsulas. The seaport was established in 1783 when Loyalists fleeing the newly independent American colonies settled here by the thousands, establishing shipbuilding and fish processing businesses—but eventually the seaport began to show its age. Then Hollywood came to town. In 1992, the motley collection of historic buildings along the waterfront was used as a setting for Fairfield, Connecticut, circa 1780 in the American Revolution movie *Mary Silliman's War.* In 1995 Shelburne again hit the big screen as the setting for 1600s Boston in *The Scarlet Letter,* an adaptation of Nathaniel Hawthorne's novel. Demi Moore and Robert Duvall may be long gone, but the two movies created an impetus for preservation. While some "historic" buildings were added to the mix, many original buildings were spruced up, power lines were buried, and generally the town came together to promote its past.

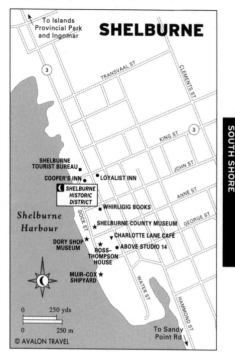

◖ SHELBURNE HISTORIC DISTRICT

Dock Street is dotted with some of Canada's oldest wooden buildings. The **Shelburne Historical Society** (902/875-3219) has done a wonderful job of breathing life into the precinct, while businesses such as a cooperage and a boatbuilder help bring the history to life. In between are grassed areas, a waterfront pathway, and kayak rentals. Admission to each of the buildings run by the Shelburne Historical Society is $3, or buy a ticket for $8 to visit all four.

Shelburne County Museum

The Shelburne County Museum (8 Maiden La., 902/875-3219; June–mid-Oct. daily 9:30 A.M.–5:30 P.M., mid-Oct.–May Mon.–Fri. 10 A.M.–5 P.M.) is the best place to make your first stop. It contains exhibits covering Shelburne's Loyalist heritage and shipbuilding

history. One highlight is the 250-year-old fire engine, believed to be the oldest in Canada.

Dory Shop Museum

First used in the mid-1800s, dories were small, skifflike wooden boats that were essential to the success of fishing the Grand Banks. Rather than fishing from the mother vessel, a dozen or more would be transported to the fishing grounds, allowing hundreds of hooks to be laid out at once. Adding to their usability, they were inexpensive to make and stackable. On the waterfront across from the county museum, the Dory Shop (11 Dock St., June–Sept. daily 9:30 A.M.–5:30 P.M.) is the last of seven once-thriving boat factories in town. The seven shops turned out thousands of handcrafted wooden fishing dories between 1880 and 1970.

The shop now houses interpretive displays and gives demonstrations on the dying art.

Ross-Thomson House and Store Museum

The Ross-Thomson House and Store Museum (9 Charlotte La., 902/875-3141; June–mid-Oct. daily 9:30 A.M.–5:30 P.M.) was built in 1785 as a Loyalist store. The last example of its kind today in Nova Scotia, it depicts the period setting with sample wares such as lumber and salted codfish, which were traded for tobacco, molasses, and dry goods. Upstairs is a military display, and outside the garden has been planted as it would have been in the late 1700s.

Muir-Cox Shipyard

At the far south end of Dock Street, this small shipyard (902/875-5310; June–Sept. daily 9:30 A.M.–5:30 P.M., Oct.–May Mon.–Fri. 8 A.M.–4 P.M.) builds boats on a custom-order basis, and you can watch men at work year-round. It operated continuously between the 1820s and the 1980s launching square-rigged barques in its earliest days and wooden racing yachts in more modern times. Inside is the Shipbuilding Interpretation Centre, with displays describing the history of the shipyard.

ACCOMMODATIONS AND CAMPING
$50-100

The centrally located **Loyalist Inn** (160 Water St., 902/875-3333; $84–89 s or d) is a late-1800s wooden hotel with 11 rooms on the top two floors and a downstairs bar and restaurant.

Better value is **Shelburne Harbour-side Cottages** (10 George St., 902/875-4555, www.shelburneharboursidecottages.com; $95 s or d). Each of two modern cottages enjoys harbor views and has cooking facilities, a separate bedroom, TV, and a deck. Extras include bike rentals ($18 per day) and kayak rentals ($25 per day).

Off historic Water Street is **Above Studio 14** (14 George St., 902/875-1333, www.studio14

.ns.ca; $95 s or d), a folksy two-bedroom suite with its own kitchen, living room, and balcony. Downstairs, owner Mary Lou Keith spends her time painting sailcloth, a Maritimes tradition dating from the days when old canvas sails were painted in nautical themes and used as floor coverings.

$100-150

Cooper's Inn (36 Dock St., 902/875-4656 or 800/688-2011, www.thecoopersinn.com; Apr.–Oct.; $100–185 s or d) is a two-story colonial beauty overlooking the harbor and next to the tourist bureau and museum. Built in 1784 by a merchant and restored and opened in 1988, the lodging has six rooms all with private baths ($100–150), and a large top-floor suite with water views ($185). Rates include a full breakfast in a cheery dining room.

◖ Whispering Waves Cottages (Black Point Rd., Ingomar, 902/637-3535 or 866/470-9283, www.whisperingwavescottages.com; $149 s or d) may be out of town, but an overnight stay at this welcoming waterfront property is as enjoyable as one could imagine. The modern cottages are stylishly furnished in wilderness, nautical, or romance themes, and each has a separate bedroom, kitchen, lounge room with a fireplace, and a deck with ocean views. Hosts Jo-Anne and Paul Goulden organize activities such as sea kayaking, fishing, and spa days. A lobster dinner, delivered to your cottage door, is a delicious extra.

Campground

Rustic and pretty **The Islands Provincial Park** (off Hwy. 3, 5 km west of Shelburne, 902/875-4304; mid-May–early Sept.; $24) faces the town across the upper harbor. It offers 64 unserviced sites with table shelters and grills, pit toilets, running water, and a spacious modern shower room.

FOOD

With an established reputation for fine dining is the **◖ Charlotte Lane Café** (13 Charlotte La., 902/875-3314; May–early Dec. Tues.–Sat. 11:30 A.M.–2:30 P.M. and 5–8 P.M.), between

Water and Dock Streets. Its Swiss owner-chef, Roland Glauser, specializes in local seafood prepared using cooking techniques from around the world. The seafood chowder is one of the best I've tasted.

The dining room at the **Loyalist Inn** on Water Street (reservations are wise, call 902/875-2343) is usually jammed with bus-tour diners. A table is easiest to get before noon, during midafternoon, or after 8 P.M. The specialty is seafood ($9–15) prepared any way you like it.

INFORMATION AND SERVICES

While Dock Street is the historic heart of Shelburne, Water Street, running parallel one block to the west, is lined with all the services of a small town, including banks and the post office.

Shelburne Visitor Information Centre (34 King St., 902/875-4547; June–Oct. daily 10 A.M.–6 P.M., July–Aug. daily 9 A.M.–7 P.M.) stocks literature and self-guided tour maps. The website www.historicshelburne.com is loaded with up-to-date information about the town. **Whirligig Books** (135 Water St., 902/875-1117) stocks a good selection of local and Nova Scotian literature.

SHELBURNE TO YARMOUTH
Barrington and Vicinity

Highway 103 takes a mainly inland route between Shelburne and Yarmouth. One place where it does come in contact with the ocean is near Barrington, just off the main highway along Highway 3, where coastal views are exquisite. In Barrington itself, the **Old Meeting House Museum** (2408 Hwy. 3, 902/637-2185; June–Sept. Mon.–Sat. 9:30 A.M.–5:30 P.M., Sun. 1–5:30 P.M.; free) is a variation on planter life. Built by 50 Cape Cod families in 1765, the New England–style church is Canada's oldest nonconformist house of worship.

Beyond Barrington, at Villagedale, is **Sand Hills Beach Provincial Park,** so named for a complex dune system where wide tidal flats extend into the ocean. Time your arrival for high tide, and the water is warm enough for swimming—in summer only, of course.

Cape Sable Island

At Barrington West, Cape Sable Island is well worth the detour. Connected to the mainland by a causeway, the island forms the southernmost point in Nova Scotia. Feared by early sailors because of its jagged shores, the island was settled by brick-making Acadians during the 17th century. The island also served as a summer base for fishermen from New England, and fishing prevails today as the community's main industry, with tourism a close second.

The island's four main beaches offer surfing, clam digging, swimming, fishing, and bird-watching. At **Hawk Beach,** on the eastern side (turn at Lower Clark's Harbour at Hawk Road and go left), you can see the **Cape Lighthouse** on a small nearby sandbar. The original tower, built in 1861, was Canada's first eight-sided structure; the present lighthouse, a protected heritage building, was constructed in 1923. At low tide on Hawk Beach you can also see the remains of a 1,500-year-old forest.

Causeway Beach (turn right at the Corbett Heights subdivision) is a prime sunbathing and fishing (for mackerel) spot. **Stoney Island Beach,** as the name implies, is not as popular with sunbathers as it is with seals, which like to sun themselves on the rocks. **South Side Beach** (turn on Daniel's Head Road in South Side) is also popular as a seal-watching and beachcombing locale.

Services and accommodations are limited. **Cape Sable Cottages** (37 Long Point Rd., Newellton, 902/745-0168, www.capesablecottages.com) are my favorite. These five spacious and modern cottages sit on a private peninsula jutting into Barrington Passage. Each cottage has water views, a separate bedroom, a living area, a kitchen, a wide deck furnished with a barbecue and outdoor furniture, and its own fire pit. Rates range $165–250 in summer (when there is also a two-night minimum). The property is open year-round, with cottages dropping to $125 in winter. Check the website for specials.

Yarmouth

Yarmouth (pop. 7,500) was the center of a ship-building empire during Canada's Great Age of Sail, when it ranked as the world's fourth-largest port of registry. Still the region's largest seaport, the town is a prosperous and orderly place supported by shipping—primarily lumber products, Irish moss, and Christmas trees—and fishing. Yarmouth's herring fleet is a major contributor to the local economy. The fleet sails at night and anchors with all its lights blazing farther up the Fundy coast, creating a sight known as "herring city." Tourism also helps the port thrive; two ferry lines bring visitors to town in numbers sufficient to establish Yarmouth as the busiest ferry landing in the province.

SIGHTS

If historic architecture interests you, take a leisurely walk along Main Street, where the commercial buildings are styled in late-19th-century Classic Revival, Queen Anne Revival, Georgian, and Italianate. At the tourist information center on Forest Street, pick up the *Walking Tour of Yarmouth* brochure, which details about two dozen points of architectural and historical interest on a self-guided four-kilometer walk.

Firefighters' Museum

The Firefighters' Museum of Nova Scotia (451 Main St., 902/742-5525; June–Sept. Mon.–Sat. 9 A.M.–5 P.M., July–Aug. Mon.–Sat. 9 A.M.–9 P.M. and Sun. 10 A.M.–5 P.M.; adult $4, child $2) is Atlantic Canada's only museum dedicated solely to firefighting equipment. Among the extensive vintage collection is an 1819 Hopwood and Tilley hand pump and other sparkling equipment.

Yarmouth County Museum

An enjoyable walk from downtown through a tree-lined residential area east of Main Street is Yarmouth County Museum (22 Collins St., 902/742-5539; June–mid-Oct. Mon.–Sat.

9 A.M.–5 P.M., Sun. 1–5 P.M., the rest of the year Tues.–Sat. 2–5 P.M.; adult $5, child $2). It showcases Canada's largest ship-portrait collection and exhibits a trove of seafaring lore, musical instruments, ship models, furniture, and more. The research library and archives store extensive records and genealogical materials.

Scenic Drive to Cape Forchu

The region's most scenic drive is to Cape Forchu, where the red and white **Cape Forchu Light Station** guides ships into the harbor. Follow Main Street north and turn left at Vancouver Street. Just past the hospital complex, turn left on Grove Road. The Faith Memorial Baptist Church marks the site where the famous Yarmouth Runic Stone, believed to have been inscribed by Leif Eriksson's men, was found. Next you come to the lighthouse (July–Aug. daily 9 A.M.–9 P.M.) perched on a stone promontory. The actual lighthouse is

© ANDREW HEMPSTEAD

Yarmouth County Museum

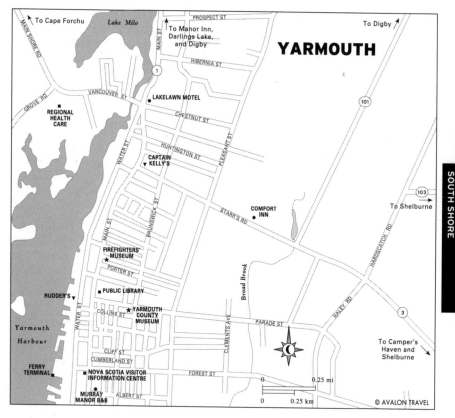

open to climb, and you get good views from the top. Beyond the parking lot, a trail leads down to **Leif Ericson Picnic Park,** overlooking the rocky coast.

ACCOMMODATIONS AND CAMPING
$50-100

If you are looking to spend less than $100 for accommodations, the **Murray Manor B&B** (225 Main St., 902/742-9625 or 877/742-9629, www.murraymanor.com; $95–139 s or d), just one block from the ferry terminal, is a good choice. In this Regency-style heritage property dating to 1820 and kept in the same family for 140 years, you find three guest rooms with a shared bath and one with

an en suite, a dining room, as well as a beautiful garden and greenhouse secluded behind a low stone wall. A unique feature is the "prayer windows," so named because you must kneel to see through them.

Churchill Mansion Country Inn (Hwy. 1, Darlings Lake, 902/649-2818 or 888/453-5565, www.churchillmansion.com; May–mid-Nov.; $80–140 s or d) was the hilltop summer home of Aaron Flint Churchill, who made his fortune in the shipping trade after establishing the Churchill Line out of Savannah, Georgia. Overlooking a lake and with distant ocean views, it was converted to an inn in the 1980s. The most expensive room is Churchill's master bedroom, with a balcony overlooking a lake. Guests can rent a bike ($10 per day), order a picnic lunch ($5), and set off to explore the local coastline. Breakfast is $6 per person and the nightly seafood buffet is $15. Darlings Lake is 15 kilometers north of Yarmouth.

North of downtown, where Vancouver Street crosses the head of Yarmouth Harbour, is the **Lakelawn Motel** (641 Main St., 902/742-3588 or 877/664-0664, www.lakelawnmotel.com; May–Oct.; $70–100 s or d). The centerpiece of this lodging is a grand 1864 mansion that holds a breakfast room and four upstairs bed-and-breakfast rooms. Spread around its perimeter is a U-shaped wing of 27 motel rooms that are a little worn but still good value.

$100-150

Chain motels include the **Comfort Inn** (96 Starrs Rd., 902/742-1119, www.choicehotels .ca; $115–145 s or d), a dependable choice with well-equipped rooms and rates that include free local calls, Internet access, weekday newspapers, and a light breakfast.

Once the home of a wealthy sea captain, **❰ Manor Inn** (Hwy. 101, 902/742-2487 or 888/626-6746, www.manorinn.com; $129–199 s or d) sprawls across five magnificent hectares 10 kilometers north of downtown. Formal English-style gardens and a grand dining room give the estate an upscale ambience, while activities such as tennis, lawn games, biking, and canoeing from the private dock keep guests busy. Guest rooms are spread through multiple buildings, including the Coach House and the original mansion. Rates include a light breakfast; check the website for American-plan meal packages.

Campgrounds

The closest campground to Yarmouth is **Campers' Haven** (5 km east of Yarmouth off Hwy. 3 in Arcadia, 902/742-4848, www .campershavencampground.com; mid-May–mid-Oct.; $15–35). The lakeside campground offers more than 200 sites ($16–27), as well as canoe rentals, a pool, a camp store, a launderette, and a recreation hall with a fireplace.

For a wilderness experience, travel a little farther out to **Ellenwood Lake Provincial Park**

(mid-June–mid-Oct.; $24), which has a beach with swimming, a short hiking trail through a mixed forest typical of the southwest region, showers, and a playground. To get there, drive 19 kilometers north of Yarmouth on Highway 101, take Exit 34, and follow the signs along Highway 340 for seven kilometers.

FOOD
Downtown

Rudder's (96 Water St., 902/742-7311; daily 10 A.M.–10 P.M.) is a large brewpub set right on the water. It's a big room that manages to maintain a warm atmosphere, with even more tables spread across a veranda facing the harbor. The menu blends traditional pub food with Nova Scotian specialties. Think maple-glazed salmon baked on a cedar plank ($21), lobster and scallop crepes ($22), and steak and lobster ($30). In summer the nightly lobster supper (4–9 P.M.; $30) is a major draw.

North of Downtown

In a two-story mansion at the north end of Main Street, **Captain Kelley's** (577 Main St., 902/742-9191) opens daily through summer at 7 A.M. for the best breakfast in town. The lunch and dinner menu features seafood dishes accompanied by local produce (mains $12–22). After your meal, ask to see the 200-year-old "captain's table" in the private dining room; it's built of solid oak and measures six meters in length.

The **❰ Commodore Dining Room** (Manor Inn, Hwy. 101, Hebron, 902/742-2487; daily for lunch and dinner) is named for the sea captain who once lived here. The room is filled with richly elegant furnishings, and service is very professional, which makes the prices a pleasant surprise. For example, you could start with scallop wraps and then order salmon topped with a maple-mustard glaze and baked on a cedar plank for just $25 combined. Wines ($24–30) are also sensibly priced.

Beyond the Manor Inn, **Churchill Mansion Country Inn** (Hwy. 1, Darlings Lake, 902/649-2818 or 888/453-5565, www.churchillmansion.com; May–Oct.; daily 6:30–9 P.M.) offers a buffet for $15. It includes salads, seafood casserole, mussels, grilled fish, vegetables, and dessert. Nonguests should make reservations.

INFORMATION AND SERVICES

Greeting visitors as they arrive by ferry is the cavernous **Nova Scotia Visitor Information Centre** (228 Main at Forest St., 902/742-5033; June–mid-Oct. daily 9 A.M.–5 P.M., July–Aug. Thurs.–Tues. 9 A.M.–9 P.M., Wed. 9 A.M.–5 P.M.), where you'll find literature and information on just about everything imaginable in the city and the province. In advance of your visit, visit www.goyarmouth.com.

The **public library** (405 Main St., 902/742-5040; Mon.–Fri. 9 A.M.–9 P.M., Sat. 9 A.M.–5 P.M.) is a good place to check your email.

The **Regional Health Centre** is at 50 Vancouver Street (902/742-1540). For the **RCMP,** call 902/742-8777. The town has seven banks downtown and at the malls, and there's also a currency-exchange counter (exchange rates are better at the banks) at the visitors center. The **post office** is at 15 Willow Street.

GETTING THERE AND AROUND

The Cat (902/742-6800 or 888/249-7245, www.catferry.com), a super-fast vehicular ferry, crosses to Yarmouth from Portland (Maine) in 5.5 hours and from Bar Harbor (Maine) in three hours. It runs three or four times weekly from each port June–mid-October. From Portland, peak-season (July–Aug.) one-way fares are adult US$99, senior US$79, child US$55, vehicle under 6.6 feet US$164. From Bar Harbor, fares are adult US$69, senior US$58, child US$48, vehicle under 6.6 feet US$115. After clearing immigration and customs at the downtown Yarmouth terminal, the information center is straight up the hill, and the main drag is off to the left. From Yarmouth it's 123 kilometers (90 minutes) to Shelburne, 340 kilometers (four hours) to Halifax, and 105 kilometers (70 minutes) to Digby.

Avis (902/742-3323) and **Budget** (902/742-9500) have desks at the ferry terminal, but reserve a vehicle before arriving.

SOUTH SHORE

FUNDY COAST

The natural beauty of Nova Scotia's Fundy coast is sublime. Sea breezes bathe the shore in crisp salt air, and the sun illuminates the seascape colors with a clarity that defies a painter's palette. Wildflowers bloom with abandon, nourished by the moist coastal air. And fog, thick as cotton, sometimes envelops the region during the summer. This is the Fundy Coast, which stretches from Yarmouth in the west to the farthest reaches of the Bay of Fundy in the east. Quietly and relentlessly, twice a day, a tidal surge that has its beginnings far away pours into the bay, creating the highest tides on the planet. Fishing boats are lifted from the muddy sea floor, and whales in pursuit of silvery herring hurry along the summertime currents, their mammoth hulks buoyed by the 100 billion tons of seawater that gush into the long bay between Nova Scotia and New Brunswick. The cycle from low to high tide takes a mere six hours. The tide peaks, in places high enough to swamp a four-story building, and then begins to retreat. As the sea level drops, coastal peninsulas and rocky islets emerge from the froth, veiled in seaweed. The sea floor reappears, shiny as shellac and littered with sea urchins, periwinkles, and shells. Where no one walked just hours ago, local children run and skip on the beaches, pausing to retrieve tidal treasures. Locals take the Fundy tides for granted. For visitors, it's an astounding show.

To a great extent, the history of the province's Fundy Coast is the story of all of Nova Scotia, and this is reflected in the region's wealth of historic and cultural wonders. France's colonial ambitions began at Port-Royal and clashed

© ANDREW HEMPSTEAD

HIGHLIGHTS

◀ **Église de Sainte-Marie:** A pocket of Acadian villages along the Fundy Coast allows visitors to immerse themselves in this uniquely French culture by trying Acadian cooking at Rapure Acadienne, visiting the local museums, and straining their necks below Église de Sainte-Marie, the tallest wooden church in North America (page 98).

◀ **Whale-Watching on the Bay of Fundy:** Use Digby Neck and the adjacent islands as a base for whale-watching trips into the Bay of Fundy (page 104).

◀ **Fort Anne National Historic Site:** After centuries of changing hands between the British and the French, the site of numerous fortifications and onetime capital of Nova Scotia is in the hands of the government as a tourist attraction (page 106).

◀ **Historic Gardens:** The name doesn't do them justice. Garden styles from the Middle Ages through to modern times have been carefully planted at this downtown Annapolis Royal attraction (page 106).

◀ **Port-Royal National Historic Site:** The oldest European settlement north of St. Augustine, Florida, has been re-created at this important national historic site (page 107).

◀ **Grand Pré National Historic Site:** This outdoor museum brings the Henry Wadsworth Longfellow story of Evangeline, a young girl caught up in the Acadian deportation, to life (page 116).

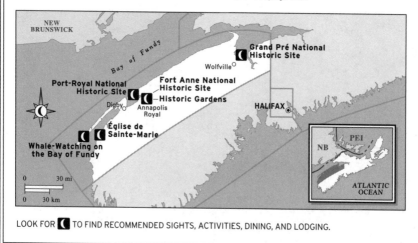

LOOK FOR ◀ TO FIND RECOMMENDED SIGHTS, ACTIVITIES, DINING, AND LODGING.

FUNDY COAST

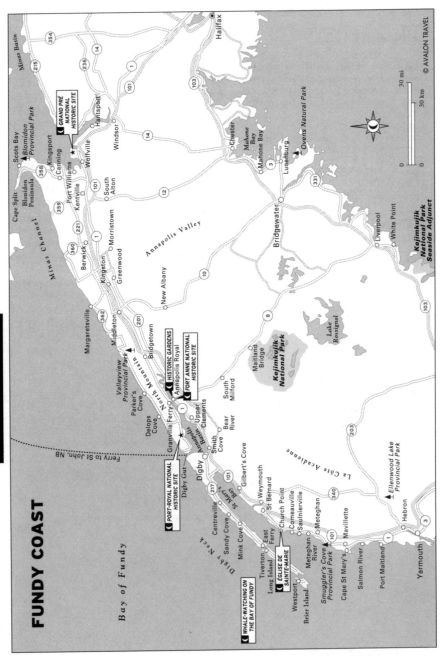

FUNDY COAST

© AVALON TRAVEL

head-on with England's quest for New World dominance, and multiple national historic sites along the coast lie in testament to these troubled times. The trim Acadian villages of La Côte Acadienne, the historic streetscape of Annapolis Royal, and the gracious towns of Wolfville and Windsor add to the appeal.

PLANNING YOUR TIME

You can drive between Yarmouth and Halifax in a single day, but you should allow a minimum of two days, which would mean you could reserve a room at one of Annapolis Royal's many historic inns. This small town is definitely the historic heart of the Fundy Coast, with sights such as **Fort Anne National Historic Site,** the **Historic Gardens,** and **Port-Royal National Historic Site** easily filling out a full day of sightseeing. For this reason, two days and two nights should be allotted for exploring the Fundy Coast. At the western end, the detour through La Côte Acadienne and stops at Acadian icons such as **Église de Sainte-Marie** add only slightly to the length of the drive. The most impressive Acadian attraction, **Grand Pré National Historic Site,** is farther east, and it deserves at least three hours of your time. At some time during your travels through the region you'll want to focus on the Bay of Fundy (digging into a plate of plump Digby scallops doesn't count). Taking the above into consideration, if you have two nights planned for the Fundy Coast, and you are traveling east from Yarmouth, spend the first morning meandering along La Côte Acadienne, order scallops for lunch in Digby, and continue to Annapolis Royal. Spend the rest of the afternoon and the first part of the next morning exploring this town before moving on to Wolfville. Spend the night, rise early for a short hike through Blomidon Provincial Park, and then move on to Grand Pré National Historic Site. You'll be back in the capital by late afternoon. With an extra day and night, plan on driving along Digby Neck and going **whale-watching.**

La Côte Acadienne

Those who zoom along Highway 101 between Yarmouth and Digby will be missing the charming La Côte Acadienne (Acadian Coast), also known as the **Municipality of Clare,** a 50-kilometer coastal stretch populated by descendants of the French who resettled here after the Acadian expulsion of 1755.

To get there, follow Highway 1 north through Yarmouth or take Highway 101 to Exit 32 to save a little time. Between Rivière-aux-Saumon (Salmon River) in the south and Weymouth in the north, the place-names, the soaring Catholic churches, and the proud Acadian flags (a French tricolor with a single yellow star) announce that you're in the largest francophone enclave in Nova Scotia.

MAVILLETTE AND VICINITY

For a look at the dynamic Fundy, check out **Mavillette Beach Provincial Park,** on the south side of Cap Sainte-Marie (Cape St. Mary's). The sign for Cape View Restaurant signals the turn from Highway 1; the road peels down to the sea and runs alongside high dunes. Boardwalks cross the dunes to the mile-long beach, where sandbars trap water into warm pools at low tide. On sunny days, beachcombers walk the expanse and hunt for unusual seashells. Though this is one of the finest beaches in all Nova Scotia, crowds are nonexistent.

Accommodations and Food

Along the beach access road you'll find **Cape View Motel and Cottages** (902/645-2258, www.capeviewmotel.ca; June–Sept.). The motel's 10 basic rooms ($80 s or d) and five cottages ($90–120) overlook sand dunes and the provincial park.

Across the road from the Cape View Motel and with wonderful views of the beach and its stunning sunsets is **Cape View Restaurant** (157

John Doucette Rd., 902/645-2519; mid-May–Oct. daily for breakfast and dinner), which dishes up breakfasts such as scrambled eggs with lobster ($13) and seafood with an Acadian twist the rest of the day (mains $12–22).

Smuggler's Cove Provincial Park

From Mavillette Beach, it's 16 kilometers north to Smuggler's Cove Provincial Park. Walkways here lead to great bluff-top views of the coast and down steep tree-lined steps to the rocky shoreline. The coastal cliffs in this area are notched with caves, which were used by Prohibition-era rumrunners. Some of the caves can be explored at low tide. The park also holds numerous picnic tables, making it an ideal lunch stop, but no campsites.

METEGHAN AND VICINITY

Settled in 1785, the seaport of Meteghan, 15 kilometers north of Mavillette, is the district's commercial hub, although the population still numbers fewer than 1,000. The main wharf is a hive of activity throughout the day, but the official attraction is **La Vieille Maison** (Old House Museum) on Highway 1 (902/645-2389; July–Aug. daily 9 A.M.–7 P.M., June and Sept. daily 10 A.M.–6 P.M.; donation). In the Robicheau family's former homestead, this museum features 18th-century furnishings and exhibits explaining the area's history, with help from bilingual guides in traditional Acadian costume. Part of the museum is operated as the **Meteghan Visitor Centre.**

Accommodations and Food

For a place to overnight, the tidy **Bluefin Motel** (7765 Hwy. 1, 902/645-2251 or 888/446-3466, www.bluefinmotel.ns.ca; $79–139 s or d) is a good choice. Situated on the south side of town, the rooms don't take full advantage of its cliff-top setting, but a few outdoor chairs can be found on a deck behind the restaurant. The view, the lobster traps strung across the adjacent lot, and scallop trawlers making their way slowly across the bay all add to the appeal. The motel restaurant is open daily from 8 A.M. for breakfast, lunch, and dinner.

A seafood cornucopia is brought in daily by the seaport's scallop draggers, herring seiners, and lobster boats. **Blue Rock Restaurant** (Hwy. 1 near the museum, 902/645-3453) is a good place for seafood dining.

North from Meteghan

The village of **Meteghan River,** north of Meteghan, is Nova Scotia's largest wooden ship–building center. One of the nicest lodgings along La Côte Acadienne is **L'Auberge au Havre du Capitaine** (9118 Hwy. 1, 902/769-2001, www.havreducapitaine.ca), a country-style inn with hardwood floors and a sitting area set around a large stone fireplace. Choose from rooms with private baths and TVs ($85–100 s or d) or larger suites with whirlpool tubs ($110 d). The inn's licensed dining room is open daily for breakfast, lunch, and dinner.

Also in Meteghan River, lobster lovers should stop in at **Wright's Lobster** (Hwy. 1, 902/645-3919; Mon.–Fri. 9 A.M.–5 P.M.), where you can buy live lobsters kept in flow-through crates at the large warehouse—perfect if you're camping or if your accommodation has cooking facilities.

Comeauville

The village of Comeauville, a bit farther north, is notable for **La Galerie Comeau** (761 Hwy. 1, 902/769-2896; June–Aug. Mon.–Sat. 10 A.M.–5 P.M., Sun. noon–5 P.M.), where artist Denise Comeau displays and sells her watercolors that reflect the region and its Acadian roots.

POINT DE L'ÉGLISE (CHURCH POINT)

This aptly named community is the last major Acadian community for northbound travelers, but it's also the most interesting.

◖ Église de Sainte-Marie

Built between 1903 and 1905, the enormous Église de Sainte-Marie (St. Mary's Church), the largest and tallest wooden church in North America, dominates this village of 490 inhabitants. The building is laid out in the shape of

The soaring Église de Sainte-Marie is the architectural highlight of La Côte Acadienne.

a cross, and its soaring 56-meter steeple has been ballasted with 40 tons of rock to withstand the winter wind. Inside, **Le Musée Sainte-Marie** (902/769-2808; June–mid-Oct. daily 9 A.M.–5 P.M.; adult $2, child free) exhibits religious artifacts and historical documents and photos. Mass takes place Sunday at 10:30 A.M.

Accommodations and Camping

Accommodations are available at **Le Manoir Samson** (1768 Hwy. 1, 902/769-2526 or 888/769-8605, www.manoirsamson.com; May–Aug.; $75–125 s or d), a red brick roadside motel where most rooms have a microwave and fridge. A light breakfast is included.

Campers can head to the full-service **Belle Baie Park** (Hwy. 1, 902/769-3160, www.bellebaiepark.ca; mid-May–Sept.), an oceanfront campground with its own beach, an outdoor pool, a playground, and a launderette. Tent sites are $20, hookups range $25–35, and the more expensive ones sit right on the edge of the ocean. Friday night events include potluck dinners and live music.

Food

Through town to the south is **◖ Rapure Acadienne** (1443 Hwy. 1, 902/769-2172; Mon.–Sat. 8 A.M.–5:30 P.M.), the most authentic place in all of Nova Scotia to try rappie pie, a traditional Acadian chicken dish with a rather unusually textured potato filling. The pies are massive (and also come with beef and clam fillings) and cost just $6, including a side of butter or molasses. Order at the inside window (where you can peek through at the big ovens) and eat at the one indoor table or the picnic tables outside.

CONTINUING TO DIGBY

The last of the Acadian communities is **Grosses Coques,** a small village immediately north of Pointe de l'Église that takes its name from the huge bar clams harvested here on the tidal flats, an important food source for early settlers.

Gilbert's Cove

A short unpaved road leads from Highway 101 to **Gilbert's Cove Lighthouse.** Built in 1904 to help vessels navigate the upper reaches of St. Mary's Bay, it has been restored and is open to the public in July and August.

Gilbert's Cove Lighthouse

FUNDY COAST

Digby and Vicinity

The port of Digby (pop. 2,300), 105 kilometers northeast of Yarmouth and 235 kilometers west of Halifax, is the terminus for the ferry from Saint John (New Brunswick) and home for the world's largest scallop fleet. The Mi'Kmaq name for the area is Te'Wapskik, meaning "flowing between high rocks," a reference to Digby Gut, a narrow opening in the Annapolis Basin to the north of town. Digby derived its English name from Admiral Robert Digby, who sailed up the Fundy in 1793 and settled the place with 1,500 Loyalists from New England. The scallop fleet ties up off Fishermen's Wharf off Water Street; be there at sunset when the pastel-painted draggers lie at anchor in a semicircle, backlit by the intense setting sun.

Lying outside the area's main roads, Digby is easily bypassed. High-speed Highway 101 lies south of Digby and routes sightseers up the St. Mary's Bay coastline into the Annapolis Valley. More scenic Highway 1, the pastoral route through the valley, starts beyond Digby to the west. Even the site of Digby's ferry terminal diverts traffic around town, and if you enter the province from New Brunswick, street signs will direct you from Shore Road to Highway 101 via Victoria Street and Highway 303.

SIGHTS AND RECREATION

A couple of worthwhile attractions are scattered along the waterfront, but the highlights are farther afield—Digby Neck and Kejimkujik National Park, both covered in this section.

Lady Vanessa

On the boardwalk in front of the Fundy Restaurant (Water St.) is the dry-docked 98-foot *Lady Vanessa*. This locally built scallop boat is open to the public (June–Sept. daily 9 A.M.–7 P.M.; $2), allowing visitors the opportunity to step aboard and experience the workplace of local fishermen. You can explore the entire boat—above and below

deck, the shucking room, the wheelhouse, and the living quarters. Interpretive panels describe the scallop fishing process, while the claws of a 45-pound lobster are one of the more eye-catching displays. A 30-minute documentary screened on board is surprisingly interesting. It is mostly underwater footage, including of a lobster entering a trap and scallops being scooped up by the dragnets.

Admiral Digby Museum

Digby's place in history is on display at the harborfront Admiral Digby Museum (95 Montague Row, 902/245-6322; mid-June–Aug. Mon.–Sat. 9 A.M.–5 P.M., Sun. 1–5 P.M.; donation), housed in a trim two-story Georgian-era residence with exhibits of old photographs, interesting maps, and maritime artifacts.

Bear River

Calling itself the "Switzerland of Nova Scotia" may be a stretch, but this small village straddling the Bear River eight kilometers south of Digby is nestled in a delightful little valley, where the trees turn glorious colors in late September. Along the main street are a motley collection of wooden buildings in various states of repair, many built on stilts above the river far below. Those that have been restored now hold craft shops.

ENTERTAINMENT AND EVENTS

Montague Row to Water Street is the place for people-watching, especially at sunset. **Club 98 Lounge** (28 Water St., 902/245-4950) in the Fundy Restaurant has a band (cover charge) or disc jockey Friday–Saturday. The lounge at the **Pines Resort** (103 Shore Rd., 902/245-2511; closed Sun.) is known for tamer pursuits, low lighting, a comfortable ambience, and finely tuned mixed drinks.

The port's famed scallops attract appropriate

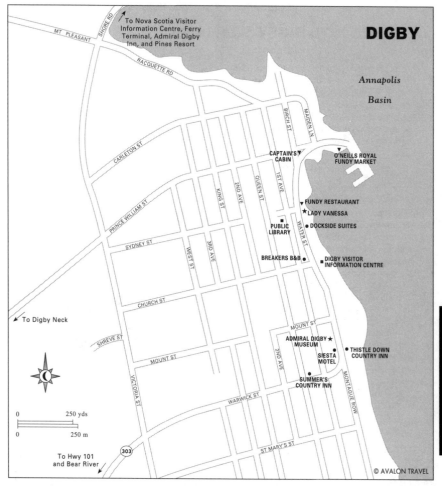

fanfare during **Digby Scallops Days** (www
.digbyscallopdays.com) with a parade, scal-
lop-shucking competitions, street vendors, the
crowning of the Scallop Queen and Princesses,
music, fireworks, and a parade of the scallop
fleet in the second week of August.

ACCOMMODATIONS AND CAMPING

Digby has a few motel rooms under $100, in-
cluding the **Siesta Motel** (81 Montague Row,
902/245-2568; $70–95 s or d), but there are no
real bargains in town.

$50-100

Two blocks from the waterfront, **Summer's
Country Inn** (16 Warwick St., 902/245-2250,
www.summerscountryinn.com; May–Oct.;
$65–95 s or d) has 11 guest rooms in an 1830s
home. Each room has a private bath and comfortable bed, although the decorations in some
are a little flowery for my tastes.

FUNDY COAST

DIGGING INTO DIGBY SCALLOPS

Digby is known for its scallops, so there is no better place to try them than this small Fundy Coast port. Unlike other bivalves (such as clams), scallops do not bury themselves in the sand. Instead, they live on the bottom of the Bay of Fundy and "swim" by quickly opening and closing their shells. The fishermen of Digby harvest scallops by dragging large wire baskets over the sea floor. They are shucked (opened) immediately and put on ice until reaching the shore.

The water temperature in the Bay of Fundy varies only slightly through the year, which, combined with the tides' creating lots of nutrient movement, creates ideal conditions for the scallops. The result is the plumpest yet most delicate and succulent meat you could imagine. As a bonus, scallops are low in fat and full of protein.

Across Nova Scotia and beyond, Digby scallops appear on menus by name. In better dining rooms they are sautéed in butter with light spices, or combined in seafood casseroles or dishes such as bouillabaisse. Local eateries such as the **Fundy Restaurant** (34 Water St., 902/245-4950; 8 A.M.-10 P.M.), which has views of the fishing fleet, get creative with scallop omelets, scallop chowder, and scallop fettuccine. At the wharfside **O'Neil's Royal Fundy Market** (Prince William St., 902/245-6528;

Mon.-Fri. 9 A.M.-5:30 P.M., Sat. 10 A.M.-5 P.M.), you can buy them fresh from the trawler and prepare them as you please back at your kitchen-equipped accommodation.

© ANDREW HEMPSTEAD

Digby is home to the world's largest fleet of scallop trawlers.

$100-150

Digby's only waterfront accommodation is **(Thistle Down Country Inn** (98 Montague Row, 902/245-4490 or 800/565-8081, www .thistledown.ns.ca; May–Oct.; $105–130 s or d), where a landscaped garden extends right to water's edge. It comprises six rooms in an Edwardian-era home and six regular motel rooms in a new addition that occupies the back half of the property. A full breakfast is included in the rates, and dinner is available with a reservation.

The **Admiral Digby Inn** (441 Shore Rd., 902/245-2531 or 800/465-6262, www.digbyns .com; mid-May–Oct.) is across the road from

the Annapolis Basin halfway between town and the ferry terminal. Better-than-average motel rooms start at $110 s or d, and for $135 you get a balcony with water views. Cottages with one and two bedrooms are $150 and $200 respectively. All rates include a light breakfast. Amenities include a restaurant, a lounge, an indoor pool, and a laundry.

Breakers Bed and Breakfast (5 Water St., 902/245-4643 or 866/333-5773, www .thebreakersbb.com; May–Oct.; $125–145 s or d, including full breakfast) is a 150-year-old two-story home across from the waterfront. The three guest rooms are extra large and furnished in keeping with a heritage theme. A covered front porch with water views and the book-filled sitting room add to the charm.

Dockside Suites (26 Water St., 902/245-4950, www.fundyrestaurant.com; $129–159 s or d) is part of the Fundy Restaurant complex. Each of the six units is air-conditioned and has a balcony with harbor views and a separate bedroom. Other in-room amenities include a TV/DVD combo and high-speed Internet access.

$150-200

Appealing to visitors looking for an old-fashioned resort experience, the baronial **Pines Resort** (103 Shore Rd., 902/245-2511 or 800/667-4637, www.digbypines.ca; mid-May–mid-Oct.; from $198 s or d) peers down over the port from the brow of a hill on the town's outskirts. The French Norman manor of stucco and stone was built in 1903 and served as a Canadian Pacific Railway hotel until the province bought it in 1965. The accommodations include more than 80 rooms in the manor and 30 cottages shaded by spruce, fir, and pine. The hotel offers a dining room of provincial renown, an 18-hole golf course (greens fees $65), an outdoor pool, a fitness center, tennis courts, hiking trails, and afternoon tea. Most guests stay as part of a package, paying, for example, $120 per person for accommodation, golf, and breakfast.

Campgrounds

Close to town is **Digby Campground** (Smith's Cove, 230 Victoria St., 902/245-1985; mid-May–mid-Oct.; $20–26). To get there, take Exit 26 from Highway 101 and follow the signs toward the ferry for three kilometers. Within walking distance of downtown, it has an outdoor pool, Laundromat, and hookups.

FOOD

Right downtown, **Fundy Restaurant** (34 Water St., 902/245-4950; 8 A.M.–10 P.M.) is a large casual restaurant overlooking the scallop fleet. Seating is inside in a main dining room, in a solarium, or out on the balcony. Digby scallops are the specialty, prepared any way you'd like them or in combination with other seafood—the Fundy (scallop) omelet ($11) is an interesting breakfast choice, while the rest of the day dishes such as scallop chowder ($9) and a platter of scallops cooked in various ways ($18) are good ways to sample this tasty treat.

One block back from the water, **Captain's Cabin** (Water St., 902/245-4868; 11:30 A.M.–10:30 P.M.) is a little more of a locals' hangout, but it still specializes in seafood. Dishes are a little less creative but a couple of dollars less expensive. A half lobster with a side of scallops is $25.

Check out ◖ **O'Neil's Royal Fundy Market** (Prince William St., 902/245-6528; Mon.–Fri. 9 A.M.–5:30 P.M., Sat. 10 A.M.–5 P.M.) for fresh seafood for those staying somewhere with cooking facilities. Otherwise, order pan- or deep-fried scallops, seafood chowder, fresh mussels and salmon, cooked lobster, and smoked cod, haddock, mackerel, and Digby chicks (smoked herring) to eat in or take out.

INFORMATION

Downtown, the **Digby Visitor Information Centre** (110 Montague Row, 902/245-5714) is open June–early October daily 9 A.M.–5 P.M. Along the road between the ferry terminal and town is the **Nova Scotia Visitor Information Centre** (237 Shore Rd., 902/245-2201; early May–Oct. daily 9 A.M.–5 P.M., until 9 P.M. daily in July and Aug.), which represents tourism regions throughout the province.

Digby Public Library (corner of 1st and Sydney Sts.; Tues.–Fri. 3–5 P.M., Sat. 10 A.M.–1 P.M.) has public Internet access.

GETTING THERE AND AROUND

The terminus of the **Princess of Acadia** is through town near the mouth of the Annapolis Basin. Operated by **Bay Ferries** (902/245-2116 or 888/249-7245, www.nfl-bay.com), the large vessel plies the Bay of Fundy between Saint John (New Brunswick) and Digby (Nova Scotia) one or two times daily throughout the year. High-season one-way fares are adult $40, senior and child $30, vehicle $100. The crossing takes 3.5 hours, and reservations are essential if you're traveling with a vehicle.

The **Acadian Lines** bus pulls into the convenience store at 77 Montague Row (902/245-2048) on its route between Digby and Halifax.

DIGBY NECK

The Digby Neck is a long spindly peninsula reaching like an antenna for almost 80 kilometers back down the Bay of Fundy from Digby. Beyond the end of the peninsula are two small islands. Off the main tourist path, the peninsula will appeal to those interested in nature and spending time in tiny coastal villages where the pace of live is much slower than elsewhere along the Fundy Coast.

Driving Digby Neck and Beyond

From Digby, Highway 217 runs down the center of Digby Neck, through the villages of **Centreville, Sandy Cove,** and **Mink Cove.** At picturesque Sandy Cove, houses cling to the shoreline while a nearby trail leads to Nova Scotia's highest waterfall. At East Ferry, a ferry departs every 30 minutes on the half hour for **Long Island.** The trip across takes just five minutes and costs $5 per vehicle inclusive of passengers. Beyond Tiverton, the main town on Long Island, a two-kilometer (30-minute) each-way trail leads along sea cliffs to **Balancing Rock.** This volcanic outcrop rises precariously from a narrow ledge, looking as if it will topple at any time.

Brier Island

A second ferry (also $5) connects Long Island to Brier Island, Nova Scotia's westernmost extremity. The island has a bustling little fishing port at **Westport** and a tourism business that revolves around spring wildflowers, summer whale-watching, and year-round bird-watching. The island's most famous inhabitant was Joshua Slocum (the two vehicle ferries are named for him and his famous sailing boat, *Spray*), who spent his childhood on the island before taking to the high seas and becoming

the first person to sail around the world solo. A small monument on a headland south of Westport commemorates the feat.

◖ Whale-Watching on the Bay of Fundy

Digby Neck is the base for a thriving whale-watching community. Companies generally offer half-day excursions between mid-June and early October, with regular sightings of finback, right, humpback, and minke whales, as well as Atlantic white-sided dolphins and porpoises. **Ocean Explorations,** based on Long Island at Tiverton (902/839-2417 or 877/654-2341), is notable for guide Tom Goodwin, a well-known biologist who takes interested visitors out into the bay aboard high-speed but stable inflatable Zodiac boats. In addition to the most common species, Goodwin searches out North Atlantic right whales when they gather in the middle of the bay (usually August). Estimated to number fewer than 300, these are the world's rarest whales, so named because they were the "right" whales to hunt. Rates are adult $59, child $40. Other operators include **Brier Island Whale and Seabird Cruises** (Westport, Brier Island, 902/839-2995 or 800/656-3660) and **Mariner Cruises** (Westport, Brier Island, 902/839-2346 or 800/239-2189).

Accommodations and Food

◖ **Brier Island Hostel** (Water St., Westport, Brier Island, 902/839-2273, www.brierisland-hostel.com; adult $18, child $9) is in a prime position across from the harbor and adjacent to a grocery store stocked with local delicacies and deli items. The lodge has just 12 beds spread through three rooms. The communal kitchen, sitting area, and wide deck are all excellent.

Between the ferry and Westport (one kilometer from each), **Brier Island Lodge** (Northern Point Rd., 902/839-2300 or 800/662-8355, www.brierisland.com; May–Oct.; $60–150 s or d) sits on a bluff overlooking the sea. The 40 motel-style rooms are spacious and bright; most have water views, and some have king beds. The lodge's pine-paneled restaurant is my favorite island dining room. You can order old-fashioned roast turkey dinner or local specialties such as smoked pollack chowder and steamed periwinkles.

Information

The website www.brierisland.org has information about the island, but before driving out along Digby Neck, stop by the **Provincial Visitor Centre** (902/742-6639; May–mid-Oct. daily 9 A.M.–5 P.M., July–Aug. daily 9 A.M.–9 P.M.) along Highway 303 between the ferry terminal and downtown Digby.

Annapolis Royal

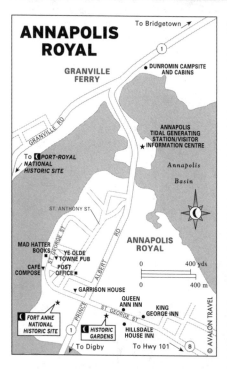

The history of Annapolis Royal (pop. 500) spans four centuries, with much of the past preserved along a main street that is lined with the finest collection of pre-1800 buildings in Canada. The town and surrounding area has 150 registered historic buildings, three national historic sites, and Canada's oldest wooden building. Add to the mix one of the world's only tidal power generating plants, Nova Scotia's largest fun park and its smallest pub, and a selection of gracious accommodations and you find a town like no other place in the province.

History

In 1605, Samuel de Champlain and the survivors of the bitter winter in New Brunswick moved across the Bay of Fundy and established the fortified Port-Royal across Annapolis Basin from modern-day Annapolis Royal. It was the first permanent European settlement north of St. Augustine, Florida. After eight years the settlement came to an abrupt end when it was attacked and destroyed by New Englanders. In the 1630s, the French governor Charles de Menou d'Aulnay built a new Port Royal on the south shore of the Annapolis Basin, attracting French settlers who came to be known as Acadians. The site would remain capital of Acadie for the next eight decades. The British captured the fort in 1710, renaming it Fort Anne and rechristening the town as Annapolis Royal in honor of their queen. It would serve as Nova Scotia's first capital until 1749, when it was succeeded by the new town of Halifax.

SIGHTS

It's easy to spend a half day wandering through Fort Anne National Historic Site and the adjacent St. George Street, which curves downhill to the waterfront. For Annapolis Royal's other attractions, you'll need a vehicle.

FUNDY COAST

Annapolis Tidal Generating Station

It may not be the town's oldest attraction, but it contains the local tourist information center, so it makes a sensible starting place for your visit. Near the head of Annapolis Basin, signposted to the right as you come into town off Highways 1 or 101, the **Tidal Power Plant** (Hwy. 1, 902/532-5769; May–mid-Oct. daily 9 A.M.–5 P.M., July–Aug. 9 A.M.–8 P.M.; free) is the only facility in North America that generates electricity from the tides. Originally built as an experiment, the plant still operates and is capable of generating 20 kilowatts of electricity (enough to power 4,000 homes). The facility harnesses the energy of the massive Fundy tides, which fill a head pond twice daily and then pass through a turbine as they flow back out toward the ocean. The plant's top floor is dedicated to describing the process, with windows allowing views down the bay and of the head pond.

◖ Fort Anne National Historic Site

This 18th-century fort and grounds, Canada's first national historic site (St. George St., 902/532-2397; mid-May–mid-Oct. daily 9 A.M.–5:30 P.M.; adult $4, senior $3.50, child $2), overlook Annapolis Basin from the heart of Annapolis Royal. Considered the key stronghold for possession of Nova Scotia, as the British knew the region—it was Acadie to the French—the site had particular importance to both parties. It has been fortified on at least eight occasions since Scots built Fort Charles in 1629. The earliest French fort, dating to 1630, was designed with a star-shaped layout. Earthwork from the French fort of 1702 remains today, impressively banked with sweeping verdant lawns. These are open to the public year-round. Interpretive boards describe features such as the parade ground, the chapel site, and a restored powder magazine. The British added an officers' garrison in 1797. This whitewashed building now houses a museum that tells the long and colorful story of the fort.

◖ Historic Gardens

The Historic Gardens (441 St. George St., 902/532-7018; mid-May–mid-Oct. daily 9 A.M.–5 P.M., extended July–Aug. daily 8 A.M.–dusk; adult $8.50, senior and child $7.50) comprise four hectares of theme gardens, a restaurant, and a gift shop. The gardens

cannon at Fort Anne National Historic Site

©ANDREW HEMPSTEAD

are undeniably beautiful, but they are also interesting. The Acadian Garden, complete with an Acadian house and outdoor oven, replicates that of the earliest European settlers. Vegetables such as beets, carrots, parsnips, onions, and cabbages are surrounded by a hedge to keep out wild animals, and off to one side is a hedge-encircled orchard of apple and pear trees. Other highlights include the Knot Garden, styled after a hedge garden of the Middle Ages; the Governor's Garden, laid out as a formal garden in the 1750s, when Annapolis Royal was the capital; and a striking Rose Garden with more than 200 varieties, including early English and modern hybrids. The gardens are at their most spectacular in summer, with roses peaking mid-July–September.

◖ Port-Royal National Historic Site

The first lasting settlement north of Florida, the 1605 fort at Port-Royal has been reconstructed at what is believed to be the original site (902/532-2898; mid-May–mid-Oct. daily 9 A.M.–5:30 P.M.; adult $4, senior $3.50, child $2). The French settlement of 1605 has been reconstructed from Samuel de Champlain's plan using 17th-century construction techniques; the rustic buildings—governor's house, priest's dwelling, bakery, guardroom, and others, furnished with period reproductions—form a rectangle around a courtyard within the palisaded compound. The original outpost boasted many historic firsts: Canada's first play, *Le Théâtre de Neptune,* was written and produced here by the young Parisian lawyer Marc Lescarbot; the continent's first social club, l'Ordre de Bon Temps (the Order of Good Cheer) was founded here in 1606; and the New World's first grain mill was built here to grind meal from the first cereal crops. The story of these is brought to life by knowledgeable staff dressed in period costume. To get to Port-Royal, cross Annapolis Basin by the generating station and turn left at Granville Ferry. It's 10 kilometers along the road (two kilometers beyond Melanson Settlement National Historic Site).

RECREATION
Hiking
Delaps Cove, 24 kilometers west of Annapolis Royal (cross Annapolis Basin, head south toward Port Royal for eight kilometers, and turn right on the unpaved road that ends at the Bay of Fundy), is a small fishing village that is the start of the **Delap's Cove Wilderness Trail,** one of the few longer hiking trails along this stretch of coast. From the wharf at the end of the road, the trail meanders southwest along the coast for 15 kilometers. It takes about eight hours round-trip, but you can hike for just an hour or so before turning around if time is an issue.

Fun Park
Upper Clements Parks (Hwy. 1, Upper Clements, 902/532-7557; mid-June–early Sept. daily 11 A.M.–7 P.M.) is Nova Scotia's largest theme park. Its style is thoroughly Nova Scotian, featuring a train ride on a historic replica, a minigolf course designed as a map of the province, and the re-creation of a fishing village. The park also has a roller coaster, flume ride, carousel, pedal boats, live entertainment, dinner theater Friday–Saturday evenings, a crafts area with demonstrations and a shop, and dining rooms. Everyone pays $8 to get through the gate, plus $3 per ride or $22.50 for everything. Tickets also include entry to the adjacent **Upper Clements Wildlife Park,** featuring indigenous wildlife of the province such as black bears, white-tailed deer, moose, and cougars, as well as farm animals and Sable Island horses.

ACCOMMODATIONS AND CAMPING
$50-100
Aside from the cabins at **Dunromin Waterfront Campground and Cabins,** few places offer rooms for less than $100 in July and August. One option is **Grange Cottage** (102 Richie St., 902/532-7993; $65 s, $75 d), where the three guest rooms share one bathroom. The rear deck has river views and the front porch is a relaxing place to cool off on hot afternoons. Rates include a full breakfast.

Swimming, hiking, wagon rides, canoeing, and lawn games fill the day at **Mountain Top Cottages** (888 Parker Mountain Rd., 902/532-2564 or 877/885-1185, www.mountaintopcottages.com; May–Oct.; $97–127 s or d), in a forested setting atop North Mountain. Seventeen simple cottages with one or two bedrooms overlook a private lake. Each has a microwave and fridge. To get there, cross Annapolis Basin at the tidal plant, follow Highway 1 through Granville Ferry, and take Parker Mountain Road off to the north (left).

$100-150

Hillsdale House Inn (519 Upper St. George St., 902/532-2345 or 877/839-2821, www.hillsdalehouseinn.ca; May–Dec.; $109–149 s or d) is on a six-hectare estate that has been graced by kings and prime ministers. The main house has 11 guest rooms and the adjacent coach house another three. Antiques fill public areas, including a cozy lounge. A cooked breakfast is included in the rates.

King George Inn (548 Upper St. George St., 902/532-5286, www.kinggeorgeinn.20m.com; mid-May–mid-Nov.; $90–160 s or d) is a ship captain's home, built circa 1868 and furnished with Victorian-era antiques. It offers eight luxurious guest rooms, including a two-room family suite. Amenities include a library, pianos, free use of bicycles, and evening tea and coffee.

Set on two hectares of landscaped grounds, **◖ Queen Anne Inn** (494 Upper St. George St., 902/532-7850 or 877/536-0403, www.queenanneinn.ns.ca; May–Oct.; $119–210 s or d) is a restored 1865 Victorian mansion with a grand mahogany staircase that sweeps upstairs to 10 guest rooms outfitted with period furnishings. Room 10 is significantly smaller than the remaining nine, which are extra large ($159–189 s or d). Behind the main house, the carriage house contains two two-bedroom units, perfect for two couples traveling together or a family. Rates include a full three-course breakfast and afternoon tea.

© ANDREW HEMPSTEAD

The Queen Anne Inn is one of many gracious accommodations in Annapolis Royal.

Campgrounds

Running right down to a private beach on the Annapolis Basin, **Dunromin Waterfront Campground and Cabins** (902/532-2808, www.dunromincampsite.com; May–mid-Oct.) is the perfect place for families. With a fort-themed playground, an outdoor pool, minigolf, lawn games, canoe rentals, and a café, the biggest problem will be dragging the children off for a day of sightseeing. The campground has 165 sites, most of them serviced ($26–38.50). Canvas tepees with shared bathrooms are $45 s or d, and cabins range from $65 for shared bathroom to $110 for a two-bedroom waterfront cottage.

Enjoying an absolutely stunning location right on the Bay of Fundy, **◖ Cove Oceanfront Campground** (Parker's Cove, 902/532-5166, www.oceanfront-camping.com; mid-May–late Oct.; $29–95) has modern facilities including a pool, a playground, a games room, and a small café. But it's the views that make this an excellent choice, with grassed terraces ensuring everyone can see the water. To get to Parker's Cove, cross the Annapolis Basin at the generating station, turn right at Granville Ferry, and then take the first left, up and over the low wooded peninsula to Parker's Cove.

FOOD

St. George Street has many dining choices, including diner-style cafés and fine-dining restaurants. If you're staying at a campground or have chosen an accommodation with cooking facilities, head over North Mountain to Parker's Cove and pick up fresh seafood such as scallops, lobster, and crab from **R. R. Shellfish** (902/532-7301), across the road from the water.

Facing Annapolis Basin from behind the main row of shops, **Café Compose** (235 St. George St., 902/532-1251; Mon.–Sat. 11 A.M.–7 P.M., Sun. 1–7 P.M.) is easy to miss. This European-style café pours good coffee and has a menu of light and sweet lunches, including delicious strudels.

Locals gather for afternoon beer and pub grub on the outdoor patio or for nightcaps in the cozy interior of English-style **Ye Olde Towne Pub** (11 Church St., 902/532-2244; Mon.–Sat. 11 A.M.–11 P.M., Sun. noon–8 P.M.), beside the outdoor Farmers Market at the bottom end of St. George Street. Built in 1884 as a bank and reputed to be the smallest bar in Nova Scotia, its meals are typical pub fare, but the portions are generous. Look to the blackboard for seafood specials.

◖ Garrison House (350 St. George St., 902/532-5501; daily from 6 P.M.) is a refined restaurant spread through three connected rooms of an 1854 inn. The chef is renowned for sourcing seasonal produce, while year-round specialties include fish cakes ($14) and Acadian jambalaya ($17). With its impressive wine list and professional service, this is the best place in town for fine dining.

INFORMATION AND SERVICES

Annapolis Royal Visitor Information Centre (Hwy. 1, 902/532-5769; May–mid-Oct. daily 9 A.M.–5 P.M., July–Aug. daily 9 A.M.–8 P.M.; free) is at the Tidal Power Plant, on the north side of downtown. Coming into town from Exit 22 along Highway 101, turn right before the historic main street.

Mad Hatter Books (213 St. George St., 902/532-2070) is an inviting bookstore that stocks a large collection of literature on local history and culture, coffee-table books, and travel guides.

The **post office** is at 50 Victoria Street. At the back of Sinclair Mews is a self-serve **laundry** (daily 9 A.M.–9 P.M.).

Kejimkujik National Park

Deep in the interior of southwestern Nova Scotia, Kejimkujik (kedji-muh-KOO-jick, or "Keji" or "Kedge" for short) National Park lies off Highway 8, about midway between Liverpool and Annapolis Royal. Encompassing 381 square kilometers of drumlins (rounded glacial hills), island-dotted lakes—legacies of the last ice age—and hardwood and conifer forests, the park and the adjacent Tobeatic Game Sanctuary are an important refuge for native wildlife and town-weary Nova Scotians.

Wildlife enthusiasts visit the park for bird-watching (including barred owls, pileated woodpeckers, scarlet tanagers, great crested flycatchers, and loons and other waterfowl) and may also spot black bears, white-tailed deer, bobcats, porcupines, and beavers. The many lakes and connecting rivers attract canoeists and swimmers in warm weather, as well as anglers (particularly for perch and brook trout). Hikers can choose from a network of trails, some leading to backcountry campgrounds; some of the campgrounds are also accessible by canoe. In winter, cross-country skiers take over the hiking trails.

© ANDREW HEMPSTEAD

The Mersey River is one of many waterways within Kejimkujik National Park.

RECREATION

The two most popular park activities are hiking and canoeing. The **Beech Grove Trail** on a two-kilometer loop starts at the visitors center and wends along the Mersey River, where it climbs a drumlin hilltop swathed in an almost-pure beech grove. The **Farmlands Trail** is another drumlin variation, and the 45-minute hike makes its way up a drumlin to an abandoned farm on the hilltop. A little further south along the park access road is the trailhead for the one-kilometer **Rogers Brook** loop, which passes through a forest of red maple and hemlock trees.

You can rent canoes, rowboats, and bicycles ($5 per hour, $24 per day) at Jakes Landing on the northeast side of large Kejimkujik Lake; the adjacent stretch of the Mersey River is placid and suitable for beginning paddlers.

ACCOMMODATIONS AND CAMPING

Within the park, **Jeremy's Bay Campground,** on the north side of Kejimkujik Lake, has 360 unserviced sites for tents and trailers ($25.50), with washrooms and showers, fire pits, and

firewood ($7), a playground, picnic areas, and an interpretive program. Another 46 wilderness sites ($18) are scattered in the woodlands with toilets, tables, grills, and firewood. A percentage of sites can be booked through the **Parks Canada Campground Reservation Service** (905/426-4648 or 877/737-3783, www.pccamping.ca) for $11 per reservation.

Hostelling International's **Raven Haven Hostel** (902/532-7320, www.hihostels.ca; mid-June–Aug.) is in South Milford, about 20 kilometers north of the park toward Annapolis Royal. Members pay $15, nonmembers $17. Family rooms are available, and you can go swimming or canoeing at adjacent Sandy Bottom Lake. Check-in is any time after 1 P.M.

INFORMATION

The **Visitor Reception Centre** (902/682-2772; mid-June–Aug. daily 8:30 A.M.–8 P.M., Aug.–mid-June daily 8:30 A.M.–4:30 P.M.) is just beyond the park entrance. This is the place to buy day passes (adult $6, senior $5, child $3) and fishing licenses ($10 per day, $35 annual) and pick up literature on the park, including hiking trail descriptions. For more information on the park, click through the links at www.pc.gc.ca.

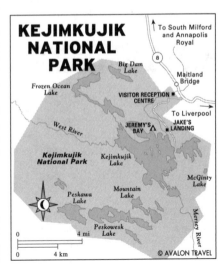

KEJIMKUJIK NATIONAL PARK

To South Milford and Annapolis Royal

Big Dam Lake
Frozen Ocean Lake
Maitland Bridge
VISITOR RECEPTION CENTRE
To Liverpool
West River
JEREMY'S BAY
JAKE'S LANDING
Kejimkujik National Park
Kejimkujik Lake
McGinty Lake
Peskawa Lake
Mountain Lake
Mersey River
Peskowesk Lake

0   4 mi
0   4 km

© AVALON TRAVEL

Annapolis Valley

The Annapolis Valley, which spreads along the Annapolis River east from Annapolis Royal, is a haze of white when its apple orchards bloom in late May to early June. The valley, extending northeast from Annapolis Royal, supports more than magnificent apple orchards, however; if you look closely, you'll also see hectares of strawberries, plums, peaches, pears, and cherries, as well as crops of hay, grain, and tobacco.

The Annapolis Valley has a legion of fans, among them the Mi'Kmaq, who first settled this region. According to Mi'Kmaq legend, Glooscap, a deity taking the form of a giant man, roamed the areas of the upper Fundy. He made his home atop the basalt cliffs of the peninsula—the lofty hook-shaped cape that finishes in sea stacks at Cape Split—and buried jewels on the Fundy beaches. (Today's tides still claw at the coastline to reveal agate, amethyst, and zeolite from Hall's Harbour to Cape Split's tip.)

ANNAPOLIS ROYAL TO CANNING

From Annapolis Royal, Highway 101 heads northeast, crossing the Annapolis River near Bridgetown and continuing east for 100 kilometers to Wolfville. You don't see a great deal from the highway, so plan to travel Highway 1 (cross the Annapolis Basin at Annapolis Royal to get going). Along this route, you pass through the villages and apple orchards now bypassed by Highway 101.

Bridgetown

About 28 kilometers from Annapolis Royal, this town has wide streets lined with grand old homes and stately trees. **James House Museum** (12 Queen St., 902/665-4530; mid-May–Sept. daily 9 A.M.–4 P.M.; free) is an 1835 residence sandwiched between modern shops along the main street. As well as predictable displays on early settlers, there's an old-fashioned tearoom.

Take Church Street north out of town and you reach **Valleyview Provincial Park** after five kilometers. This small park sits atop North Mountain, an ancient ridge of lava that forms a cap over softer shale and sandstone that has been gouged away to the south, forming the Annapolis Valley. From the park, views extend across the valley to the province's remote interior. The park campground (mid-June–mid-Oct.; $24) has just 30 sites, but it only ever fills on summer weekends. It has toilets and drinking water but no showers.

Kentville

The commercial hub of the Annapolis Valley is Kentville (pop. 6,000), 120 kilometers east of Annapolis Royal. The town is on the north side of Highway 101 (take Exits 14 or 13 from the west and Exit 12 from the east) and at the junction of Highway 12, which cuts south through the Nova Scotia interior to Mahone Bay and Lunenburg. In the historic heart of town is **King's County Museum** (37 Cornwallis Ave., Mon.–Fri. 9 A.M.–4 P.M.; free), which contains an art gallery and small theater within a two-story red brick courthouse.

On the outskirts of town, you'll find a couple of inexpensive motels, including **Allen's Motel** (384 Park St., 902/678-2683, www.allensmotel.ns.ca; mid-Mar.–mid-Dec.; $70–105 s or d), two kilometers west of downtown. Here, 10 rooms are separated from the highway by well-tended gardens and a picnic area with a gas barbecue.

South Mountain Park (Hwy. 12, South Alton, 902/678-0152 or 866/860-6092, www.southmountainparkcampground.com; $33–38, cabins $70) fills with holidaying families through its mid-May to mid-October season. A few kilometers south of Kentville, it's not really set up for quick overnight stays. But if you have children and are looking for a break from touring, it's a great place to kick back for a few days. The activities offered could easily fill a week of fun—everything from fishing to tennis and wagon rides to walking paths. Amenities include a par 3 golf course, games room, TV room, library, Internet access, Olympic-size outdoor pool, and more, lots more. On the downside, campsites offer little privacy.

Starr's Point

Prescott House Museum (1633 Starr's Point Rd., 902/542-3984; June–mid-Oct. Mon.–Sat. 9:30 A.M.–5:30 P.M., Sun. 1–5:30 P.M.; adult $4, senior $3, child $2) harks back to the valley's orchard beginnings, when horticulturist Charles Ramage Prescott imported species to add to the provincial store of fruit trees. His profits built this Georgian-style homestead. The restored mansion, constructed circa 1812, displays period furnishings and sits amid beautiful gardens. Its special events celebrate the fall harvest. It's along Highway 358, which leads north from Greenwich (Exit 11 from Highway 101).

Canning

The east end of the Annapolis Valley has a smattering of emerging boutique wineries, including **Blomidon Estate Winery** (10318 Hwy. 221, 902/582-7565; June–Oct. daily 10 A.M.–5 P.M.). This winery was the first in Nova Scotia to produce classic varietals such as chardonnay, pinot noir, and shiraz. The winery and a small cellar door are two kilometers east of Canning along Highway 221.

BLOMIDON PENINSULA

The Blomidon Peninsula is the sphincter-shaped northern end of North Mountain. Extending into the Minas Channel and with Minas Basin to its back, it features more fantastic Fundy scenery and a couple of good campgrounds. From Exit 11 of Highway 101, it's 40 kilometers to the end of the road.

The Look-Off

On the north side of Canning, **Look-Off Family Camping** (Hwy. 358, 902/582-3022, www.lookoffcamping.com; May–Sept.) lives up to its name with a long list of activities—think hayrides, bingo, and fitness classes—and

workshops such as kite-making and cookie painting. Other facilities include a café open daily at 9 A.M., a playground, a pool, and a launderette. Unserviced sites around the shaded edge of the campground are $25, hook-ups are $30, and camping cabins (no linen supplied) are $60 s or d. The namesake Look-Off (a Nova Scotian term for a lookout) is across the road and has wonderful views across the bucolic Annapolis Valley.

Blomidon Provincial Park

This dramatically positioned 759-hectare park is along the eastern side of the Blomidon Peninsula, facing Minas Basin. To get there, turn off Highway 358 three kilometers north of the Look-Off and follow the secondary road north for 14 kilometers. The red shale and sandstone that make the park so striking was laid down millions of years ago and then eroded by glacial and water action to form 180-meter-high bluffs that are topped by coastal forest. Fundy tides sweep up to the cliff face twice daily, but as the water recedes, you can walk along the red-sand beach, searching for semiprecious stones such as amethyst and agate. The uplands area is covered in forests of sugar maple, beech, and birch, yet also present are alpine plants such as maidenhair.

The best place for a walk is along the beach, but check at the park office (902/582-7319) or information boards for tide times. Four official trails wind their way through the park. The best views are from the Look-Off Trail, an easy one-kilometer walk to a lookout high atop the cliffs. The 5.6-kilometer **Jodrey Trail** fringes the cliffs while the **Interpretive Trail** passes information boards describing the forest and its inhabitants. The main day-use area is where the access road enters the park. It's one of the few places along the Fundy Coast where the water gets warm enough for swimming.

Beyond the day-use area, the access road climbs to the campground (early June–early Oct.; $24), where sites are spread through the forest on two short loops. Facilities include showers, a playground, and drinking water.

To Cape Split

At the tip of the Blomidon Peninsula is Cape Split. To get there, continue north on Highway 358 from the Look-Off to Scots Bay, where there's a small provincial park with a pebbly beach fronting Minas Channel. The road ends just beyond Scots Bay, from where it's 13 kilometers on foot to Cape Split. It's a long way to walk (and make the return trek) in one day, but there is no elevation gain and the rewards are total wilderness and sweeping views from the cliff top at the end of the trail.

Wolfville and Vicinity

At the eastern end of the Annapolis Valley, the genteel town of Wolfville (pop. 3,700) began with the name Mud Creek, an ignoble tribute from the founding New England planters who wrestled with the Fundy coastal area once farmed by early Acadians. Now the town sits in the lushest part of the Annapolis Valley, and you won't want to miss it. Highway 1 runs through town as Main Street, where large houses with bay windows and ample porches sit comfortably beneath stately trees. Acadia University's ivy-covered buildings and manicured lawns lie along Main and University.

The town, just six blocks deep, has an uncomplicated layout alongside Highway 1 and Highway 101.

SIGHTS
Along the Main Street

Wolville's refined nature is apparent to anyone walking along the main street, which is dotted with grand stone buildings and, at the eastern end, stately trees.

Randall House Museum (259 Main St., 902/542-9775; mid-June–mid-Sept. Mon.–Sat. 10 A.M.–5 P.M., Sun. 1:30–5 P.M.; donation) is a historic home (built in 1815) with period furnishings and local artifacts from the 1760s to the 20th century.

Acadia University Art Gallery (Beveridge Arts Centre, at Highland Ave. and Main St., 902/585-1373; summer Tues.–Sat. 1–4 P.M., the rest of the year daily 1–4 P.M.; free) has a fine-arts collection of local and regional works, highlighted by Alex Colville's oils and serigraphs.

Wolfville Waterfront

Most visitors miss Wolfville's waterfront, but the town does have one, one block north of the main street across Front Street. Trails and a small park have been developed at the mouth of the Cornwallis River, which was once lined with busy shipyards. Views extend across the Minas Basin to the red cliffs of Blomidon Provincial Park.

Along Front Street to the west is **Robie Tufts Nature Centre,** which is a series of covered interpretive boards describing the flora and fauna native to the area. The main purpose of the structure is to provide a home for chimney swifts, which make their home in the red brick chimney rising through the roof.

SHOPPING

The **Harvest Gallery** (462 Main St., 902/542-7093) displays the work of local artists. Especially eye-catching are the colorful oil paintings of Jeanne Aisthorpe-Smith.

Although apples get all the glory, lots of other farming happens in the Annapolis Valley. **Gaspereau Valley Fibres** (830 Gaspereau River Rd., 902/542-2656) highlights the local wool industries, with knitting, weaving, and spinning, as well as the raw materials sold as-is. The shop is on a farm on the south side of Highway 101; to get there from town, take Gaspereau Road south.

ACCOMMODATIONS AND CAMPING

Most Wolfville accommodations are grand heritage homes, so there are no bargains.

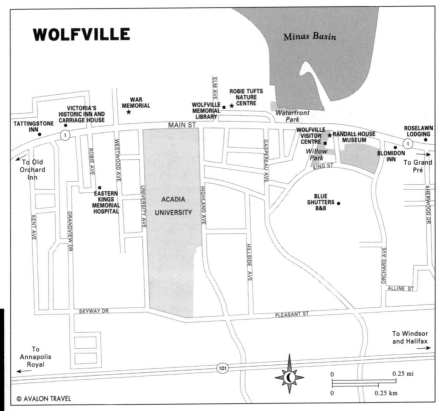

WOLFVILLE

Minas Basin

ELM AVE

ROBIE TUFTS
NATURE
★ CENTRE

WAR
MEMORIAL
★

VICTORIA'S
HISTORIC INN AND
CARRIAGE HOUSE

WOLFVILLE
MEMORIAL ▪ ★
LIBRARY

*Waterfront
Park*

TATTINGSTONE
INN

① MAIN ST

WOLFVILLE
VISITOR ★ RANDALL HOUSE
CENTRE   MUSEUM

ROSELAWN
LODGING

①

To Old
Orchard
Inn

ROBIE AVE

WESTWOOD AVE

GASPEREAU AVE

*Willow
Park*

KING ST

BLOMIDON
INN

To Grand
Pré

EASTERN
KINGS
MEMORIAL
HOSPITAL

KENT AVE

GRANDVIEW DR

UNIVERSITY AVE

ACADIA
UNIVERSITY

HIGHLAND AVE

HILLSIDE AVE

BLUE
SHUTTERS ▪
B&B

SHERWOOD DR

ORCHARD AVE

ALLINE ST

SKYWAY DR

PLEASANT ST

To Windsor
and Halifax
→

To
Annapolis
Royal
←

101

0   0.25 mi

0   0.25 km

© AVALON TRAVEL

$50-100

On the hill behind the information center, **Blue Shutters Bed and Breakfast** (7 Blomidon Terr., 902/542-3363; $80–110 s, $100–125 d) has three well-equipped guest rooms. Each has an en suite bathroom, TV/DVD combo, wireless Internet, and an electric fireplace. Rates include a full breakfast.

Roselawn Lodging (32 Main St., 902/542-3420, www.roselawnlodging.ca) is a modest motel on the east side of downtown. Facilities include an outdoor pool, launderette, barbecues and picnic tables, a tennis court, and a playground. The 28 motel rooms ($80–120 s or d) are clean and comfortable, and 12 adjacent cottages come with kitchens ($100–150 s or d).

$100-150

If you're a garden lover, you won't want leave the expansive grounds of ◖ **Blomidon Inn** (127 Main St., 902/542-2291 or 800/565-2291, www.blomidon.ns.ca; $100–270 s or d), which is surrounded by more than one hectare of cacti, roses, rhododendrons, azaleas, ponds, a croquet lawn, and a terraced vegetable garden that doubles as an outdoor eating area. The home itself, built in 1882 by a shipbuilder, reflects the wealth of its original owner. Mahogany and teak dominate, and local antiques are found throughout public areas and the 29 guest rooms. The least expensive rooms are on the small side, but all have en suite bathrooms. Rates include a continental breakfast and afternoon tea. Tennis courts, a restaurant, and a lounge round out this elegant accommodation.

A registered historic property (1893), **Victoria's Historic Inn and Carriage House** (600 Main St., 902/542-5744 or 800/556-5744, www.victoriashistoricinn.com; $108–245 s or d) combines a grand Victorian house with an adjacent carriage house. Rooms vary in character greatly; my favorite is the Hunt Room ($138 s or d), on the upper floor of the carriage house, which has a smart green and burgundy color theme and a vaulted cathedral ceiling. Like the other rooms, it has an en suite four-piece bathroom, TV, telephone, bathrobes, and a CD player. Rates include a cooked breakfast and afternoon tea.

Dating to 1874 and within walking distance of downtown, **Tattingstone Inn** (630 Main St., 902/542-7696 or 800/565-7696, www.tattingstone.ns.ca; $118–178 s or d) is casually formal with 10 guest rooms spread through the main house and adjacent carriage house. All are decorated with antiques and some have whirlpool tubs. The inn also offers a music room, dining room, steam room, heated outdoor pool, and tennis court. Rates include a cooked breakfast.

The **Old Orchard Inn** (153 Greenwich Rd., 902/542-5751 or 800/561-8090, www.oldorchardinn.com) is a sprawling resort near Exit 11 of Highway 101. It comprises more than 100 motel-style guest rooms ($150–195 s or d) and 29 cabins (May–Oct.; $150–225 s or d) spread through the forest. Tennis courts, an indoor pool, saunas, spa services, hiking trails, and a stone patio with sweeping valley views add to the appeal. The resort also has a dining room and lounge.

FOOD

For a small town, Wolfville has a surprising number of eateries. If you're in town on a Saturday, it's worth browsing the **Wolfville Farmers Market.** In summer it's outdoors (Robie Tufts Nature Centre, Front St.; mid-May–Sept. 8:30 A.M.–1 P.M.) while the rest of the year, everything is moved indoors (Acadia Student Union Building, Highland Ave.; Oct.–mid-May 8:30 A.M.–1 P.M.).

Cafés

Just Us (450 Main St., 902/542-7731; Mon.–Fri. 7 A.M.–9 P.M., Sat. 8 A.M.–6 P.M., Sun. 10 A.M.–5 P.M.) pours organic coffees and a wide range of teas from the front of a historic theater building, with seating spread through the lobby. Meals are very inexpensive ($4 for soup and sandwich), and the muffins are baked fresh daily. A little farther along, the **Coffee Merchant** (472 Main St., 902/542-4315; daily 8 A.M.–10 P.M.) has some of the best coffee concoctions in town.

Restaurants

In a restored 1860 home one block from Main Street, the kitchen at **◖ Tempest** (117 Front St., 902/542-0588; daily for lunch and dinner and Fri.–Sat. until 10:30 P.M.) prepares the most creative and well-presented cooking in the Annapolis Valley, although it's also a little more expensive than other local restaurants. The menu features cuisine from around the world that makes use of local seafood and produce. The origin of dishes is truly global—Indian butter chicken, lobster risotto, potato-crusted haddock, and the highlight for me, lobster and corn chowder. Starters range $7–15 while mains are $18–31. Lunch is an excellent deal, with most dishes under $10. The tree-shaded patio fills on warmer evenings and jazz musicians play on Friday night.

The dining rooms at the local inns are good bets for meals. One of the best of the dining rooms associated with local accommodations is the **Acadian Room** (Old Orchard Inn, 153 Greenwich Rd., 902/542-5751; daily 7 A.M.–9 P.M.), which draws diners to its large restaurant with stunning views and good food. Before 11 A.M., the French toast with whipped cream and blueberry sauce is a delight. Local fare such as cedar-plank salmon basted with dark rum and maple syrup is an evening standout. Most dinner mains are less than $20. The wine list allows the opportunity to taste Nova

Scotian wine by the glass. Sunday brunch (Oct.–May 11 A.M.–2 P.M.; $18) is a grand affair, with a huge array of hot and cold foods laid out on a buffet table.

INFORMATION AND SERVICES

At the east end of town is **Wolfville Visitor Centre** (Willow Park, Main St., 902/542-7000; May–mid-Oct. daily 9 A.M.–5 P.M.). **Wolfville Memorial Library** (21 Elm St., 902/542-5760; Tues.–Sat. 11 A.M.–5 P.M., Sun. 1–5 P.M.) is a red brick building that was once the local railway station. As with most public libraries through Nova Scotia, public Internet access is free.

Box of Delights Bookshop (328 Main St., 902/542-9511; Mon.–Sat. 9 A.M.–5:30 P.M., Sun. noon–5 P.M.) has a good collection of Canadiana and Acadian history and field guides. In business since the 1970s, the **Odd Book** (112 Front St., 902/542-9491; Mon.–Thurs. 9:30 A.M.–5:30 P.M., Fri. 9:30 A.M.–9 P.M., Sat. 9:30 A.M.–5 P.M., Sun. 1–5 P.M.) is where locals go to search out hard-to-find used and antiquarian books.

Eastern Kings Memorial Hospital is at 23 Earnscliffe Ave. (902/542-2266). Call the **police** at 902/542-3817 or the **RCMP** at 902/679-5555.

Banks and the **post office** are along Main Street. **Wile's** (210 Main St.; daily 8 A.M.–10 P.M.) has coin-operated laundry machines.

GETTING THERE AND AROUND

Acadian Lines stops up at the university twice daily on the route between Digby and Halifax. Buy tickets at the information desk (15 Horton Ave., 902/585-2110).

GRAND PRÉ

Continue east through Wolfville on Highway 1 for six kilometers (or take Exit 10 from Highway 101) to reach this small village that was the epicenter of one of the most tragic events in Canadian history, the expulsion of the Acadians from their homeland. First settled

Grand Pré National Historic Site

in 1680 by an Acadian family who moved from the confines of nearby Port Royal, Grand Pré grew to become the largest Acadian settlement in Nova Scotia. The main attraction is Grand Pré National Historic Site, but also worth visiting is **Grand Pré Wines** (Hwy. 1, 902/542-1753; Mon.–Sat. 10 A.M.–6 P.M., Sun. 11 A.M.–6 P.M.), where grapes are grown on 60 hectares of former Acadian farmland. In the main building you'll find a restaurant, wine shop, and crafts corner. Winery tours ($6) are offered through summer daily at 11 A.M., 3 P.M., and 5 P.M.

◖ Grand Pré National Historic Site

Commemorating the Acadian deportation, this living museum (2242 Grand Pré Rd., 902/542-3631; mid-May–mid-Oct. daily 9 A.M.–6 P.M.; adult $7.80, senior $6.60, child $4) brings Acadian history and the deportation to life. It wasn't until Henry Wadsworth Longfellow wrote the poem *Evangeline* in 1847 that the English-speaking world became aware of the expulsion, but by then nothing remained of Grand-Pré (Great Meadow), the setting for the story of the Acadian heroine separated from her lover by the deportation.

In 1922 an interested benefactor with Acadian roots built a small stone church on the presumed site of Grand Pré, and this was the genesis for the historic site of today. Visitors enter through a large museum complex, where there's a bookstore and gift shop, along with information panels describing Acadian life, the deportation, and the return of the Acadians to Nova Scotia. Outside are sprawling grounds crisscrossed by pathways that lead to vegetable gardens, a blacksmith shop, an orchard, a lookout over the diked farmland, and a statue of Henry Wadsworth Longfellow. In the middle of the site is a statue of Evangeline, who was born at Grand Pré and whose life has become an icon of the struggle of her people. Directly behind the statue is the 1922 church. It houses an exhibit of paintings that showcase the history of the people, a copy of the original expulsion order that was read to a congregation within the original church, as well as stained-glass windows with a story to tell. Guided tours of the grounds (included with admission) are highly recommended. A guide is also stationed within Église Saint-Charles to lead you through the story of each painting.

Accommodations and Food

The best choice of accommodations are in nearby Wolfville, but the centrally located **Evangeline Inn and Motel** (11668 Hwy. 1, 902/542-2703 or 888/542-2703, www .evangeline.ns.ca; May–Oct.) provides comfortable accommodations right at the turnoff to the historic site. Choose from motel rooms ($75–95 s or d) or rooms in the adjacent boyhood home of Sir Robert Borden, prime minister of Canada for nine years early last century ($95–115 s or d). All guests have use of a landscaped pool. Also on the grounds is a café open daily for breakfast and lunch, where cooked breakfasts are less than $5 and dishes such as haddock chowder with a warmed scone on the side are $4–7.

Across the road from the entrance to Grand Pré National Historic Site is **Le Panier D'Evangéline** (2208 Grand Pré Rd., 902/542-1543; Tues.–Fri. 8 A.M.–8 P.M., Sat.–Sun. 10 A.M.–8 P.M.), a large country-style café serving healthy foods, local and organically grown whenever possible. The freshly squeezed juices are especially good.

WINDSOR

If you've toured along the South Shore and then traveled along the Fundy Coast, the temptation may be to stay on the highway and give Windsor, just 60 kilometers northwest of Halifax, a miss. But this gracious town on the banks of the Avon River is well worth the short detour from busy Highway 101. To get there

HOLY PUMPKINS!

Windsor may be famous as the birthplace of hockey, but no attraction is bigger than the pumpkins grown on the south side of town at **Howard Dill Enterprises** (400 College Rd., 902/798-2728). Dill is renowned in the giant pumpkin-growing business for developing seeds that go on to produce some of the world's largest pumpkins, some of which grow to over 700 kilograms (1,540 pounds).

You won't find the pumpkins grown from Dill's seeds on grocery-store shelves. They are used for fall fairs and pumpkin-growing competitions, and as jack-o-lanterns by folks with strong porches. Most of the company's business is done online; through the website www.howarddill.com you can order the precious seeds and books such as How to Grow World Class Giant Pumpkins and How To Grow World Class Giant Pumpkins Volume II, as well as download growing tips. At Dill's farm, visitors are encouraged to drop by and see his own pumpkin patch, where even the smallest pumpkins are in the 180- to 230-kilogram (400- to 500-pound) range leading up to the late September–early October harvest.

from the main highway, take Exit 6, which leads into downtown. Before town is a small **information center** (902/798-2690; mid-May–mid-Oct. daily 9 A.M.–5 P.M.).

Fort Edward National Historic Site

Dating to 1750, Fort Edward National Historic Site (King St., 902/542-3631; mid-June–late Sept. daily 10 A.M.–6 P.M.; free) preserves the last 18th-century blockhouse in Nova Scotia. Fort Edward was one of the main assembly points for the deportation of the Acadians from the province in 1755. Although the building is open only during summer, touring the grounds will give a good feel for the location of the fort and the chance to see earthen mounds where the rest of the fort once stood.

Historic Homes

Haliburton House (414 Clifton Ave., 902/798-5619; June–mid-Oct. Mon.–Sat. 9:30 A.M.–5:30 P.M., Sun. 1–5:30 P.M.; adult $3, child

$1.50) was owned by 19th-century author, humorist, and historian Judge Thomas Chandler Haliburton, who was born in Windsor in 1796. Among the sayings that originated in Haliburton's writings are "It's raining cats and dogs," "barking up the wrong tree," "Facts are stranger than fiction," and "quick as a wink." The Victorian mansion on 10 hectares is open to the public, as are the surrounding gardens. For hockey fans, his written memories of childhood have special meaning. In them, he reminisced about children "playing ball on ice" behind Haliburton House, which is the earliest mention of the game of ice hockey.

On Ferry Hill, **Shand House** (389 Avon St., 902/798-8213; June–mid-Oct. daily 9:30 A.M.–5:30 P.M., Sun. 1–5:30 P.M.; adult $3, child $1) is another vintage beauty and marks the wealthy Shand family's prominence in Windsor. When it was built in the early 1890s, the Queen Anne–style mansion was one of the first residences in the area fitted with electric lights and indoor plumbing.

Nova Scotia's oldest remaining blockhouse, protected within Fort Edward National Historic Site

© ANDREW HEMPSTEAD

CENTRAL NOVA SCOTIA

This chapter encompasses a wide swath of Nova Scotia extending north from Halifax to Truro (the geographical center of the province) and then west to the New Brunswick border and east to the causeway leading to Cape Breton Island. This region, at once the most traveled and least known part of the province, is perfect for those looking for low-key attractions as varied as ancient fossils, beautiful beaches, and remote parks.

The region can roughly be divided into manageable sections—each very different in look and feel. The TransCanada Highway slices through the region's northwest corner and extends to Cape Breton Island in the east. But this route promises little besides uninterrupted speed. Detour south to explore an area that was once the realm of Glooscap, the Mi'Kmaq god

who roamed this part of Nova Scotia as a man as large as Gulliver among the Lilliputians. A legend relates that Glooscap slept stretched out over the region's northern portion and used Prince Edward Island as his pillow. While the Northumberland Strait has long been the domain of vacationing locals—attracted by warm water and long stretches of beautiful beach—other visitors on a fast track often see the region as a flash of landscape from the TransCanada Highway. The other option for reaching Cape Breton Island from Halifax is to drive along the Eastern Shore, which is as rugged as the Northumberland Strait shore is tame. This super-scenic road unfurls itself at a leisurely pace, and it's worth slowing down and taking two or three days to travel its length. Passing tiny fishing ports reminiscent of seafaring life

HIGHLIGHTS

◖ Watching the Tidal Bore: The tidal bore phenomenon occurs in only a few places in the world. Locals call it the Total Bore, and I'll admit it's not exactly exciting, but it's unusual enough to be worth timing your visit to Truro to coincide with the twice-daily tidal bore (page 124).

◖ Balmoral Grist Mill: Surrounded by rich green foliage, the reflection of this bright red building in an adjacent pond creates a scene of tranquility (page 132).

◖ Hector Heritage Quay Museum: Step aboard a full-size replica of the *Hector*, upon which Pictou's first settlers arrived, to get a taste of the hardships that were endured crossing the Atlantic Ocean (page 133).

◖ Arisaig: The unassuming cliffs at Arisaig are filled with fossils that have helped scientists understand the evolution of life on earth 400 million years ago (page 137).

◖ Taylor Head Provincial Park: Marine Drive passes dozens of protected areas, but Taylor Head stands out for its ease of access and interesting geology (page 142).

◖ Sherbrooke Village: History comes alive at this living museum. For the full effect, join the Hands on History program by dressing up in period costume (page 144).

◖ Canso Islands National Historic Site: The focus of this attraction is Grassy Island, home to a thriving fishing community in the early 1700s. But the best part for budget-conscious travelers will be the price – just $5 including a boat trip (page 146).

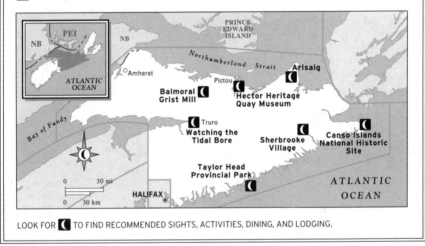

LOOK FOR ◖ TO FIND RECOMMENDED SIGHTS, ACTIVITIES, DINING, AND LODGING.

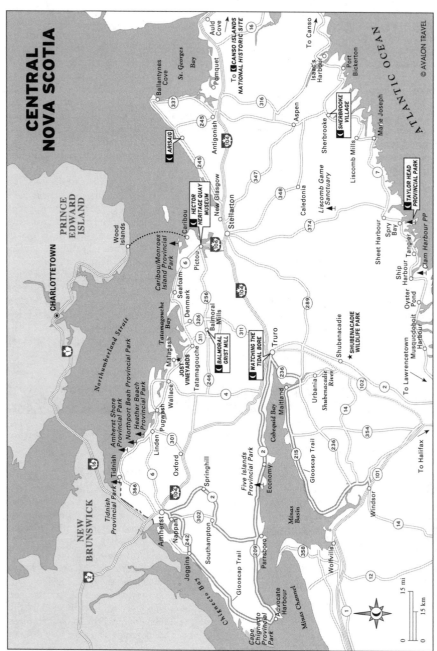

CENTRAL NOVA SCOTIA

© AVALON TRAVEL

decades ago and rock-bound coves where the forest grows right down to the sea, the road's services are few and far between (Canso, with a population of 1,000, is the largest town), so plan ahead by making accommodation reservations and keeping your gas tank full.

PLANNING YOUR TIME

Central Nova Scotia is not a destination like Cape Breton Island, where you would plan your visit around an itinerary that lasted a certain length of time. Instead, you will surely find yourself passing through central Nova Scotia on more than one occasion—for example driving from New Brunswick through to Halifax and then again on the way to Cape Breton Island. If you've been touring through New Brunswick, you'll already be well aware of the massive Fundy tides. In central Nova Scotia, you can **watch the tidal bore** at Truro. Along Northumberland Strait, beaches lapped by warm water will tempt you to linger while historic attractions such as **Balmoral Grist Mill** and Pictou's **Hector Heritage Quay Museum** keep the past alive. From Halifax, you could plan on spending two days reaching

Cape Breton Island via the above-mentioned attractions, which would also allow time for a detour to **Arisaig,** a fossil hot spot protected by a small provincial park. If you have an extra day or two, consider taking Marine Drive to or from Cape Breton Island. The distance (320 kilometers) is deceiving when planning how long the drive will take. Add a ferry trip to a winding, often narrow road that passes through dozens of small townships, and you should expect the journey to take at least six hours. From Canso it will take another 90 minutes to reach Port Hastings, the gateway to Cape Breton Island. But of course, this estimate of 7.5 hours to complete the Marine Drive is sans stops, and if you're only interested in reaching Cape Breton Island from Halifax, the Highway 102/104 route via Truro takes around half as long. Leaving Halifax in the morning, an ideal scenario would be to spend one night en route and plan on reaching Cape Breton Island later the following day. This would allow time to explore **Taylor Head Provincial Park,** to step back in time at **Sherbrooke Village,** and to take the boat trip to **Canso Islands National Historic Site.**

Halifax to Truro

As you head north from Halifax, suburbia is quickly left behind as divided Highway 102 speeds north to Truro, which is easily reached in an hour from downtown. The original route between these two cities (Highway 2) may look appealing on the map, but the scenery is no different from what you'll see from Highway 102—it simply takes longer. If you've traveled the Fundy Coast from west to east, take Highway 22 from Windsor as a shortcut, or Highway 215, also from Windsor, to follow the Bay of Fundy to its head.

SHUBENACADIE

If you're willing to try something new or you have an animal-loving family, there

are two good reasons to take Exit 10 from Highway 102.

Riding the Tidal Bore

The **Shubenacadie River,** which drains into the Bay of Fundy at Cobequid Bay, is not just a good place to view the tidal bore but also to *ride* it. **Tidal Bore Rafting Park** (Urbania, Hwy. 215, 902/758-4032 or 800/565-7238, www.tidalboreraftingpark.com) operates two- and four-hour Zodiac raft excursions May–September. You board the rafts at low tide and head downstream, just in time to catch the tidal bore back upriver. The driver rides the wave, and then doubles back to blast through its face, finding rapids along the way to keep the adrenaline pumping. Rates range $60–75. Departures are dependent on the tides; check the website for times.

Shubenacadie Wildlife Park

Upstream of Highway 102 (signposted from Exit 11), families will enjoy Shubenacadie Wildlife Park (902/758-2040; mid-May–mid-Oct. daily 9 A.M.–7 P.M., mid-Oct.–mid-May Sat.–Sun. 9 A.M.–3 P.M.; adult $4.25, child $1.50), a zoological facility operated by the provincial government. Throughout the spacious grounds are Canadian animals you are unlikely to see in the wild (fishers, mink, and more), ones that you don't want to meet face to face (bears, cougars, bobcats, and lynx), and those you'll see only at Christmas (reindeer). The Sable Island horses may look like regular horses, but they are one of the world's few wild horse populations.

Accommodations and Camping

◖ **Rafters Ridge Cottages** (Urbania, Hwy. 215, 902/758-4032 or 800/565-7238, www .raftersridgecottages.com; $145–190 s or d) is part of the Tidal Bore Rafting Park complex, so it's no surprise that many guests come for the rafting (booked as part of an accommodation package). Enjoying a riverside location, you can also rent canoes or hang out around the outdoor pool. Lodging is in one- and two-bedroom cottages. The cottages have decks, barbecues, and pleasant views across a lightly treed hillside.

In the vicinity of the rafting park and also right on the Shubenacadie River is **Wide Open Wilderness Campground** (Urbania, 902/261-2228 or 866/811-2267, www.wowcamping .com; mid-May–mid-Oct.). You can watch the tidal bore, walk marked hiking trails, relax around the pool, or try your hand at the horseshoe pits. Campsites are $20–26, and cabins are $60 s or d.

MAITLAND

If you've been moseying eastbound along the Bay of Fundy and don't particularly want to detour back through Halifax, turn at Windsor (take Exit 5 from Highway 101) and follow Highway 215 along the edge of Minas Basin to Maitland, crossing the Shubenacadie River to meet busy Highway 102 at Truro.

Maitland, at the mouth of the Shubenacadie River, was where Canada's largest wooden ship, the three-masted *William D. Lawrence,* was built. Documentaries, ship portraits, and memorabilia are kept at the shipbuilder's former homestead, the **Lawrence House Museum,** which overlooks Cobequid Bay (8660 Hwy. 215, 902/261-2628; June–mid-Oct. Mon.–Sat. 9:30 A.M.–5:30 P.M., Sun. 1–5:30 P.M.; adult $3.25, senior and child $2.25). The actual 1874 launching is commemorated on the middle Saturday of each September with a parade of period-dressed locals, a symbolic launch, and seafood suppers hosted throughout the village.

TRURO

Situated at the convergence of the province's major expressways and served by VIA Rail, Truro (pop. 12,000) is called the hub of Nova Scotia. It is the province's third-largest town, with an economy based on shipping, dairy products, and the manufacture of clothing, carpets, plastic products, and wines. Truro's academic side includes a teachers' college in town and an agricultural college on the outskirts.

Town Sights

The access road leading into 400-hectare **Victoria Park** (corner Brunswick St. and Park Rd.) ends at a wide-open day-use area where beds of tulips flower through June, a colorful highlight of the town. At other times of year the park is still worth visiting—forests of spruce, hemlock, and white pine are spliced with hiking trails that lead along a deep canyon and past two waterfalls.

In a quiet residential area, **Colchester Society Museum** (29 Young St., 902/895-6284; June–Sept. Mon.–Fri. 10 A.M.–5 P.M., Saturday 2–5 P.M.; adult $4, child $2) does a fine job entwining exhibits on Fundy eccentricities and the area's natural history.

CENTRAL NOVA SCOTIA

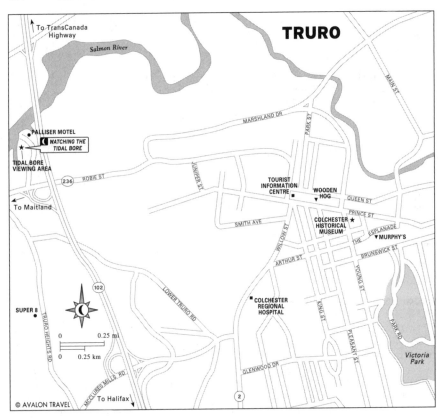

☾ Watching the Tidal Bore

Tidal bores only occur in a few places in the world, and one of the most accessible is the **Salmon River,** which flows through Truro. Best described as a small wave, the bore is particularly high along the Salmon River as it is at the head of Cobequid Bay, where the incoming tide pushing up the Bay of Fundy is forced into a narrow funnel. At Truro, the lead wave travels up the river as it pushes toward town beneath the Highway 102 overpass. If you want a close-up look at the tidal bore, take Robie Street west out of town toward Highway 102 and turn off on one of the roads leading to the river. Tidal-bore arrival times are listed in the *Truro Daily News* and at the town's visitor information center (902/893-2922).

Accommodations

Lodgings in Truro are plentiful and reasonably priced. Motels line all the main routes into town, and you shouldn't have a problem finding a room at short notice.

Occupying a prime site for watching the tidal bore, the **Palliser Motel** (902/893-8951; May–Oct.; $79–99 s or d) is west of downtown off Robie Street (Highway 2), or take Exit 14 from Highway 102. It's on the banks of the Salmon River, and the bore-watching area is lit at night. The rooms are basic and old-fashioned, but rates include a breakfast buffet at the motel restaurant.

As usual, the **Super 8** (85 Treaty Trail, 902/895-8884 or 877/508-7666, www.super8truro.com; $140 s or d) is close to a main artery and is filled with clean, comfortable air-conditioned rooms packed with amenities. Here you also get an indoor pool with a waterslide and hot tub. A light breakfast is included, and you can walk next door to the Capricorn Restaurant for dinner. Call for last-minute specials.

Food

In a nondescript strip mall near the heart of downtown, 【 **Murphy's** (the Esplanade, 902/895-1275; daily 11 A.M.–8 P.M.) serves some of the best-priced seafood anywhere in this part of the province. I had the deep-fried haddock and chips—cooked to perfection— for just $8. A variety of fish is offered—pan-fried, poached, or "Texas style"—amid bright nautical-themed decor.

Another favorite is the **Wooden Hog** (627 Prince St., 902/895-0779; Mon.–Fri. 9 A.M.–10 P.M., Sat. 11 A.M.–10 P.M.). While locals often stop by just for coffee and one of the many delicious pastries, the lunch and dinner menu provides good value, with all dinner mains less than $20 (including poached salmon smothered in hollandaise sauce for $14).

Many motels have in-house dining rooms, including the **Palliser Motel Restaurant** (off Robie St., 902/893-8951), where you can combine inexpensive dining with tidal bore–watching.

© ANDREW HEMPSTEAD

At the Truro Tourist Information Centre ask for a brochure detailing the tree-trunk sculptures scattered around the town.

Information

At the **Truro Tourist Information Centre** (Victoria Sq., Court St., 902/893-2922; Apr.–mid-Oct. daily 9 A.M.–5 P.M.), ask for a map of the tree-trunk sculptures scattered through town and check your email at the public computer terminal. Driving out from Victoria Square and ending up heading out of town in the right direction can be confusing, so get the staff to point the way.

Glooscap Trail

Named for the mighty Glooscap, a mythical Mi'Kmaq legend who controlled the tides, this region is far enough from the main highway that it is missed by most visitors, which is a shame, because it is dotted with interesting seaside villages, has beaches that occasionally give up precious gemstones, and has been the site of some amazing dinosaur discoveries. According to the tourist brochures, the Glooscap Trail extends along the Bay of Fundy from as far west as Windsor, but in the name of organization, this section divulges the best of Highway 2, which follows the coast west from Truro to Cape Chignecto and then north to Amherst.

TRURO TO PARRSBORO

Take Exit 14A from Highway 102 and you'll quickly find yourself on Highway 2, heading west along Cobequid Bay. En route to Parrsboro are a string of small fishing villages,

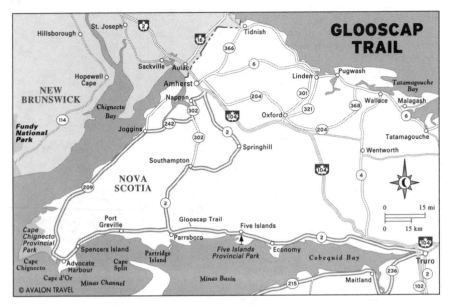

lookout points, and a couple of spots where beach access is possible at low tide.

Five Islands Provincial Park

As the name suggests, Five Islands Provincial Park does protect five islands, but it also encompasses more than 600 hectares of the mainland between Economy and Parrsboro. Along the park's coastal extremes are high cliffs and beaches, the latter giving up gems such as agate, amethyst, and jasper as the huge Fundy tides sweep across the bay. The five-kilometer (round-trip; allow 90 minutes) **Red Head Trail** reaches almost a dozen lookouts, including the Old Wife, a point of land that enjoys views across to the five islands.

PARRSBORO

The sea's erosive force has opened a window on the ancient world along the coastlines of Chignecto Bay and Minas Basin. Archaeological digs have yielded 100,000 fossilized bone fragments of ancient dinosaurs, crocodiles, lizards, sharks, and primitive fish.

Learn about local geology at Parrsboro Rock and Mineral Shop and Museum.

Sights

FUNDY GEOLOGICAL MUSEUM

Cross the bridge from downtown via Two Island Road to reach Fundy Geological Museum (162 Two Islands Rd., 902/254-3814; June–mid-Oct. daily 9:30 A.M.–5:30 P.M.; adult $5, senior and child $3.50). It highlights the Bay of Fundy, with displays describing how the tides have eroded the bedrock to expose numerous geological wonders, such as precious gemstones, and the fossilized remains of dinosaurs.

PARRSBORO ROCK AND MINERAL SHOP AND MUSEUM

Parrsboro Rock and Mineral Shop and Museum (39 Whitehall Rd., 902/254-2981, May–Dec. Mon.–Sat. 9 A.M.–9 P.M., Sun. 9 A.M.–5 P.M.) is famed local geologist Eldon George's pride. The museum displays dinosaur, reptile, and amphibian footprint fossils. The shop stocks fossil and gem specimens, rock-hound supplies, books, and maps.

OTTAWA HOUSE

Through town, beyond the mineral shop, is Ottawa House (902/254-2376; June–Sept. daily 10 A.M.–5 P.M.; donation), a 21-bedroom waterfront home dating to 1775. All that remains on the beach in front of the home are broken-down pylons, so it's hard to believe that this was once an important shipbuilding port. Now cared for by the local historical society, Ottawa House has two floors of historic displays and a tearoom.

Linked to the mainland by a narrow strip of rocky beach that begins below Ottawa House, archaeological evidence points to Mi'Kmaq occupation of Partridge Island 10,000 years ago. A rough road ends just before the island, from where a hiking trail winds to the summit and views across the Minas Basin to Cape Split (allow 30 minutes round-trip).

Accommodations and Camping

Riverview Cottages (3575 Eastern Ave., 902/254-2388 or 877/254-2388, www.riverviewcottages.ca; mid-Apr.–mid-Nov.; $60–90 s or d) lie along Farrells River on the

Ottawa House

© ANDREW HEMPSTEAD

east side of town. They are older and only a few have cooking facilities, but canoes are available for guest use, and the price is right.

Within walking distance of downtown, the **Maple Inn** (2358 Western Ave., 902/254-3735, www.mapleinn.ca) subtly combines two historic homes into an accommodation with 11 regular rooms and a spacious two-bedroom suite. The building was originally a hospital, and so the inn has special meaning to those visitors returning to the town where they were born (Room 1 was the delivery room). The inn is surrounded by well-tended gardens, while inside is a lounge with a TV and a library of books. Rates are $90–170 including a full breakfast served in a cheery dining room.

Dating to a similar era is **Gillespie House Inn** (358 Main St., 902/254-3196 or 877/901-3196, www.gillespiehouseinn.com; May–Oct.; $99 s, $119 d). The rooms ooze Old World charm and each has an en suite bathroom. The Elderkin Room has a wooden sleigh bed and looks over the front garden, which catches the morning sun.

Food

As you cruise the main street, **Glooscap Restaurant** (758 Upper Main St., 902/254-3488, daily breakfast, lunch, and dinner) is obvious, but a better choice is the 【 **Harbour View Restaurant** (476 Pier Rd., 902/254-3507, summer daily 11 A.M.–9 P.M.), which has uninterrupted water views from off Two Island Road. It's a friendly place, with all the usual seafood choices, including daily specials that are sourced from seasonal seafood. The lobster dinner ($25) is a favorite.

WEST TO CAPE CHIGNECTO

At Parrsboro, most travelers head north to Springhill on Highway 2, but Highway 209 along Minas Channel makes for a pleasant drive. It's 50 kilometers to the last village of any consequence, Advocate Harbour. At the halfway mark is Port Greville, once home to four shipbuilding companies. Today, take Wagstaff Street to the cliff edge and you can peer down at the river mouth that 100 years ago would have been filled with ships in various stages of construction. Across the water, Cape Split is plainly visible.

Advocate Harbour

At Spencers Island, Highway 209 turns inland to Advocate Harbour, a quiet corner of the province first visited by Europeans in 1604 when Samuel de Champlain came ashore. Just before town, take the signposted road to Cape d'Or, where a light-keeper's residence has been converted into 【 **The Lighthouse at Cape d'Or** (902/670-0534, www.capedor.ca; May–mid-Oct.; $80–110 s or d). Perched on high cliffs overlooking the Bay of Fundy, this four-room lodge is a wonderful place to kick back and do absolutely nothing at all. One room has an en suite bathroom while the other three share two bathrooms, and the common room is stocked with books and board games. The attached restaurant (cash only) serves light lunches and creative dinners in the $16–30 range.

Cape Chignecto Provincial Park

As the crow flies, this park isn't far from the TransCanada Highway or the city of Saint John (New Brunswick), but it is a world away from civilization, protecting an arrow-shaped headland jutting into the Bay of Fundy. Cliffs up to 185 meters high are lapped by the world's highest tides, which pour into Chignecto Bay on one side and Minas Basin on the other. No roads penetrate the park. Instead, from the end of the road at Red Rocks, just beyond the village of West Advocate and 46 kilometers from Parrsboro, a hiking trail leads around the cape and loops back through the forested interior. Most backpackers complete the circuit in three days, packing their own food and water and pitching their tents at backcountry campgrounds. Cabins along the way at Arch Gulch and Eatonville provide an alternative to camping (call 902/392-2085 for reservations). All hikers should be experienced in backcountry travel and totally self-sufficient.

JOGGINS

This town on the Chignecto Bay coast is 40 kilometers southwest from Amherst. From Parrsboro, take Highway 2 north to Southampton and then follow Highways 302 and 242 north and then west for 38 kilometers.

Joggins Fossil Cliffs

Declared a UNESCO World Heritage Site in 2008, the sea cliffs here have yielded thousands of fossils from the Carboniferous period (350 million to 280 million years ago). Plants are most common, but a forest of upright petrified tree stumps is what the site is best known for. First discovered in the 1850s, the hollow stumps contained the fossilized remains of *Hylonomous,* the earliest reptile ever discovered. It is supposed that these 30-centimeter-long critters fell inside and were unable to escape. The site has also revealed a two-meter arthropod with 30 sets of legs, as well as dinosaur footprints.

In conjunction with the UNESCO designation, the opening of the **Joggins Fossil Centre** (100 Main St., off Hwy. 302, 902/251-2727; mid-May–mid-Nov. daily 9:30 A.M.–5:30 P.M.;

adult $8, senior and child $6) in 2008 cemented the town as an important stop in central Nova Scotia. In addition to displays of ferns, fish scales, reptile footprints, and gastropods, visitors can watch lab technicians at work. Daily two-hour guided tours to Coal Mine Point ($10 per person) are dependent on the tides.

SPRINGHILL

The sultry voice of crooner Anne Murray is known the world over, but the folks in the small town of Springhill, on a slight rise just off Highway 104, take special pride in this local girl who has gone on to sell 50 million albums and win more awards than any other female vocalist.

Anne Murray Centre

You probably already guessed that Springhill would provide a home for the Anne Murray Centre (36 Main St., 902/597-8614; mid-May–mid-Oct. daily 9 A.M.–4:30 P.M.; adult $7.50, senior and child $5.50). The museum pays tribute to the beloved local warbler who hit the Top 40 in the 1970s with "Snow Bird" and is still going strong. Exhibits include photos, clothing, and other memorabilia, and an audio-visual display catalogs her career.

AMHERST AND VICINITY

Amherst (pop. 9,000) is built on high ground above Amherst Marsh—part of the larger 200-square-kilometer Tantramar Marshes—on the isthmus joining Nova Scotia to the mainland of Canada. The fertile marshes were first diked and farmed by the Acadians in the 1600s and are still productive today, mainly as hayfields.

Sights

Amherst is at its architectural best along Victoria Street, where the profits of industry and trade were translated into gracious

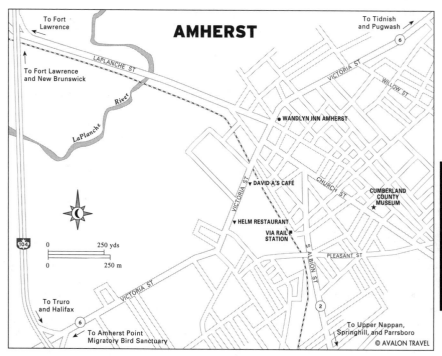

THINKER'S LODGE

Recognized mostly for its delightful name, Pugwash (from the Mi'Kmaq word *pagweak,* meaning "shallow water"), 50 kilometers east of Amherst, is best known as the origin of the **Pugwash Conferences on Science and World Affairs** (www .pugwash.org). The first of these took place in 1955 in Pugwash after Albert Einstein called for a meeting to discuss the dangers of a nuclear war. Cyrus Eaton, who had made his fortune in the United States as an industrialist, offered to sponsor the event on the condition it was held in his hometown of Pugwash, Nova Scotia. And so in 1957 it came to be that 13 Cold War nuclear scientists, including three from the USSR, met at what became known as the Thinker's Lodge, a large but otherwise unremarkable residence on the Pugwash foreshore. It was the first of many such gatherings, which now take place annually in London, Washington, Rome, Tokyo, and even still in Pugwash. Weapons of mass destruction are discussed, but topics have broadened to include breaking down international borders, the environment, and economic prosperity. To get to Thinker's Lodge, follow Durham Street to its eastern end and turn right down Water Street.

houses and commercial buildings garnished in Tudor, Gothic, and Queen Anne Revival styles. A few blocks south of the historic district, **Cumberland County Museum** (150 Church St., 902/667-2561; Feb.–Dec. Tues.–Fri. 9 A.M.–5 P.M., Sat. noon–5 P.M.; adult $3) is in an 1838 residence. The museum does an impressive job of tracking the past with exhibits on early Acadian settlements, Amherst's Anglo background, and spicy tidbits relating to Russian revolutionary Leon Trotsky, who was interned in an Amherst POW camp in 1917.

Amherst Point Migratory Bird Sanctuary, a few kilometers from town at the end of Victoria Street, spreads out over 190 hectares with trails through woodlands, fields, and marshes, and around ponds. The sediment-rich Cumberland Basin lures 200 bird species, including Eurasian kestrels, bald eagles, hawks, and snowy owls.

Accommodations

If you've just arrived in Nova Scotia by highway from New Brunswick, the **Fort Lawrence Inn** (La Planche St., 902/667-3881) is a basic but convenient choice on the western outskirts of Amherst. It charges $55–85 for older motel rooms and has a restaurant, a lounge, and laundry facilities. To get there, take the Nova Scotia Visitor Information Centre exit and continue east along La Planche Street for a few hundred meters.

Wandlyn Inn Amherst (Victoria St. off Hwy. 104 at Exit 3, 902/667-3331 or 800/561-0000, www.wandlyninns.com; from $90 s or d), the town's largest lodging, has 88 air-conditioned rooms, a restaurant, a café, a lounge, and an indoor pool.

Food

David A's Café (125 Victoria St., 902/661-0760; Mon.–Sat. for lunch and dinner) has a surprisingly varied menu for a small-town restaurant, with local produce and seafood prominent in most dishes.

The dining room at the **Wandlyn Inn** (Victoria St., 902/667-3331; daily 7 A.M.–2 P.M. and 5–9 P.M.) has inspired offerings by a creative chef who likes flamed steak with shrimp sauce and Caesar salad tossed at the table. Entrées range $15–29.

Information

The **Nova Scotia Visitor Information Centre** (902/667-8429; daily 8:30 A.M.–4:30 P.M., May–Sept. 8 A.M.–8 P.M.) is a large complex west of downtown. Adjacent is a promenade describing driving routes through the province, with picnic tables overlooking Tantramar Marshes. In a rail carriage on the same side of town, the **Amherst Tourist Bureau** (51 La Planche St., 902/667-0696; May–Aug. Mon.–Sat. 10 A.M.–6 P.M.) specializes in the region, with lots of information for those heading south to the Glooscap Trail.

Sunrise Coast to Pictou

The quickest way to reach Pictou from Amherst is to take Highway 104 via Truro, but Highway 6 is more scenic. Throughout the region, the land dips and sweeps in manicured farmlands extending to the red beaches and cliffs of Northumberland Strait. The villages are small, and the backcountry roads are scenic. This is rural Nova Scotia at its best. Allow three hours plus stops.

TIDNISH AND VICINITY

Highway 366 branches off Highway 6 a few kilometers northeast of Amherst and reaches the Northumberland Strait at Tidnish, which lies right on the provincial border between Nova Scotia and New Brunswick.

Tidnish Dock Provincial Park

Across the Tidnish River from town is Tidnish Dock Provincial Park. This small day-use park protects the northern terminus of an ambitious railway construction project that was designed to transport vessels across the isthmus between the Bay of Fundy and Northumberland Strait. The initial proposal had been for a canal link, but the government decided constructing a rail line would be easier. The plan called for the construction of hydraulic presses at either end to lift the boats into cradles that were to be pulled across the 28-kilometer rail line by locomotives. In 1891, after nearing completion, the entire project was abandoned. The park protects remains of the dock and a short length of the rail bed.

Continuing East Along Highway 366

Head east from Tidnish to **Amherst Shore Provincial Park.** From the day-use area, a short trail follows Annebelles Brook to a short beach, while on the other side of the highway is a campground (mid-May–mid-Sept.; $24) with flush toilets, showers, and fire pits. Continue east for seven kilometers to **Northport Beach Provincial Park,** renowned for its excellent beach and water warmed by shallow sandbars. Next up, and equally popular for swimming, is **Heather Beach Provincial Park.**

PUGWASH

Recognized mostly for its delightful name, Pugwash (from the Mi'Kmaq word *pagweak,* meaning "shallow water") lies at the mouth of Pugwash Basin 50 kilometers east of Amherst. Durham Street (Highway 6) is the main drag. Here you find a summer-only information center and the usual array of small-town businesses. Across the water to the south of downtown is a salt mine. Current production is 90,000 tons annually (10 percent of Nova Scotia's total mineral value). The best opportunity to get an idea of the operation's scope is to watch the freighters being loaded at the downtown dock.

Accommodations and Food

Downtown, the Irish-themed **Shillelagh Sheila's Country Inn** (10340 Durham St., 902/243-2885, www.shillelaghsheilasinn .com; June–mid-Oct.; $65–75 s or d) has a distinctive green and red exterior and four guest rooms with older furnishings. Breakfast is included, and dinner is offered with notice.

Hidden Jewel Café (10163 Durham St., 902/243-4059; Mon.–Sat. 9:30 A.M.–5 P.M.) has tables along a covered veranda and a menu of healthy choices.

PUGWASH TO PICTOU

It's 110 kilometers between Pugwash and Pictou along Highway 6, but there are many worthwhile detours; the first, Gulf Shore Road, starts from downtown Pugwash.

Along Gulf Shore Road

From downtown's Durham Street, Gulf Shore Road spurs north and then follows the edge of Northumberland Strait in an easterly direction before rejoining Highway 6 at Wallace. About four kilometers from Pugwash is **Gulf Shore**

© ANDREW HEMPSTEAD

Toney River is one of many fishing villages between Pugwash and Pictou.

Picnic Park, a day-use area with fireplaces and picnic tables spread across a grassed area that slopes to a red-sand beach.

Near where Gulf Shore Road loops south to Wallace is **Fox Harb'r Golf Resort and Spa** (1337 Fox Harbour Rd., 902/257-1801 or 866/257-1801, www.foxharbr.com). While the resort and its facilities wouldn't look out of place in Arizona or the Atlantic Coast, it's certainly unique in rural Nova Scotia. At $225 for a round of golf, the greens fee is too high for a humble travel writer such as myself (no, we don't get everything for free), but I'm told it's a beautiful course. Other facilities include an Olympic-size indoor pool, spa services, guided kayaking, and formal dining (jacket required) in the Great Room. Guests soak up pure luxury in suites (from $325 s or d) contained within 12 chalets that line the fairways and look out over Northumberland Strait.

Jost Vineyards

About 34 kilometers west of Pugwash, Jost Vineyards (902/257-2636; mid-June–mid-Sept. daily 9 A.M.–6 P.M., the rest of the year daily 9 A.M.–5 P.M.) is signposted off Highway 6. The creation of the Jost (pronounced "yost") family from Europe's Rhineland, this 18-hectare vineyard produces fine white wines that are sold throughout the province, including at many better restaurants. The best-known blends are the Jost ice wines. To produce this style, grapes are left on the vines until after the first frost, and then gently pressed to produce just a few drops of concentrated juice from each grape. The result is an intensely sweet wine that is perfect as an after-dinner treat. Free guided tours are given daily in summer at noon and 3 P.M., and a deli is stocked with picnic treats—the perfect compliment to Jost wines.

◖ Balmoral Grist Mill

Best known for its gristmill, Balmoral Mills lies along Highway 311 south of Tatamagouche 10 kilometers and 38 kilometers north of Truro. Nestled at the base of a wooded vale, bright red Balmoral Grist Mill (660 Matheson Brook Rd., 902/657-3016; June–mid-Oct. Mon.–Sat. 9:30 A.M.–5:30 P.M., Sun. 1–5:30 P.M.; adult $3.25, senior and child $2.25) is a photographer's ideal setting. Wheat, oats, and barley are still ground using 19th-century methods at this historic gristmill-cum-museum built in 1874. Milling demonstrations are at 10 A.M. and 2 P.M. The mill is busiest the first Sunday in October—an Open Day drawing a crowd of hundreds with activities such as milling demonstrations and popular taste testing of oatmeal cakes.

Seafoam

At this coastal village 24 kilometers east of Tatamagouche, you find the ◖ **Seafoam Campground** (Harris Ave., 902/351-3122; mid-May–Sept.; $18), a large facility with direct access to the beach and warm swimming water. Amenities include lawn games, a playground, showers, and a laundry. On the west side of the campground, a side road leads to an abandoned dock, where a concrete wall has created a natural barrier for shifting sand. The result is a wide stretch of beach, perfect for lazing away a few hours on a warm summer day.

Pictou

Pictou (PIC-toe), 160 kilometers west of Amherst and 14 kilometers north of Exit 22 from Highway 104, is a historic port town on Northumberland Strait. It is also the ferry gateway to Prince Edward Island, meaning plenty of traffic passes through.

Nearly everything in Pictou happens at the waterfront, which is home to the main museum, restaurants, and historic accommodations. Some of the older buildings have a distinct Scottish vernacular style, designed to reflect local lineage. The residential streets also have numerous fancier styles; you'll see examples of stone Gothic and Second Empire designs along Water, Front, and Church Streets.

History

In 1773, 33 families and 25 unmarried men arrived from the Scottish Highlands aboard the *Hector,* and Pictou (pop. 3,800) quickly became known as the "birthplace of New Scotland." The flamboyant Presbyterian minister and doctor Thomas McCulloch, en route to ministerial duties on Prince Edward Island, arrived here with his family by accident in 1803 when a storm blew his ship into Pictou Harbour. Local immigrants asked him to stay, and McCulloch agreed. In addition to providing medical care to the immigrants, McCulloch tried to reform the province's backward educational system.

SIGHTS
◖ Hector Heritage Quay Museum

At the heart of the downtown waterfront, Hector Heritage Quay Museum (33 Caladh Ave., 902/485-6057; mid-May–late Oct. Mon.–Sat. 9 A.M.–6 P.M., Sun. noon–6 P.M.; adult $5, senior $4, child $2) is home to a three-floor interpretation center detailing the Scottish immigrants' arrival and early years. An elevated outdoor walkway overlooks the harbor. Admission includes access to the *Hector,* a replica of the sailing ship that transported Scottish settlers from across the Atlantic.

Take time to look over the *Hector.* The three-masted black-and-off-white replica is a splendid vessel, wide-hulled and round-ended.

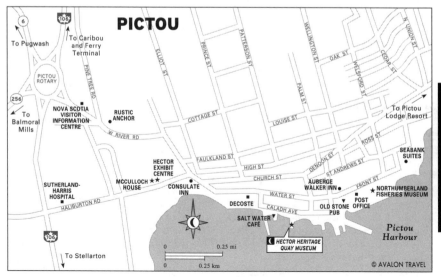

CENTRAL NOVA SCOTIA

© ANDREW HEMPSTEAD

Climbing aboard this replica of the *Hector* is a highlight of visiting Pictou.

From the shape of the ship, though, you'll easily see that the voyage from Scotland was not so splendid. The ship's hull is unusually wide, and indeed the *Hector,* owned by the Dutch and chartered by the Scots for the voyage, was built as a freighter and modified only slightly to carry human cargo. Remarkably, the 200-plus immigrants from the Highlands survived, and Nova Scotia owes its Scottish heritage to those seaworthy voyagers.

Northumberland Fisheries Museum

This fascinating museum (71 Front St., 902/485-4972; mid-June–mid-Oct. Mon.–Fri. 10 A.M.–5 P.M., Sun. noon–5 P.M.; adult $5, senior $4, child $2) is within a red brick railway station, away from the redeveloped waterfront precinct and easy to miss. Displays tell the story of the local fishing industry through a vintage lobster boat, an aquarium holding local marine species, a mock fisherman's bunkhouse, period photos, and other memorabilia.

Hector Exhibit Centre

The next two attractions are east of downtown along Old Haliburton Road. The Hector Exhibit Centre (86 Old Haliburton Rd., 902/485-4563; mid-May–mid-Oct. Tues.–Sat. 8:30 A.M.–4:30 P.M.) showcases fine arts as part of the national arts exhibit circuit. The site is also one of the province's best genealogical libraries. Admission to the exhibits is $1; admission to the genealogical library is $5 first visit, $2 subsequent visits.

McCulloch House

A path leads uphill from the Hector Exhibit and Research Centre to McCulloch House (100 Old Haliburton Rd., 902/485-1150; June–mid-Oct. Wed.–Sat. 9:30 A.M.–4:30 P.M.; $1), the early 1800s home of Thomas McCulloch. With distant water views, it holds period antiques and a small library. The print of a Labrador falcon downstairs was a gift to McCulloch from artist-naturalist John James Audubon.

ENTERTAINMENT AND EVENTS

The local performing arts scene is based at **deCoste** (Water St., 902/485-8848), a modern waterfront entertainment complex that puts on upward of 100 shows each year. In July and August, the center hosts the Summer Sounds of Nova Scotia series. These concerts highlight top Celtic dancers, singers, and fiddlers, who hit the stage Tuesday–Thursday at 8 P.M. Tickets are generally under $20.

The **Hector Festival** (902/485-8848, www.decostecentre.ca) celebrates the 1773 arrival of Pictou's Scottish ancestors through five mid-August days. Most of the action takes place along the waterfront, including concerts, pipe bands, Highland dancing, and workshops. The second Sunday in August is the final day and also the highlight. A reenactment of the historic landing takes place at 4 P.M., drawing thousands to the waterfront. This is followed by a *ceilidh* (Celtic music concert).

© ANDREW HEMPSTEAD

Hector Heritage Quay Museum

ACCOMMODATIONS AND CAMPING

Pictou has cheap motels such as the **Rustic Anchor Motel** (132 W. River Rd., 902/485-4423, www.rustyanchormotel.com; $60 s, $65 d), but I encourage you to take advantage of the wonderful choice of historic lodgings, many within walking distance of the waterfront and all well priced.

$50-100

Right on the water and within walking distance of downtown, the **Consulate Inn** (157 Water St., 902/485-4554 or 800/424-8283, www.consulateinn.com) dates to 1810. It's a historic building styled in Scottish and Georgian vernacular that was once the U.S. consulate. The restored inn has five guest rooms ranging from the low-ceilinged Lower Garden Suite ($80 s or d) to the spacious Harbour View Suite, which has a kitchen and private balcony ($140). In a modern annex are five additional guest rooms, with the largest,

the Bermudiana Suite ($160), providing excellent value. All rooms have en suite bathrooms, and a self-serve–style breakfast is included in the rates.

The three units at **Seabank Suites** (68 Front St., 902/485-4274 or 866/877-2988, www.seabanksuites.com; May–Dec.; $95–140 s or d) have private entrances and full kitchens. The 1854 home, built for a local shipping merchant, has been thoroughly modernized, with rooms also featuring TV/DVD combos.

The restored 1876 **Auberge Walker Inn** (34 Coleraine St., 902/485-1433 or 800/370-5553) has 11 guest rooms ($79–159 with a light breakfast), some with harbor views, and a fully licensed dining room.

$100-150

Dating to the 1920s, **Pictou Lodge Resort** (Braeshore Rd., 5 km east of town, 902/485-4322 or 800/495-6343, www.pictoulodge.com; mid-May–mid-Oct.; $139–423 s or d) sits on a 67-hectare oceanfront estate overlooking Northumberland Strait. The roomy lodge has

© ANDREW HEMPSTEAD

Reserve a room at the Consulate Inn and you'll be close to everything in Pictou.

been restored with rustic comforts and features a long outside porch, dining in the high-ceilinged rotunda, and a nearby pond with canoes. The 59 guest units include six three-bedroom chalets, 21 suites of various sizes and configurations, and 20 standard motel rooms. All units have private baths, and many have fireplaces, kitchens, and separate living rooms. Resort amenities include canoe rentals, a driving range, an outdoor pool, and a playground.

Campground

Caribou/Munroes Island Provincial Park (mid-June–mid-Oct.; $24) has 87 campsites (Loop B is closest to the beach), cooking shelters, flush toilets, and fire pits. It fronts a long red-sand beach, which at low tide links Munroes Island to the mainland. The park is six kilometers west of town, signposted from Highway 6.

FOOD

For waterfront ambience, head to the **Salt Water Cafe,** next to Hector Heritage Quay Museum (67 Caladh Ave., 902/485-2558; daily 11 A.M.–8:30 P.M.). Sit inside or out on the screened deck while enjoying the house specialty—seafood, moderately priced. The **Old Stone Pub** (38 Dept St., 902/485-4546; daily from 11 A.M.) has an inviting Scottish ambience, but the menu takes from many countries—lobster bruschetta, lasagna, and spaghetti and meatballs are all under $20.

Several local lodgings offer excellent public dining rooms. **The Vines** (Consulate Inn, 157 Water St., 902/485-4554; daily for dinner) has intimate dining June–September. The specialty is seafood, with some beef and chicken dishes. Five kilometers out of town, the dining room at the (**Pictou Lodge Resort** (Braeshore Rd., 902/485-4322; mid-May–mid-Oct. daily for lunch and dinner) is a woodsy, old-fashioned space. You'll enjoy strait views from an intimate setting, with tables centered around a massive stone fireplace. The menu features entrées such as ginger-fried chicken, sauced poached salmon, and smoked trout, with prices ranging $18–29.

INFORMATION AND SERVICES

At the Pictou Rotary (where Highway 106 meets Highway 6), the **Nova Scotia Visitor Information Centre** (902/485-6213 or 800/565-0000; mid-May–mid-Oct. daily 8 A.M.–9 P.M.) is primarily in place for those arriving in Nova Scotia via the ferry from Prince Edward Island, but it is also a good source of local information. The website www.townofpictou.com will help plan your trip.

Sutherland-Harris Hospital is at 1059 Haliburton Road (902/485-4324). Locals do their banking in style at architecturally resplendent places; the **Bank of Nova Scotia** is in a Second Empire–style building at the corner of Front and Colerain Streets (902/485-4378). The **post office** is at 49 Front Street.

GETTING THERE

If you're combining your travels through Nova Scotia with a visit to Prince Edward Island, you have the choice of driving across the

Confederation Bridge or catching the ferry. From Caribou, a short drive north of Pictou, **Northumberland Ferries** (902/566-3838 or 800/565-0201, www.nfl-bay.com) operates 5–9 sailings May to mid-December daily to the eastern side of Prince Edward Island. Taking just longer than one hour, the fare is $61 round-trip per vehicle, regardless of the number of passengers (you pay when leaving the island).

Pictou to Cape Breton Island

The TransCanada Highway promises little besides uninterrupted speed on its route across the northeastern mainland. The best vistas, beaches, camping, and other attractions lie off the expressway, along the strait's coastal roads between Tatamagouche and Cape Breton. Shallow pools of seawater among sandbars turn warm in the sun, making for comfortable wading and swimming at Rushton's **Beach Provincial Park, Tatamagouche Bay,** and **Melmerby Beach Provincial Park,** east of Pictou.

CAPE GEORGE SCENIC DRIVE

The route to fossil hunting at Arisaig and Cape George's ruggedly beautiful eastern coastline lies along Highways 245 and 337 between New Glasgow and Antigonish. From Exit 27 east of New Glasgow, allow half a day to reach Antigonish, which is enough time to spend time at the sights detailed here.

◖ Arisaig

Like many other places in Nova Scotia, Arisaig, 57 kilometers northeast of New Glasgow, is an unassuming place that is much more interesting than the casual visitor may imagine. The cliffs on the west side of the village tell the story of a 4-million-year period of life on earth 400 million years ago—one of the only places in the world where such a long period of time is exposed in a single layered cliff line. Four hundred million years ago, this area was a shallow sea, and as the layers of sediment built up on its floor, brachiopods (shells), nautiloids (related to squid), trilobites (ancient crabs), crinoids (a filter-feeder that attached itself to the sea bed), and bryozoans (coral) were buried. As ocean levels dropped, cliffs were formed along the shoreline, and as erosion broke the sediment down further, fossils from the Silurian Period were exposed, perfectly preserved in bands of rock that represent specific time periods all those millions of years ago. Added to the mix is the upper cliff face, which is topped with up to four meters of sand and gravel left behind when glaciers retreated across the area at the end of the last ice age. Geologists have studied the site since the mid-1800s, and as the erosion process continues and more fossils are uncovered, interest continues. You can walk to the cliffs from the wharves of Arisaig, but

© ANDREW HEMPSTEAD

Cape George Lighthouse is the high point of the Cape George Scenic Drive.

the official access is from **Arisaig Provincial Park,** on the east side of the town. From the park, steps descend steeply to the beach far below, ending near Arisaig Brook, where the largest concentration of fossils is found. It is illegal to dig at the cliff face, but scavenging through fallen rock is permitted.

Cape George

At Malignant Cove, Highway 337 branches north from Highway 245 and climbs steadily before peaking at an elevation of 190 meters at Cape George. The setting is a bicyclist's favorite scene and a just reward after the steep coastal climb. The panorama from the lighthouse at the cape's tip takes in the manicured farmlands of the Pictou–Antigonish highlands to the south as well as the misty vision of Prince Edward Island across the strait.

Along Cape George's eastern side, Highway 337 peels down from the peak alongside St. Georges Bay. Nestled below the cape is **Ballantynes Cove.** From the town wharf, a rough walking trail climbs back to the lighthouse. The 1.8-kilometer route takes less than one hour each way and makes reaching the cape more satisfying than simply driving to its summit.

ANTIGONISH

First impressions of Antigonish (An-tee-guh-NISH), from a Mi'Kmaq name meaning "place where the branches are torn off by bears gathering beechnuts," are not promising. Main Street is a thicket of fast-food restaurants and service stations—but the town is not without its charms. Dig deeper and you'll find a bustling university town with nearby beaches and hiking trails, a good choice of places to stay and eat, and two popular festivals.

Sights

In a downtown railway building dating to 1908, **Antigonish Heritage Museum** (20 E. Main St., 902/863-6160; Mon.–Fri. 10 A.M.–5 P.M.; free) tells the town's story through donated items and historical photographs. Farther along the main street is the **County Courthouse** (168 Main St.), still in use even though it has been designated a

National Historic Site. Although no tours are offered, the landscaped grounds of gracious **St. Francis Xavier University** (take Exit 32 north from Highway 104) are pleasant for a stroll, especially in summer when the campus is deserted.

Festivals and Events

The second week of July, the town hosts the **Antigonish Highland Games** (902/863-4275, www.antigonishhighlandgames.com)—the longest-running in North America, celebrated since 1863. Highlights include Celtic music, pipe bands, dancing, heavy sports such as caber tossing, and a kilted golf tournament. Throughout July and August, the **Festival Antigonish** (800/563-7529), Nova Scotia's largest and most successful professional summer theater program, features a variety of drama, musicals, comedies, cutting-edge improv, and children's entertainment at the university campus.

Accommodations

Maritime Inn Antigonish (158 Main St., 902/863-4001 or 877/768-3969, www.maritimeinns.com; $125–175) is open year-round. It has 32 units and a dining room, lounge, and café. **Antigonish Victorian Inn** (149 Main St., 902/863-1103 or 800/706-5558, www.antigonishvictorianinn.ca; $125–170 s or d) is a splendid bed-and-breakfast occupying a William Critchlow Harris–designed Queen Anne–style mansion. Each of the 12 guest rooms has a private bath and TV. Rates include full homemade breakfast.

Food

Antigonish offers a surprising number of good dining options. **Sunshine on Main** (332 Main St., 902/863-5851; Sun.–Thurs. 7 A.M.–9 P.M., Fri.–Sat. 7 A.M.–10 P.M.) has a homey atmosphere and a good menu of inexpensive healthy fare, including a number of choices for vegetarians and tasty thin-crust pizza.

Being close to the university, **Piper's Pub** (33 College St., 902/863-2590; daily from 11 A.M.) is a popular student hangout. The typical pub grub is well priced (mains $10–16), and bands play Saturday night.

Marine Drive

From Halifax, it's 320 kilometers along the Eastern Shore to Canso, at the eastern tip of mainland Nova Scotia. From this point, it's another 80 kilometers to the Canso Causeway, gateway to Cape Breton Island. It is a scenic alternative to the TransCanada Highway via Truro—longer and beyond the main tourist path, but with interesting stops around every bend.

LAWRENCETOWN

If you have enough time to take the Marine Drive, you have enough time to kick off the drive by following Cole Harbour Road from Exit 7 of Highway 111 in Dartmouth to **Lawrencetown Beach,** one of Canada's best-known surf spots. Easily reached in 30 minutes from Dartmouth, this long stretch of sand backed by high dunes is an enjoyable stop even if you don't plan to take to the water.

Surfing at Lawrencetown Beach

The waves of "L-town," as it's known to locals, break along the length of the beach and off a rocky headland that breaks the main beach in two. They are best November–May, when winter swells provide large and consistent waves. These waves also coincide with the coldest ocean temperatures—and I mean *cold.* Even with water temperatures of 0°C (32°F) and air temperatures that drop to –20°C (–4°F), it's not unusual to see footprints leading down a snow-covered beach to the breakers beyond. Summer is not devoid of waves. They are just likely to be smaller and less consistent. Hardy locals swim in the ocean in the warmer months, when water temperatures rise to 15°C (59°F), but for surfing, be prepared with a wetsuit. The beach's southern headland provides an ideal vantage point for watching the action.

From an unlikely spot in the heart of downtown Halifax, **DaCane Surf Shop** (5239 Blowers St., 902/431-7873, www.hurricane-surf.com) rents surfboards ($25 for 24 hours), wetsuits ($20), gloves and booties ($10), and bodyboards ($15). The company also has a rental outlet behind the dunes at Lawrencetown Beach Provincial Park (June–Sept.); three-hour rates are surfboards, $20; wetsuits, $20; booties and gloves, $15; bodyboards, $15. Surf lessons are $90 per hour.

Accommodations

Room rates at **Seaboard Bed and Breakfast** (2629 Cromwell Rd., East Lawrencetown, 902/827-3747 or 866/599-8094, www .seaboardbb.com; $100–115 s or d) have been creeping up, but this converted farmhouse one kilometer from the beach is still a relaxing place to spend one or more nights. Bikes are available for guest use, as is a canoe tied up at Porters Lake, which lies directly across the road. Other amenities include games such as bocce ball and horseshoes, a library with a fireplace, and a TV room. Rates include a

© ANDREW HEMPSTEAD

Lawrencetown Beach is Nova Scotia's premier surf spot.

FABLED SABLE ISLAND

COURTESY OF SABLE ISLAND GREEN HORSE SOCIETY

Just less than 200 kilometers off Nova Scotia's eastern coastline is a 40-kilometer-long sliver of sand that was known for generations of seafarers as the Graveyard of the Atlantic and is today inhabited by a herd of horses that have taken on almost mythical proportions.

The island is made up entirely of sand. The sand is part of a terminal moraine left behind by the receding ice cap at the end of the last ice age 11,000 years ago. Hardy marram grass stabilizes the central part of the island, while seals and birds are also native. The island's most famous residents are horses; they were introduced in the late 1700s, some say to feed shipwreck victims, while others claim they were aboard ships that came to grief. Today, Sable Island is home to about 300 horses. They are of special interest since they are one of the world's few truly wild horse populations, without feral intruders (such as domestic horses gone wild), and are free to roam, feed, and reproduce without human interference.

Since Sable Island was first mapped in the late 1500s, more than 350 vessels have been wrecked along its fog-shrouded shore (the last was a small yacht, the *Merrimac*, in 1999). In 1801 a station manned with a lifesaving crew was established on the island. This government-operated service soon expanded to five stations and continued until 1958. Today, the island has a year-round population of fewer than 20 people – mostly scientists who study the weather and monitor the island's environment.

The island is under the control of the Canadian Coast Guard, with Sable Island Station jointly funded by provincial and federal agencies. Aside from those in the scientific and government communities, about 50 or so intrepid travelers visit Sable Island each year. If you'd like to visit, the first step is to obtain permission from the Canadian Coast Guard. Once permission is granted, make accommodation arrangements in the staff quarters of **Sable Island Station** (not always available) and arrange fixed-wing air charters from Halifax through **Maritime Air** (902/873-3330, www.maritimeair.com). The charter company is charged a $500 landing fee (which of course will be passed on to you). The best source of island information is the website of the **Sable Island Preservation Trust** (www.sabletrust.ns.ca), which includes a visitor guide.

breakfast made up of homemade bread, jam, waffles, and more.

Ocean views from **Moonlight Beach Inn** (Hwy. 207, north end of Lawrencetown Beach, 902/827-2712, www.moonlightbeachinn.com; $139–350 s or d) are nothing short of stunning. The three guest rooms are decorated in a nautical theme, and each has a private deck, jetted tub, and TV/VCR combo, while thoughtful extras include binoculars and beach towels. The largest of the three rooms is massive and has a huge private deck with sweeping water views. Rates include a full breakfast.

MUSQUODOBOIT HARBOUR TO TANGIER

With just 900 people, Musquodoboit Harbour is nevertheless the largest community between Dartmouth and Canso. The only real attraction in town is **Musquodoboit Harbour Railway Museum** (Hwy. 7, 902/889-2689; summer only; free), housed in a 1918 railway station and three vintage rail cars. The **tourist**

information center is in the same building. Five kilometers south of Musquodoboit Harbour on Petpeswick Road, **Martinique Beach Provincial Park** protects the southern end of Nova Scotia's longest beach. The beach is often windy, but it's still a relaxing place for a long, easy walk.

Salmon River Bridge

Cross the bridge for which this village, 13 kilometers east of Musquodoboit Harbour, is named and you reach a neat little lodge nestled between a forested hill and the river. Dating to 1850 and operating as a guesthouse since 1920, **Salmon River House Country Inn** (9931 Hwy. 7, 902/889-3353 or 800/565-3353, www.salmonriverhouse.com) has seven guest rooms ($108–144 s or d), all with en suite bathrooms and some with water views, and a riverfront cottage ($144) with a fireplace. Part of the inn is the **Lobster Shack** (Apr.–Nov. daily 8 A.M.–9 P.M.), a seafood restaurant with seats that spill outside to a large riverfront

© ANDREW HEMPSTEAD

CENTRAL NOVA SCOTIA

Salmon River House Country Inn is one of the best-located lodgings along the Marine Drive.

deck. Lobsters kept in the tank are often larger than five pounds, but there's a wide choice of other seafood, including supercreamy lobster chowder.

Drive three kilometers beyond Salmon River Bridge and then four kilometers north to reach ◖ **Webber Lakeside Park** (Upper Lakeville, 902/845-2340 or 800/589-2282, www.webber-slakesideresort.com), which is filled with fun things to do such as lake swimming, a floating dock, canoe and boat rentals, a playground, and a games room with table tennis. The two-bedroom cottages ($145 s or d) have kitchens and wide decks, and the campground (mid-May–mid-Oct.; $25–34) has full hookups and hot showers. Being just an hour's drive from Halifax, this place fills up every summer weekend, so you'll need reservations.

Oyster Pond

Turn south off Highway 7 just beyond Salmon River Bridge to visit the small but interesting **Fisherman's Life Museum** (58 Navy Pool Loop, 902/889-2053; June–mid-Oct. Mon.–Sat. 9:30 A.M.–5:30 P.M., Sun. 1–5:30 P.M.; adult $3.25, senior and child $2.25). Rather than a collection of artifacts, this museum within a small homestead re-creates the life of a fisherman, his wife, and their 13 children who lived a simple self-sufficient lifestyle.

Clam Harbour Provincial Park and Vicinity

This park along the south-facing side of Clam Bay protects a long stretch of hard white sand. The beach has supervised swimming in summer, as well as change rooms and picnic areas, but no camping (from the end of the access road, turn right to reach the nicest picnic area, where tables are nestled in windswept coastal forest).

Members of the Murphy family have lived in Murphy Cove for seven generations, involved through time in everything from rum-running to fishing. Now they operate ◖ **Murphy's Camping on the Ocean** (291 Murphy's Rd., 902/772-2700; mid-May–mid-Oct.), which sprawls across a grassy headland. The campground has all the usual facilities—showers,

boat and kayak rentals, a laundry, a playground, and more—but it's Brian's evening storytelling, boat tours (two hours for $17.50), clam-digging trips, and free mussel bakes that make this place stand apart. Tent camping is $20, hookups $25, or rent trailers for $75 s or d.

TANGIER

Tangier is best known for the smokehouse of ◖ **J. Willy Krauch and Sons** (signposted off Hwy. 7, Tangier, 902/772-2188; Mon.–Fri. 8 A.M.–6 P.M., Sat.–Sun. 10 A.M.–6 P.M.), whose smoked salmon you'll find in better restaurants throughout the province. Willy Krauch was a Danish immigrant who settled in Tangier in the 1950s. Following a Scandinavian recipe that Krauch's sons still use, the fish is cold-smoked (salted and then smoked at low temperatures for one week), creating a divine-tasting treat of the most delicate texture. The smokehouse's retail shop stocks smoked salmon, mackerel, and eel, ready to eat or packed to travel. If you've planned well by bringing crackers and cheese from the city, stop by for a selection of salmon and continue to Taylor Head Provincial Park for a seafood snack by the seaside.

Coastal Adventures (84 Mason's Point Rd., 902/772-2774, www.coastaladventures .com) pushes off into the cove on full-day kayak excursions that include a visit to uninhabited islands; $110 per person includes lunch. Kayak rentals are $50 per day for a single and $75 for a double. The same people operate ◖ **Paddler's Retreat Bed and Breakfast** ($50–80 s, $55–75 d), which is an excellent spot to plan to spend one and more nights. Most guests staying in this restored 1860s fisherman's home do so as part of a kayaking instruction package or before or after participating in a day trip. Three of the four rooms share bathrooms while the fourth has an en suite bathroom and private entrance. Rates include a full breakfast.

TANGIER TO SHERBROOKE
◖ **Taylor Head Provincial Park**

Turn off at Spry Bay, 15 kilometers beyond Tangier, to reach this interesting ocean park protecting a narrow peninsula extending six

Psyche Cove, Taylor Head Provincial Park

kilometers to Taylor Head. The west-facing side of the spit is rugged and windswept, with stunted white spruce trees clinging precariously to the rocky ground, while the east side is characterized by sandy coves lapped by calm waters. A five-kilometer unpaved road from Highway 7 hugs the west side of the peninsula before crossing to protected Psyche Cove. At the end of the road is a series of small parking lots with beach access. You can walk along the beach back toward the mainland to Bob Bluff or head in the opposite direction to a headland with sweeping views up and down the peninsula and of island-dotted Mushaboom Harbour. Taylor Head itself is four kilometers from the end of the road. If you return via rocky Spry Bay, you'll have walked 10 kilometers (allow four hours).

Spry Bay to Liscomb Mills
Marine Drive between Spry Bay and Liscomb Mills passes a string of fishing villages with delightful names such as Ecum Secum (a Mi'Kmaq word of unknown origin) and Spanish Ship Bay (named for a nearby headland that resembles a Spanish galleon). Linked

to Highway 7 by a short bridge, Sober Island's name has a more cynical origin (the first residents bemoaned the lack of alcohol).

In Liscomb Mills, **Liscombe Lodge** (Hwy. 7, 902/779-2307 or 877/375-6343, www.signatureresorts.com; mid-May–late Oct.; from $170 s or d) boasts an idyllic setting along the Liscomb River. Amenities include an indoor pool, sauna, hot tubs, a fitness center, hiking trails, tennis courts, a marina with boat, canoe, and fishing-equipment rentals, and a comfortable dining room overlooking the river.

SHERBROOKE
Highway 7 leaves the coast at Liscomb, turning north to Sherbrooke, from where Highway 7 continues north to Antigonish and the Marine Drive spurs east, continuing along the Eastern Shore as Highway 316. Sherbrooke (pop. 400) was founded at the farthest navigable point of the St. Mary's River in the early 1800s. By 1869 gold had been discovered in the area, and the town was booming. In addition to mining, mills were established to process lumber

historic Sherbrooke Village

for export, and local farms depended on the town for services. But by 1890 the gold rush was over, and the population began slipping.

◖ Sherbrooke Village

By the late 1960s Sherbrooke was a shadow of its former self. Gold rush–era buildings remained in varying states of disrepair, but the only visitors were anglers chasing salmon along the river. At this point, a local trust stepped in, and under the guidance of the Nova Scotia Museum an ambitious restoration project took place. Today, Sherbrooke Village (902/522-2400; June–mid-Oct. daily 9:30 A.M.–5 P.M.; adult $10, senior $8, child $4.25) is a unique historical setting, comprising more than 80 restored buildings that are integrated with the town itself. About 20 buildings are open to the public, including an ambrotype photography studio, the colonnaded courthouse, a jail, a water-powered sawmill, the Sherbrooke Hotel, a drug store, a blacksmith shop, a church, and a farmyard. The site is brought alive by costumed interpreters who wander the village streets, tend to their crops, and go about operating each business as folks would have done in the late 1800s. To fully immerse yourself in the experience, consider participating in the Hands on History program (July–Aug. only). For $30 per person, the costume department will dress you in period clothing, and you can spend the day helping in the kitchens, trying your hand at pottery, or learning skills from the blacksmith. The Courthouse Concert Series (888/743-7845 or check the schedule at www.sherbrookenow.ca) takes place 2–3 nights a week through the summer season; entertainment varies from traditional Celtic *ceilidhs* to musical comedies. Starting time is usually around 7:30 P.M. The main parking lot and entrance are off Court Street (turn left at the end of the modern-day main street).

Accommodations and Food

For overnight stays, Sherbrooke offers several choices. **St. Mary's River Lodge** (21 Main St., 902/522-2177, www.riverlodge.ca; Apr.–Dec.;

$75–106 s or d) is across the road from the river and steps from Sherbrooke Village. It has seven guest rooms, each with an en suite bathroom. A cooked breakfast is included in the rates. On the east side of town, a 10-minute walk from the village, is **Sherbrooke Village Inn** (7975 Hwy. 7, 902/522-2235 or 866/522-3818, www.sherbrookevillageinn.ca; May–Oct.). The medium-size motel rooms are plain but comfortable ($80 s, $95–100 d) and self-contained units are $110 s or d.

In the Sherbrooke Hotel, within the historical village, the ◖ **What Cheer Tea Room** (June–mid-Oct. daily 11 A.M.–9 P.M.) is a countrified restaurant with friendly staff and basic but tasty dishes that will set you up for more historical sightseeing. You can try traditional rural dishes such as Acadian chicken pot pie ($14), or big city favorites such as a veggie burger on focaccia ($9). **Sherbrooke Village Inn Restaurant** (7975 Hwy. 7, 902/522-2235, www.sherbrookevillageinn.ca; May–Oct. daily 7:30 A.M.–9 P.M.) is a small wood-paneled restaurant on the east (Halifax) side of town. The emphasis is on simple presentations of local seafood. You could start with fish chowder ($5.50) and then choose between dishes such as deep-fried scallops and strip loin ($20) or a lobster from the tank (usually around $25). The homemade pie with ice cream (it was blueberry the night I visited) is $6.

SHERBROOKE TO CANSO

It's only a little more than 100 kilometers between Sherbrooke and Canso, but the drive will take at least two hours, plus any time you wait for the ferry at Country Harbour.

Nova Scotia Lighthouse Interpretive Centre

There could be no better location for a lighthouse display than in a restored light-keeper's home at the end of a windswept, often fog-enshrouded peninsula—which is exactly where this museum (Lighthouse Rd., Port Bickerton, 902/364-2000; mid-June–Sept. daily 10 A.M.–8 P.M.; adult $2) is situated. Built in 1901 and deactivated in 1962, the two-building complex, originally **Point Bickerton Lighthouse,** now holds a display describing the lonely life of Nova Scotian light-keepers and their families, the original foghorn, and a directory of Nova Scotia's lighthouses. Stairs lead to an observation tower. Outside, a trail leads past clumps of tasty blueberries and cranberries to a sandy beach. From the turn-off in Port Bickerton, 25 kilometers beyond Sherbrooke and seven kilometers before the ferry across Country Harbour, it's three kilometers to the interpretive center, the last two along an unpaved road.

Country Harbour

The Country Harbour ferry, along Highway 316 seven kilometers north of Port Bickerton, departs the east side (Halifax side) of the bay on the half hour and the west side on the hour. During the laughably named "rush hour" (9–10 A.M. and 5–6 P.M.), ferries operate more frequently. The ferry has room for just 12 passenger vehicles or a limited number of trucks and RVs. The fare is $5 (cash only), which is paid to the attendant upon loading. From the west side of the bay, it's 86 kilometers to Canso. Aside from the short detour to Tor Bay, it's worth slowing down to admire the village of Issacs Harbour, which on a calm day is reflected across the bay of the same name from Goldboro.

Tor Bay

Named for granite knolls that dot the region, Tor Bay is lined by three small communities established by Acadians after their deportation by the English in 1755. For visitors, the highlight is **Tor Bay Provincial Park,** on an isthmus along a peninsula that forms the southern boundary of the bay. This small day-use park encompasses one of the few sandy beaches this far east along the Marine Drive. A boardwalk leads to the beach, from where a short trail leads to a rocky headland where covered interpretive boards describe the geology that led to the creation of the beach.

CANSO

The remote town of Canso, 320 kilometers along Marine Drive from Halifax, is the jumping-off point to an interesting historic site that

© ANDREW HEMPSTEAD

CENTRAL NOVA SCOTIA

After a century of guiding ships, Port Bickerton Lighthouse is now a museum.

protects Canada's oldest fishing village. In more recent times, Canso was an important link in trans-Atlantic communications. The most striking reminder of this era is the 1884 **Hazel Hill Cable Station,** just before town. It was from here that the distress signal from the sinking *Titanic* and news of the 1929 stock market crash were transmitted to the rest of the world.

◖ Canso Islands National Historic Site

Archaeological digs point to European settlement as early as the 1500s on this small island one kilometer offshore from Canso. Their time on the island was only temporary, and no obvious signs of this era remain today. Two hundred years later, the French and British were fighting for control of North America, with ownership of the Canso Islands in dispute even after the signing of the Treaty of Utrecht in 1713. In 1718 the French were displaced, and the same year, fearing a reprisal attack by the French, the British built a small fort on Grassy Island to protect access to cod stocks that were being harvested at the amazing rate of 10 million pounds per year. Grassy Island grew into a prosperous community, complete with wealthy merchants who built solid stone homes. The village was destroyed by a French invasion from Louisbourg in 1744 and was never rebuilt.

The site comprises a visitors center (Union St., 902/366-3136; June–mid-Sept. daily 10 A.M.–6 P.M.; $5 donation) on the Canso waterfront and the island itself. Mainland exhibits include a scale model of the settlement, fragments of French pottery dated to the early 1700s, and a short documentary. Boats run on demand between the visitors center and the island. Once safety regulations are described, the small craft is off, and you'll be on the island within 15 minutes. A mowed trail passes eight information boards describing the settlement and what remains—cellar pits, mounds of rubble from residences, and terraced vegetable plots—before looping back down to the dock. Allow around 30 minutes to walk the trail. If visitation is slow, the boat will be waiting at

Not much remains of early settlements at Canso Islands National Historic Site, but what does is a poignant reminder of the past.

the wharf for your return; otherwise, expect a wait of up to 30 minutes while it transports more visitors across. The only services on the island are pit toilets and a shelter, so bring warm clothes and water. The suggested donation to the visitors center includes the boat ride to the island.

Stan Rogers Folk Festival

On the first weekend of July, the population of Canso increases 10 times as music fans descend on the town for "Stanfest" (888/554-7826, www.stanfest.com), a folk-music festival of 50 acts from around the world performing on six stages. In addition to the music, there are a food fair, craft show, and beer garden. Most visitors camp at the Acoustic Campground, set up by the organizers within walking distance of the main stage. Other temporary campgrounds take the overflow, with shuttle buses running to the grounds and to showers at the local high school. A camping pass is $60 and entry to the concert is $100 for the entire weekend.

Accommodations and Camping

Canso is most definitely not a tourist town. The **Last Port Motel** (Hwy. 16, 902/366-2400) is just before town. It offers basic rooms in the $60–70 range as well as a restaurant open daily at 7 A.M. A much better option is ◖ **DesBarres Manor Inn** (90 Church St., 902/533-2099, www.desbarres-manor.com; $199–259 s or d), 56 kilometers east in Guysborough. Dating to 1837, the three-story inn has been beautifully restored, and the grounds remain in immaculate shape. The 10 guest rooms are stylish and come with niceties like 600-thread-count sheets on super-comfortable mattresses, plus luxurious bathrooms. Rates include a gourmet continental breakfast, with dinner available with advance reservations.

Ten kilometers before Canso along Highway 16 is **Seabreeze Campground and Cottages** (230 Fox Island Rd., Fox Island, 902/366-2352; mid-May–mid-Oct.), where modern facilities, full hookups, and views across Chedabucto Bay keep the 51 campsites full through July and August. One- and two-bedroom cottages ($90 and $110 respectively) have basic cooking facilities, a lounge area with TV, and separate bedrooms. Other resort amenities include coin-operated showers, a laundry, firewood sales, a playground, canoe rentals, and even a lobster pound (where you can buy live lobster).

Food

You can get a meal in the restaurant at the **Last Port Motel** (Hwy. 16, 902/366-2400; daily 7 A.M.–10 P.M.), but a better choice is **Canso Rose Family Restaurant** (20 Telegraph St., 902/366-2189; daily from 8 A.M.), a sparsely decorated but cheerful room attached to the local pharmacy. A cooked breakfast is just $6, *including* coffee, while the rest of the day fish cakes with baked beans is $6, fish-and-chips is $9, and a chicken stir fry is $11.

Information

Whitman House (1297 Union St., 902/366-2170; June–Sept. daily 9 A.M.–5 P.M.; donation), a handsome three-story 1885 house with displays illustrating local history, doubles as an information center.

CAPE BRETON ISLAND

"I have traveled around the globe," wrote Alexander Graham Bell, perhaps Cape Breton Island's most renowned transplant. "I have seen the Canadian and American Rockies, the Andes and the Alps, and the Highlands of Scotland; but for simple beauty, Cape Breton outrivals them all."

Linked to the mainland by a two-lane causeway, nearly every coastal and inland backcountry road on the western half of the island leads eventually to the Cabot Trail, the scenic highway rimming the unforgettable landscape of northwestern Cape Breton. The 294-kilometer route of steep ascents, descents, and hold-your-breath switchbacks has no official beginning or end, nor, unlike every other highway in the province, is it numbered. From the south, enter the route from Highway 395 near Whycocomagh or from Exit 7 of the TransCanada Highway, eight kilometers west of Baddeck. The latter option is most scenic, passing through the Margaree River Valley.

In the far northern part of the island, magnificent Cape Breton Highlands National Park stretches from coast to coast, as wild and remote as the Highlands of Scotland. Green, steeply pitched highlands begin at the sea in the south and sweep north, cut by salmon-filled rivers. As the elevation increases, the Acadian and boreal forests give way to a taiga tableland of windswept stunted trees.

The Northumberland Strait opens into the Gulf of St. Lawrence on the western coast, while the Atlantic washes the opposite shore. The 1,098-square-kilometer Bras d'Or Lakes forms the island's heart. The saltwater "Arm of

HIGHLIGHTS

◖ Glenora Distillery: Tucked into a quiet glen along the remote west coast is North America's only single-malt whiskey distillery, complete with a restaurant and guest rooms for those looking to linger longer (page 154).

◖ Alexander Graham Bell National Historic Site: Dedicated to one of the world's most prolific inventors, this museum will interest all ages (page 155).

◖ Boat Tours on Bras d'Or Lakes: Sail back in time aboard Alexander Graham Bell's beautiful yacht *Elsie* (page 157).

◖ Driving the Cabot Trail: This spectacular 300-kilometer circuit traverses varying landscapes, but the highlight is the section through Cape Breton Highlands National Park – the main reason for visiting the island (page 162).

◖ Golfing Highland Links: Where else can you walk the fairways of one of the world's finest golf courses knowing that what you've paid to play is less than at many regular city courses (page 166)?

◖ Gaelic College of Celtic Arts and Crafts: No, you don't need to sign up for a course. Instead, take in music recitals and demonstrations such as weaving (page 168).

◖ Celtic Colours International Festival: Hosted at venues across Cape Breton Island, this October festival draws crowds for the opportunity to enjoy traditional music while soaking up the colors of fall (page 169).

◖ Fortress of Louisbourg National Historic Site: It may be a little off the tourist path, but sprawling across 10 hectares of a remote headland is a reconstruction of a French town destroyed by the British 250 years ago (page 172).

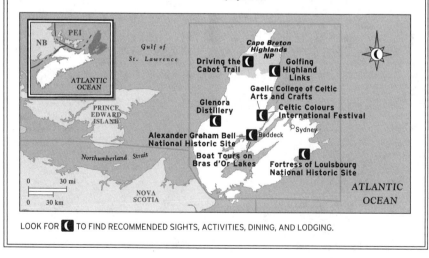

LOOK FOR ◖ TO FIND RECOMMENDED SIGHTS, ACTIVITIES, DINING, AND LODGING.

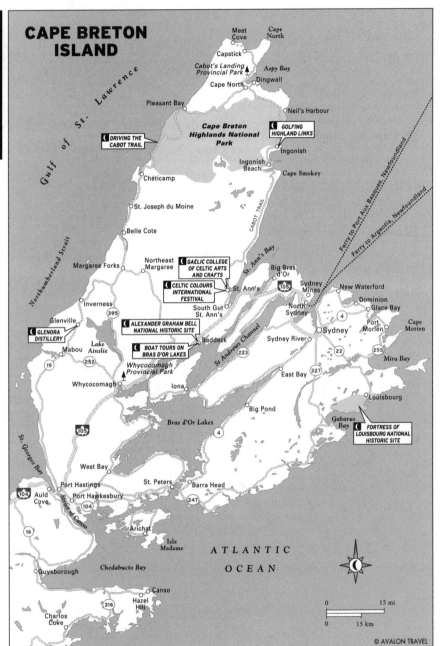

CAPE BRETON ISLAND

Gulf of St. Lawrence

Meat Cove
Cape North
Capstick
Cabot's Landing Provincial Park
Aspy Bay
Dingwall
Cape North
Pleasant Bay
Neil's Harbour

Cape Breton Highlands National Park

DRIVING THE CABOT TRAIL

GOLFING HIGHLAND LINKS
Ingonish

Chéticamp

Ingonish Beach
Cape Smokey

St. Joseph du Moine

CABOT TRAIL

Belle Cote

Northumberland Strait

Margaree Forks
Northeast Margaree

St. Ann's Bay

GAELIC COLLEGE OF CELTIC ARTS AND CRAFTS

Big Bras d'Or

Ferry to Port Aux Basques, Newfoundland
Ferry to Argentia, Newfoundland

CELTIC COLOURS INTERNATIONAL FESTIVAL
St. Ann's

Sydney Mines
New Waterford

Inverness
395

South Gut St. Ann's

105
North Sydney
Dominion
Glace Bay

Glenville

ALEXANDER GRAHAM BELL NATIONAL HISTORIC SITE

St. Andrews Channel

4
Port Morien
Cape Morien

GLENORA DISTILLERY
Mabou

Baddeck

Sydney River
Sydney

22

Lake Ainslie

BOAT TOURS ON BRAS D'OR LAKES

223

255
Mira Bay

19
252

Whycocomagh Provincial Park

Whycocomagh
Iona

East Bay
327

Louisbourg

105

Bras d'Or Lakes

Big Pond

Gabarus Bay

FORTRESS OF LOUISBOURG NATIONAL HISTORIC SITE

St. Georges Bay

West Bay
4

Port Hastings
St. Peters
Barra Head

104
Auld Cove

Port Hawkesbury
104

247

16

Arichat

Isle Madame

ATLANTIC OCEAN

Guysborough

Chedabucto Bay

Canso

Hazel Hill

316

Charlos Cove

0   15 mi
0   15 km

© AVALON TRAVEL

Gold," though barely influenced by tidal cycles, is an inland arm of the Atlantic consisting of a sapphire-blue main lake with numerous peripheral channels, straits, and bays.

PLANNING YOUR TIME

Although you can fly into the airport at Sydney, most visitors drive to Cape Breton from Halifax, reaching the causeway linking the island to the mainland in less than four hours. From the causeway, a choice of routes present themselves, including the little-traveled route up the west coast, which passes the **Glenora Distillery.** The geographic and tourist hub is Baddeck. Plan to spend at least one full day at this resort town, which is enough time to visit the **Alexander Graham Bell National Historic Site** and take a **boat tour on Bras d'Or Lakes.** Baddeck is also a good starting point for beginning the **Cabot**

Trail, a 300-kilometer highway that loops through the wilderness of **Cape Breton Highlands National Park.** The park scenery is the highlight of the drive, but along the way, plan on browsing the **arts and crafts of Chéticamp** and **golfing at Highland Links.** If your travels correspond with the October **Celtic Colours International Festival,** plan on taking in as many concerts as you can. At other times of the year, St. Ann's **Gaelic College of Celtic Arts and Crafts** is the place to immerse yourself in Celtic culture. To hit all the highlights—those detailed above—you should allow yourself at the very least three days from Halifax, but preferably four or five. The main reason for veering from the Cabot Trail is to visit the **Fortress of Louisbourg,** a lesser-known but impressive attraction that re-creates a French town from the mid-1700s.

Port Hastings to Baddeck

Canso Causeway, easily reached in four hours from Halifax, links Cape Breton to the mainland. From this point, Highways 104 and 105 (the TransCanada) and Highway 19 fan out across the island from here. Highway 19 follows the west coast up to Mabou and Inverness, and then links up with the Cabot Trail in the Margaree Valley. The TransCanada Highway lies straight ahead, leading through the center of the island to Baddeck and on to Sydney. The endless stream of buses packed with tourists makes a beeline along this route, connecting with the Cabot Trail at Baddeck. Highway 4 branches off to the east (or take the more direct Highway 104 for the first 28 kilometers), passing the turnoff to Isle Madame, and then following Bras d'Or Lakes, en route to Sydney.

PORT HASTINGS

The main reason to stop in Port Hastings, the gateway town to Cape Breton Island, is to load up with brochures at the well-stocked **Nova**

Scotia Visitor Information Centre, on the right as the TransCanada Highway crosses to the island (902/625-4201; May–Dec. daily 9 A.M.–5 P.M.). Behind the center, views extend back across to the mainland, and information boards describe the processes involved in constructing the causeway.

Accommodations

Through town toward Port Hawkesbury, **EconoLodge MacPuffin Motel** (Hwy. 4, 902/625-0621 or 800/867-2212, www.macpuffin.com; Apr.–late Dec.; $89–149 s or d) has 46 air-conditioned rooms, each with comfortable beds, coffeemakers, and high-speed Internet access. Bonuses include an indoor pool, playground, fitness room, and free breakfast.

ISLE MADAME

Take Highway 104 for 30 kilometers east from Port Hastings, and then Highway 320 south over Lennox Passage Bridge to reach this

© ANDREW HEMPSTEAD

Arichat Church, Isle Madame

43-square-kilometer island. Settled by French fishermen in the early 1700s, this was one of the first parts of the province to be settled, and it's one of the oldest fishing ports in North America. Isle Madame has four main communities—**Arichat, West Arichat, Petit Grat,** and **D'Escousse.**

The wooded island is a popular weekend getaway, with two provincial parks (**Lennox Passage** to the north and **Pondville Beach** on the east side) and plenty of picnicking, swimming, and vista spots. In Arichat, on the waterfront, **LeNoir Forge Museum** (902/226-9364; May–Sept. daily 10 A.M.–6 P.M.; donation) is a restored working 18th-century forge open to visitors.

L'Auberge Acadienne Inn (High Rd., Arichat, 902/226-2200, www.acadienne .com) is designed as a 19th-century Acadian-style inn, with eight inviting rooms, one with a jetted tub, in the main building ($105 s, $115 d) and nine adjacent motel units ($85 s, $95 d). The dining room serves Acadian dishes in a casual country-style atmosphere.

BRAS D'OR LAKES SCENIC DRIVE

It's an easy two-hour drive (148 kilometers) from the Canso Causeway to Sydney via Highway 4 along the southeastern shore of Bras d'Or Lakes. The highway steers away from the lake until passing St. Peters, with nearby **Dundee Resort** (902/345-2649 or 800/565-1774, www.capebretonresorts.com; mid-May–Oct.), a destination in itself. The resort, 12 kilometers from Highway 4, is set on 223 hectares overlooking Bras d'Or Lakes. It features an 18-hole golf course (greens fees $55), an outdoor pool, a marina with all manner of watercraft for rent, an Arcade Activities Centre, summer programs for the kids, and a restaurant. Motel rooms, most with balconies, range $139–199, while cottages with limited cooking facilities and up to three bedrooms are $129–219.

St. Peters and Vicinity

This small town lies 12 kilometers beyond the

turnoff to Isle Madame and 55 kilometers from Port Hastings.

Photography buffs should check out the **MacAskill House Museum** (7 MacAskill Dr., 902/535-2531; mid-June–Sept. daily 10 A.M.–6 P.M.; donation), in the restored childhood home of Wallace MacAskill, one of the world's preeminent marine photographers. The museum exhibits a collection of his best photographs as well as historic cameras.

Overlooking Bras d'Or Lakes, 1.5 kilometers east of St. Peters, **Joyce's Motel and Cottages** (tel. 902/535-2404, www.joyces-motel.com; mid-May–mid-Oct.; $65–110 s or d) offers the choice of regular motel rooms or larger one-bedroom cottages. Attractions include a laundry, boating, fishing, and an outdoor swimming pool. **Battery Provincial Park** (off Hwy. 4 1 km east of town, 902/535-3094; mid-June–early Sept.) has hiking trails and ocean views. Rates are $24 for the 52 open, wooded, unserviced campsites.

Big Pond

From St. Peters, the run to Sydney takes a little more than an hour, with Highway 4 paralleling Bras d'Or Lakes for much of the way. A good halfway-point lunch stop is **Rita's,** in a converted schoolhouse at Big Pond (902/828-2667; summer daily 9 A.M.–7 P.M.). Owned by singer Rita MacNeil, who grew up in Big Pond and who continues to promote Cape Breton Island around the world, the café serves her own blend of tea, sandwiches, and salads in a country setting. An adjacent room is devoted to her distinguished career.

HIGHWAY 19: THE CEILIDH TRAIL

This is the least traveled of the three routes north from the Canso Causeway. Highway 19 hugs the coastline and passes many small villages that haven't changed much in decades. This stretch of coastline is a bastion of Celtic music, hence the nickname Ceilidh Trail. Natalie MacMaster and the Rankins, as well as a new generation of stars headed by

FIDDLING THE NIGHT AWAY

A *ceilidh* (KAY-lee) was originally an informal gathering, usually on a Friday or Saturday night, that would bring together young people who would dance the night away to lively Celtic music in a local hall. These social gatherings originated in Gaelic-speaking regions of Scotland and Ireland, with the tradition introduced to the New World by immigrants in the 1700s. Although nightclubs and pubs may have replaced the *ceilidh* in popularity in the city, along the west coast of Cape Breton Island and in other rural areas they remain an important part of the social scene. Most important, the music has retained its original roots, with progressive dancing in which the woman moves along a ring from man to man or everyone dancing in formation (similar to line dancing). The most skilled dancers break away from the formations to step dance.

Highway 19 is known as the Ceilidh Trail, and for good reason, as *ceilidhs* take place in towns and villages along the route year-round. Everyone is welcome, with many of the summer events especially tailored for visitors. At Mabou, the Mabou Community Hall fills with the sound of fiddle music every Tuesday through summer while the following night, the foot-stomping fun happens down the road at the local museum. Passing through on Thursday? Then plan for a lively evening of entertainment at the Inverness Fire Hall *ceilidh*.

Christine Crowley, were all born and raised in the area.

Mabou

A 60-kilometer drive north up Highway 19 from the Canso Causeway, the town of Mabou (pop. 400) is the center of Gaelic education in Nova Scotia (the language is taught in the local school) and the location of Our Lady of Seven Sorrows Pioneers Shrine. The Mabou

Gaelic and Historical Society Museum, or **An Drochaid** (902/945-2311; July–Aug. daily 9 A.M.–5 P.M.) focuses on crafts, local music and poetry, genealogical research, and Gaelic culture.

The Mabou Mines area, near the coast, has some excellent hiking trails into a roadless section of the **Mabou Highlands.**

◖ Glenora Distillery

The Glenora Inn and Distillery (Glenville, 9 km north of Mabou, 902/258-2662 or 800/839-0491, www.glenoradistillery.com; mid-June–Oct.), is North America's only single-malt whiskey distillery (it can't be called Scotch whiskey as it's not from Scotland). The final product is marketed as Glen Breton Rare, with 250,000 liters distilled annually. Built in 1990 using impressive post-and-beam construction and traditional copper pots for the distilling process, the complex is open for tours through summer on the hour 9 A.M.–5 P.M. The cost is $7 per person. Better still, it's also a country inn with nine comfortable rooms ($155–170) and six spacious log chalets ($205–295). Also at the distillery is **Glenora Dining Room and Pub** (daily 7–9 A.M., 11 A.M.–3 P.M., and 5–10 P.M.), which serves light breakfasts and hearty lunches and dinners, the latter two accompanied by live Celtic music.

Inverness

This Scottish settlement (pop. 2,000), the largest town along Highway 19, has decent beaches and the **Inverness Miners' Museum** (62 Lower Railway St., 902/258-2097; June–Sept. Mon.–Sat. 9 A.M.–7 P.M.; adult $2, child $1), which focuses on the region's mining history.

Ten kilometers north of Inverness on Highway 19 is ◖ **MacLeod's Beach Campsite** (Dunvegan, 902/258-2433, www.macleods .com; June 15–Oct. 15), which slopes down to a delightful beach that rarely gets crowded. Amenities include washrooms, showers, fire pits, a store, a launderette, a games room, volleyball, basketball, horseshoes, and more. Tent sites are $25, hookups $28.

HIGHWAY 105 TO BADDECK

From the Canso Causeway, it's 90 kilometers to Baddeck along Highway 105 (TransCanada Highway). This is the main route north to Sydney and the Cabot Trail.

Iona

Nine kilometers northeast of Whycocomagh, Highway 223 crosses Little Narrows to Iona, and then follows the shoreline of St. Andrews Channel all the way to Sydney. It's the least traveled of the many up-island highways, but no less interesting than the other options. The route is posted as Bras d'Or Lakes Drive.

Set on 16 hectares overlooking the narrow body of water between Bras d'Or Lakes and St. Andrews Channel, Iona's **Highland Village** (Hwy. 223, 902/725-2272; June–mid-Oct. daily 9:30 A.M.–5:30 P.M.; adult $9, senior $7, child $4) features 10 historic buildings as well as many examples of working farm equipment.

Baddeck and Vicinity

Baddeck (from *abadak,* or "place near an island," as the Mi'Kmaq called it, referring to Kidston Island just offshore) lies on the misty wooded shore of St. Patrick's Channel, a long inlet of Bras d'Or Lakes. Halfway between the Canso Causeway and Sydney, Baddeck also marks the traditional beginning and ending point for the Cabot Trail.

SIGHTS AND RECREATION

Many visitors plan a stop in Baddeck for its heritage accommodations and fine dining, but there are also a few things to see and do, including a National Historic Site that everyone should visit.

◖ Alexander Graham Bell National Historic Site

At the east end of Baddeck (within walking distance of downtown) is Alexander Graham Bell National Historic Site (902/295-2069; June daily 9 A.M.–6 P.M., July–mid-Oct. daily 8:30 A.M.–6 P.M.; adult $7.80, senior $6.55, child $3.90), a tremendously satisfying museum with displays on Bell's life, family, and seemingly inexhaustible curiosity about science. The multimedia exhibits include working models of Bell's first telephones and a full-size reproduction of his speed-record–setting HD-4 hydrofoil, but some of the most interesting displays are information panels describing how Bell's interest in teaching the deaf to speak led

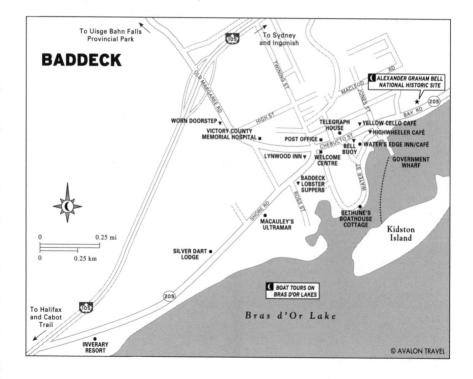

ALEXANDER GRAHAM BELL

© ANDREW HEMPSTEAD

Alexander Graham Bell National Historic Site

Once a major shipbuilding center, Baddeck claims as its most famous resident not a sailor but an inventor – Alexander Graham Bell. The landscape, language, and people all reminded the Scotsman of his native land. He built a grand summer home, Beinn Bhreagh (Ben Vreeah), across the inlet from Baddeck (it is still owned by his descendents and is not open to the public). While the telephone is his most famous invention, Bell possessed an intellectual curiosity that is almost impossible to comprehend in today's world.

At Beinn Bhreagh, he studied heredity by breeding sheep and seeking to increase twin births. Even when separated from the rest of the world at Baddeck, he maintained friendships in high places – after the attempted assassination of President Gar-field in 1881, Bell was hastily commissioned to invent an electromagnetic device to find the bullet. When his son died after experiencing breathing problems, he developed a breathing device that was the prototype of the iron lungs used to help polio victims. More than anything else, Bell was captivated by flight. He tested propeller-driven kits as early as the 1890s, and in 1909, four years after the Wright Brothers' famous flight, the great inventor took to the air over Bras d'Or Lakes in the **Silver Dart.** But he wasn't done yet: In 1919, at the age of 72, Bell and his estate manager, Casey Baldwin, invented the hydrofoil, which set a water-speed record of more than 70 miles per hour. Bell died three years later and was buried at Beinn Bhreagh.

to the invention of the telephone. The inventor always had a soft spot for children, and the love of the younger generation is reflected in Children's Corner, a large space where kids of all ages can make and decorate kites, do experiments, and generally have fun in an educational environment. Allow at least two hours, more if you have children.

Kidston Island

A free ferry runs from Government Wharf out to Kidston Island, just 200 meters from the mainland, which has a beach with supervised swimming. The wooded island also has numerous short walking trails, including one that leads to a lighthouse that has been guiding vessels on Bras d'Or Lakes for more than a century. The ferry operates every 20 minutes July–August Monday–Friday 10 A.M.–6 P.M., Saturday–Sunday noon–6 P.M.

◖ Boat Tours on Bras d'Or Lakes

Built by Alexander Graham Bell, *Elsie* is a sleek 55-foot yacht that has spent its entire life sailing the calm waters of Bras d'Or Lakes. Now operated by Cape Breton Resorts (902/295-3500 or 800/565-5660), *Elsie* sails mid-June to mid-October daily at 10:30 A.M. and 2:30 P.M. from the Inverary Resort marina on the south side of town. The trips last three hours and cost $65 per person.

A less expensive option (adult $25, child $10) are 90-minute trips aboard **Amoeba** (902/295-2481), a 67-foot concrete-hulled yacht built by the current owner's father during a 10-year period. Departures are from Government Wharf three or four times daily mid-May through mid-October. In addition to enjoying the lake, you'll pass Alexander Graham Bell's estate and often spot bald eagles perched atop shoreline trees.

ACCOMMODATIONS AND CAMPING
$50-100

Owned by the same family for five generations, **Telegraph House** (479 Chebucto St., 902/295-1100 or 888/263-9840; $80–119 s or d) combines basic rooms in the grandly historic original 1861 home with a row of modern motel units. The lodge has two historic links of note—it was once home to a telegraph office that sent some of the first trans-Atlantic messages, and Alexander Graham Bell was a frequent guest. The room that Bell called his own looks exactly like it would have in the 1880s ($109 s or d); others have been given a modern look while retaining the historic feel through antique furnishings. Amenities include a library, a sitting room, and a dining room open daily for breakfast, lunch, and dinner. Telegraph House is also one of the few downtown accommodations open year-round.

Don't expect room service at the delightful **Bethune's Boathouse Cottage** (49 Water St., 902/295-2687; mid-May–mid-Oct.; $90–110), a converted boathouse that enjoys a waterfront location with gardens that extend to the water's edge. The cottage has a separate bedroom, bathroom, TV, outdoor barbecue, and a dock where a rowboat is tied up for guest use.

$100-150

A 10-minute walk from town, the ◖ **Worn Doorstep** (43 Old Margaree Rd., 902/295-1997; $115 s or d) has four delightful en-suite rooms, each with a private entrance, air-conditioning, basic cooking facilities, and a TV. Rates include breakfast delivered to your room.

Water's Edge Inn (22 Water St., 902/295-3600 or 866/439-2528, www.thewatersedgeinn.com; May–mid-Oct.; $140–170 s or d) is across the road from the lake and also within easy walking distance of downtown restaurants. Four of the six rooms have lake views and private balconies. All six are heritage-themed yet stylishly outfitted with modern touches such as air-conditioning and TV/DVD combos. The in-house café is also highly recommended.

Named for Alexander Graham Bell's famous airplane, **Silver Dart Lodge** (257 Shore Rd., 902/295-2340 or 800/565-8439, www.silverdartlodge.com; mid-May–mid-Oct.; $135–200 s or d) sits on a 40-hectare hillside overlooking the lake. Amenities include a heated outdoor pool and putting green, as well as lake cruises, boat rentals, a beach, and hiking trails.

Oatcakes and hot drinks (no extra charge) are served for early risers, followed by a buffet breakfast ($12 per person). Picnic lunches are available with notice, and the restaurant is also open for dinner.

Direct water access is a major draw at **(Inverary Resort** (Exit 8 from Hwy. 105, 902/295-3500 or 800/565-5660, www .capebretonresorts.com; May–Nov.; $110–350), a large complex that offers accommodations varying from homely bed-and-breakfast–style rooms to modern two-bedroom suites. Down on the waterfront, rent canoes and kayaks from the activity center, or go for a sailing trip aboard Alexander Graham Bell's yacht *Elsie*. Elsewhere on the grounds are an indoor pool, game rooms, a playground, spa services, two dining rooms, and a pub.

Campgrounds

Bras d'Or Lakes Campground (5 km west of Baddeck on Hwy. 105, 902/295-2329, www .brasdorlakescampground.com; mid-June–Sept.) has 95 unserviced and two-way-hookup sites ($25–39, cabins $59–89 s or d). On Bras d'Or Lakes, it has showers, washrooms, a launderette, Wi-Fi Internet throughout, a pool, and a recreation area.

In the vicinity, **Adventures East Campground** (between Exits 7 and 8 of Hwy. 105, 902/295-2417 or 800/507-2228, www .adventureseast.ca; early June–mid-Oct.; campsites $26–30, cabins $115–140 s or d) has all the necessary amenities—showers, laundry, a pool, fishing, a restaurant, and tours.

FOOD

Cafés and restaurants line Baddeck's main street, but be aware that most open only through the warmer months, and by mid-October, choices become very limited.

Casual Dining

For breakfast, sandwiches, pizzas, and light meals, the **(Yellow Cello Cafe** (525 Chebucto St., 902/295-2303; May–Oct. daily 8 A.M.–10:30 P.M.) is centrally located and well priced, with an indoor dining room and

veranda in front. The calzones are delicious, the beer selection is good, and the people-watching can't be beat. Expect a wait in peak summer season, when live musicians grace the small indoor stage.

For the best coffee in town, head to the **Highwheeler Café** (486 Chebucto St., 902/295-3006; May–mid-Oct. daily 6 A.M.–9 P.M.). This café has an in-house bakery, so you know everything is fresh, including inexpensive yet healthy sandwiches made to order.

After a boat tour or a trip to Kidston Island, **Water's Edge Cafe** (22 Water St., 902/295-3600; June–Oct. daily 11 A.M.–5 P.M.) is the perfect place to eat a healthy bite to eat. The *tikka* (chicken curry) is as spicy as it should be and the seafood chowder is as creamy as you'd expect. Almost everything is under $12.

Lakeside Café (Exit 8 from Hwy. 105, 902/295-3500; Apr.–Nov. daily from 11 A.M.) is set on the waterfront within the Inverary Resort complex. The food is simple and unsurprising, but the prices are reasonable and the setting a delight when the sun is shining and you find yourself seated at an outdoor table.

Herring Choker Deli (Hwy. 105, 902/295-2275; daily 8 A.M.–8 P.M.) overlooks the water from 10 kilometers west of town. Instead of greasy cooked breakfasts, tuck into a scrambled egg, ham, and cheese wrap ($5). The lunch-time highlight is the thick gourmet sandwiches packed with goodies on bread baked each morning.

Lobster Supper

Lobster suppers originated as local gatherings held in church basements and community halls. Today, they have become a little more commercialized, but they are still a fun and inexpensive way to enjoy this succulent seafood treat. One of the few regularly scheduled in Nova Scotia (Prince Edward Island is a hotbed of lobster suppers) is **Baddeck Lobster Suppers** (Ross St., 902/295-3307; mid-June–mid-Oct. daily 4–9 P.M.). A one- to 1.5-pound lobster with all-you-can-eat chowder, mussels, trimmings, dessert, and nonalcoholic drinks costs $30 per person. Substitute salmon for lobster and pay $21–25.

Other Restaurants

Watching the sun set over Bras d'Or Lakes from a window table at the **⟨C⟩ Bell Buoy Restaurant** (536 Chebucto St., 902/295-2581; mid-May–June daily dinner only, July–mid-Oct. daily lunch and dinner) is worth the price of dinner alone. A menu highlight is the seafood chowder ($10), which comes chock-full of haddock, salmon, mussels, and even lobster, as well as a slab of homemade oatmeal bread as a side. Mains vary from pastas (from $14) to whole lobsters ($34).

Of many local lodges with dining rooms that welcome nonguests, none is better than the **Lynwood Inn** (24 Shore Rd., 902/295-1995; mid-May–mid-Oct. noon–8:30 P.M.), a grand 1868 home that has been converted into an inn and restaurant. The smallish dining room is tastefully decorated in Victorian-era style. The menu is less expensive than you may imagine, with most seafood mains less than $20.

INFORMATION AND SERVICES
Information

At the east end of the main street, the **Baddeck Welcome Centre** (corner Chebucto St. and Shore Rd., 902/295-1911, www.visitbaddeck.com; June–Sept. daily 9 A.M.–5 P.M.) is indeed welcoming. Friendly staff will help out with finding accommodations and, as always, love handing out maps and brochures.

Public Internet access is offered at **Cape Breton Regional Library** (526 Chebucto St., 902/295-2055; Mon.–Fri. 1–5 P.M., Thurs.–Fri. also 6–8 P.M., Sat. 10 A.M.–noon and 1–5 P.M.).

Services

You'll find a couple of banks with ATMs along Chebucto Street, as well as the local **post office.** For emergencies, dial 911 or **Victoria County Memorial Hospital** (902/295-2112).

MARGAREE RIVER VALLEY

Eight kilometers west of Baddeck (back toward the Canso Causeway), the Cabot Trail branches off the TransCanada Highway northwest through the hills and into the valley of the Margaree River, a renowned salmon-fishing stream and the namesake of seven small communities.

The peak time for fishing is mid-June to mid-July and September to mid-October; many guides are available locally. Near North East Margaree, **Margaree Salmon Museum** (60 E. Big Intervale Rd., 902/248-2848; mid-June–mid-Oct. daily 9 A.M.–5 P.M.; adult $2, child $1) tells the story of the river and its fishy inhabitants.

Accommodations and Camping

Even though it's away from the ocean, the Margaree River Valley is a popular spot to get away from it all. Near the village of Margaree Valley, **Normaway Inn** (691 Eygpt Rd., 902/248-2987 or 800/565-9463, www.normaway.com; $99–269 s or d) is typical of the many accommodation options. This elegantly rustic 1920s resort is nestled on 100 hectares in the hills. The main lodge has nine guest rooms, and the grounds hold 19 one- and two-bedroom cabins. Activities include nightly films or traditional entertainment, tennis, walking trails, bicycling, weekly barn dances, and fiddling contests. The dining room (open for breakfast and dinner) serves dishes of Atlantic salmon, lamb, scallops, and fresh fruits and vegetables. The Normaway is about 30 kilometers along the Cabot Trail from Highway 105, and then three kilometers along Egypt Road.

On Lake O'Law, **The Lakes Resort** (902/248-2360 or 888/722-2112; May–Oct.; $98–110 s or d) comprises eight two-bedroom cottages overlooking the lake. Each cottage has a bathroom, microwave, living area, and outdoor barbecue. Recreational opportunities include boating, fishing, canoeing, minigolf, and go-karting while the resort restaurant specializes in lobster dinners. To get there, turn off the Cabot Trail at North East Margaree.

Chéticamp

Along the Cabot Trail 90 kilometers north and then east of Baddeck, Chéticamp is an Acadian fishing village (pop. 1,000) set along a protected waterway that opens to the Gulf of St. Lawrence. Deep-sea fishing and whale-watching charter boats leave from the central Government Wharf, and the entrance to Cape Breton Highlands National Park is five kilometers north of town.

The village was first settled by Acadians expelled from the Nova Scotia mainland in the 18th century. Today, the weeklong **Festival de l'Escaouette,** in early August, celebrates aspects of Acadian culture with a parade, arts and crafts, and music.

SIGHTS

The first stones for **St. Pierre Catholic Church** were laid in 1893, but it took almost 20 years to finish. Its tower pierces the sky at a height of more than 50 meters and can be seen from far up and down the coast. On the south side of town, the **Acadian Museum** (744 Main St., 902/224-2170; mid-May–mid-June daily 9 A.M.–6 P.M., mid-June–Sept. daily 9 A.M.–9 P.M., Oct. daily 9 A.M.–6 P.M.; donation) displays artifacts from early settler days, with an emphasis on the sheepherding past, including weaving, spinning, and rug-hooking demonstrations.

RECREATION

At Government Wharf, **Whale Cruisers** (902/224-3376) operates two vessels, the *Whale Cruiser* and the *Bonnie Maureen III,* which take guests out on three-hour whale-watching trips three times daily July to mid-September and less frequently in May, June, and late September. Fare is adult $35, child $15.

One of the major cottage industries of this area is the production of hooked rugs, a craft developed by Acadians centuries ago. In the late 1930s, a group of Chéticamp women formed a rug-hooking cooperative that still

Each morning, the docks of Chéticamp come alive as crab fishermen begin unloading their catch.

© ANDREW HEMPSTEAD

thrives. The Co-op Artisanale de Chéticamp gives demonstrations and displays its wares at the Acadian Museum. You can also see beautiful hooked rugs and tapestries at **Les Trois Pignons** (15584 Main St., 902/224-2612; mid-May–mid-Oct. daily 9 A.M.–5 P.M., the rest of the year weekdays only; adult $5, senior and child $4), a striking red-roofed building at the northern end of Chéticamp (the building also houses the visitors information center).

A number of galleries and shops hereabouts also sell locally produced folk arts—brightly colored, whimsical carvings and paintings of fish, seabirds, fishermen, boats, or whatever strikes the artists' fancy. One kilometer north of the visitors center, the **Sunset Art Gallery** (902/224-2119) features the colorfully painted woodcarvings of William Roach.

ACCOMMODATIONS

If you're traveling on a budget, a choice of older, inexpensive motels along the main street makes Chéticamp a good base for day trips into Cape Breton Highlands National Park. Best of the bunch is **Fraser's Motel and Cottage** (902/224-2411; mid-May–mid-Oct.; $50–80 s or d), near the main wharf.

Overlooking the ocean a few kilometers south of town, **Chéticamp Outfitters Inn B&B** (13938 Cabot Tr., Point Cross, 902/224-2776; Apr.–mid-Dec.; $60–110 s or d) is a large, modern home with six guest rooms and common areas that include a deck with sweeping ocean views. The less expensive rooms share two bathrooms, while all rates include a full breakfast. The hosts operate a charter fishing business, so this is a good base for anglers.

Behind the main street and linked to the local golf course by a short trail, **Cabot Trail Sea and Golf Chalets** (902/224-1777 or 877/244-1777, ww.seagolfchalets.com; mid-May–mid-Oct.) is a complex of spacious and modern freestanding units, each with a bathroom, kitchen, deck, and barbecue. Rates range $149–299 for up to four people.

FOOD

At the north end of town, **Hometown Kitchen** (15559 Main St., 902/224-3888; daily from 8 A.M.) is right on the water but doesn't really take advantage of the location. The food is good, though, with generous portions and inexpensive prices. Expect lots of seafood.

Dine at the **Restaurant Acadien** (774 Main St., 902/224-3207; May–Oct. daily 7 A.M.–10 P.M.) for authentic Acadian food: *fricot* (souplike stew), meat pies, fresh fish, blood pudding, and butterscotch pie. Entrées range $12–22. **Evangeline** (15150 Main St., 902/224-2044; daily 6:30 A.M.–midnight) is a family restaurant specializing in homemade soups and meat pies.

INFORMATION

On the north side of town, **Chéticamp Visitor Information Centre** (15584 Main St., 902/224-2642; mid-May–mid-Oct. daily 9 A.M.–5 P.M.) has information on tours, accommodations, and campgrounds. For national park information, continue north through town to the large visitors center complex.

Cape Breton Highlands National Park

Protecting a swath of wilderness at the northern tip of Cape Breton Island, this national park is one of the finest in Canada. While outdoor enthusiasts are attracted for opportunities to hike and bike, anyone can enjoy the most spectacular scenery simply by driving the Cabot Trail, which spans the length of the park from Chéticamp in the west to Ingonish in the east.

The Land

Heath bogs, a dry rocky plateau, and a high taiga 400 meters above sea level mark the interior of the 950-square-kilometer park. Rugged cliffs characterize the seacoast on the west side, where the mountains kneel into the Gulf of St.

Lawrence, and gentler but still wildly beautiful shores define the eastern side. Nova Scotia's highest point, 532-meter White Hill, is simply a windswept hump, far from the nearest road and with no formal access trail reaching it.

Typical Acadian forest, a combination of hardwoods and conifers, carpets much of the region. Wild orchids bloom under the shade of thick spruce, balsam fir, and paper birch. The **Grand Anse River** gorge near MacKenzie Mountain is the Acadian forest's showpiece. Its terrain—with sugar maples, yellow birches, and rare alpine-arctic plants—has been designated an international biological preserve. The park is also a wildlife sanctuary for white-tailed deer, black bears, beavers, lynx, mink,

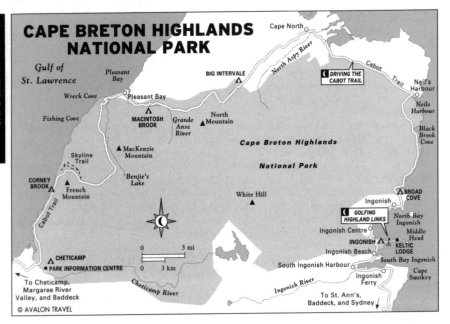

red foxes, snowshoe hare, and more than 200 bird species, including eagles and red-tailed hawks.

Park Entry

Cape Breton Highlands National Park is open year-round, though campgrounds and the two information centers operate only mid-May–October. A **National Parks Day Pass** is adult $7.80, senior $6.80, child $3.90 to a maximum of $19.60 per vehicle. It is valid until 4 P.M. the day after its purchase. Passes can be bought at both park information centers, Chéticamp and Ingonish campgrounds, or at the two park gates.

◖ DRIVING THE CABOT TRAIL

The Cabot Trail extends well beyond park boundaries along its 300-kilometer length, but the most spectacular stretch is undoubtedly the 110 kilometers through the park between Chéticamp and Ingonish. By allowing a full day for the drive, you will have time to walk a trail or two, stop at the best lookouts, and even head out on a whale-watching trip. This section describes the drive itself, with recreational opportunities discussed below. You can of course follow the Cabot Trail in either direction, but I've laid out the drive from Chéticamp to Ingonish (clockwise), meaning you pass the main park information center at the beginning of the drive and that you're driving on the safer inland side of the road the entire way.

Thousands of outdoor enthusiasts tackle the Cabot Trail under pedal power each summer. The trip is not particularly long, but it is very strenuous in sections, and lack of a wide shoulder can make for some hair-raising moments.

Chéticamp to Pleasant Bay

Make your first stop out of Chéticamp the **Park Information Centre** (902/224-2306; mid-May–mid-Oct. 9 A.M.–5 P.M., extended July–Aug. 8 A.M.–8 P.M.). Pick up a map, ask about hiking opportunities, browse the natural history displays, and hit the highway. You can pay for park entry here or at the tollgate a little farther up the road.

This is the most impressive stretch of one of the world's most spectacular drives, with the highway clinging to the shoreline and then climbing steeply along oceanfront cliffs to a viewpoint 18 kilometers north of the information center.

Continuing Around the Cape

From Pleasant Bay, the park's northwestern corner, the highway turns inland and wraps upward to 455-meter-high **French Mountain.** From this point, a level stretch barrels across a narrow ridge overlooking deeply scooped valleys. The road climbs again, this time to **MacKenzie Mountain,** at 372 meters, and then switchbacks down a 10–12 percent grade. Another ascent, to **North Mountain,** formed more than a billion years ago, peaks at 445 meters on a three-kilometer summit. The lookout opens up views of a deep gorge and the North Aspy River.

Cape North and Vicinity

The northernmost point on the Cabot Trail is Cape North, the name of a small service town (as well as a geographical feature to the north). Here a spur road leads 22 kilometers north to Meat Cove. Although outside the park, this road traverses complete wilderness before reaching the open ocean at St. Lawrence Bay. En route, **Cabot's Landing Provincial Park,** the supposed landing site of English explorer John Cabot, offers a sandy beach on Aspy Bay (good for clam digging) and a picnic area and marks the starting point for hikes up 442-meter-high Sugar Loaf Mountain.

The East Coast to Ingonish

From Cape North, it's 45 kilometers east and then south to the resort town of Ingonish. Aside from tucking into a seafood feast at Neil's Harbour, you should make time for a stop at **Black Brook Cove.** Backed by a short stretch of beach, the cove is an extremely popular spot for picnicking and swimming. To escape the

© ANDREW HEMPSTEAD

Black Brook Cove is a protected bay with safe swimming.

summertime crowd, walk to the north end of the beach and follow the Jack Pine Loop through open coastal forest.

RECREATION
Hiking

The park offers 26 established hiking trails, varying from simple strolls shorter than half a kilometer to challenging treks leading to campgrounds more than 20 kilometers away. Many of the trails are level; a few climb to awesome viewpoints. Some hug the rocky shoreline; others explore river valleys. No matter what your abilities may be, you'll be able to enjoy the park at your own speed. For details on hiking in the park, look for the book *Walking in the Highlands,* for sale at Les Amis du Plein Air, the bookstore within the Park Information Centre.

The following hikes have been arranged in a clockwise direction.

On the light side, the self-guiding **Le Buttereau Trail** leads 1.9 kilometers to wildflowers and good bird-watching opportunities.

The trailhead is just north of the park gate north of Chéticamp.

For the more hardy, the seven-kilometer (two hours one-way) **Skyline Loop** climbs a headland, from which the lucky can spot pilot whales; along the way, look for bald eagles, deer, and bears. The trail begins where the Cabot Trail heads inland at French Mountain.

On overcast or wet days, **Benjie's Lake Trail** provides an ideal break from driving. From a trailhead six kilometers beyond the start of the Skyline Loop Trail, this easy walk takes about 30 minutes each way.

Serious backpackers gravitate to the **Fishing Cove Trail** (16 km round-trip), a rugged journey to a campground and beach. You can reach the end of the trail in two hours, but allow at least three for the strenuous return trip back up to the highway.

Whale-Watching

One of two whale-watching spots in Nova Scotia (the other is the Bay of Fundy), a number of operators depart daily through summer from Pleasant Bay. The region boasts a high success rate when it comes to spotting pilot, humpback, and minke whales, simply because of the high numbers close to the coastline. Tours last about 90 minutes and cost a reasonable $30 per person. Operators based at Pleasant Bay include **Captain Mark's** (902/224-1316 or 888/754-5112) and **Fiddlin' Whale Tours** (866/688-2424). Both have booths along the harbor, but you should book by phone in advance for July and August sailings.

ACCOMMODATIONS AND CAMPING

As it's a national park, there are no hotel accommodations within the park boundary. Instead, visitors stay at Chéticamp for its Acadian heritage, at Ingonish for its beaches and golfing, or at one of the following choices in between the two.

Under $50

The only backpacker lodge on Cape Breton Island is **Cabot Trail Hostel** (23349 Cabot Tr.,

902/224-1015; $26 per person), within walking distance of Pleasant Bay, 38 kilometers north of Chéticamp on the park's western side. The facility is small but friendly and comfortable, with 18 dorm beds in two rooms and an adjacent bunkhouse. Guests have use of communal washrooms, two kitchens, a deck with barbecue, and Internet access.

$100-150

Just more than 40 kilometers north of Chéticamp, the Cabot Trail exits the park for a short distance at Pleasant Bay. Here, the distinctively pink **Midtrail Motel & Inn** (23475 Cabot Tr., 902/224-2529 or 800/215-0411, www.midtrail.com; mid-May–Oct.; from $109 s or d) offers 20 bright but basic motel rooms, some with ocean views, and a family-friendly seafood restaurant.

Set on 25 hectares of oceanfront property, **The Markland** (Dingwell, 902/383-2246 or 800/872-6084, www.marklandresort.com; May–mid-Oct.) is 52 kilometers north of Ingonish (signposted off the Cabot Trail between Cape North and South Harbour). Although it is a resort, the emphasis is on the outdoors, with most guests spending their time on the adjacent beach or lazing around the outdoor pool. Regular rooms go for $149 s or d, and the much larger and private chalets are $249–299. The resort restaurant features the freshest of fresh seafood combined with seasonal produce such as fiddleheads and wild mint.

Campgrounds

Cape Breton Highlands National Park is the most popular camping destination in Nova Scotia. Parks Canada operates seven campgrounds within the park.

Chéticamp Campground (5 km north of Chéticamp) is behind the main park information center. Amenities include showers, flush toilets, kitchen shelters, playgrounds, and an outdoor theater hosting a summer interpretive program. Only some sites have fire pits. Tent sites are $25.50 per night, serviced sites $38.20. Chéticamp Campground is the park's only

Corney Brook Campground sits right on the ocean.

campground that accepts reservations. Sites can be reserved through the **Parks Canada Campground Reservation Service** (905/426-4648 or 877/737-3783, www.pccamping.ca) for $11 per reservation. If you're traveling in the height of summer and require hookups, this booking system is highly recommended.

Continue north from the park gate for 10 kilometers to ◀ **Corney Brook Campground** (mid-May–early Oct.; $23.50), which is not much more than a parking lot with 20 designated sites, but it has incredible ocean views that more than make up for a lack of facilities. Beyond Pleasant Bay, the 10 sites at **MacIntosh Brook Campground** (mid-May–early Oct.; $21.50) fill quickly. Ten kilometers farther east is **Big Intervale Campground** (mid-May–early Oct.; $18), also with 10 sites. Neither of these two campgrounds have drinking water. With 256 sites, **Broad Cove Campground** (mid-May–early Oct.; $27.40), on the ocean just north of Ingonish, is the park's largest campground. Campers have use of showers, flush toilets, kitchen shelters, playgrounds, and an outdoor theater. **Ingonish Campground** (late June–early Sept.; $27.40) is within a finger of the park that extends to the ocean along the Ingonish coastline. Although it's close to the resort town of Ingonish, the wooded setting is quiet and private and within walking distance of a sandy beach with safe swimming. It has showers, flush toilets, and kitchen shelters.

INFORMATION

Turn right as soon as you cross into the park for the excellent **Park Information Centre** (902/224-2306; mid-May–mid-Oct. 9 A.M.–5 P.M., extended July–Aug. 8 A.M.–8 P.M.). It features natural-history exhibits, weather reports, an activities schedule, and helpful staff. Part of the complex is **Les Amis du Plein Air** (902/224-3814), a surprisingly large bookstore with more than 1,000 titles in stock.

Parks Canada also operates a smaller information center in Ingonish for those entering the park from the east. It's open mid-May–mid-October 9 A.M.–5 P.M., extended to 8 A.M.–8 P.M. in July and August.

Ingonish and Vicinity

Ingonish (pop. 500), 110 kilometers east of Chéticamp and 100 kilometers north of Baddeck, is a busy resort center at the eastern entrance to Cape Breton Highlands National Park. The town is a lot more than somewhere simply to rest your head: It is fringed by beautiful beaches, has one of Canada's premier golf courses, and offers a delightful choice of seafood restaurants. Simply put, if you are allowing yourself some rest time on your Nova Scotia travels, this is the place to book two or more nights in the same accommodation.

SIGHTS AND RECREATION

Ingonish has no official attractions as such. Instead, beach lovers gather on **Ingonish Beach,** where a lifeguard watches over swimmers splashing around in the shallow water that reaches enjoyable temperatures July–August.

Drag yourself away from one of Canada's finest beaches and you'll find the **Freshwater Lake Loop,** a two-kilometer circuit that encircles a shallow lake where beavers can often be seen hard at work in the evening. The trailhead is the parking lot at Ingonish Beach.

Even if you're not a guest at the Keltic Lodge, the grounds are a pleasant place for a stroll. Beyond the end of the lodge access road, a walking trail leads two kilometers to the end of Middle Head Peninsula.

◖ Golfing Highland Links
Highland Links (3 km north of Ingonish Beach, 902/285-2600 or 800/441-1118) is generally regarded as one of the world's top 100 golf courses, and relative to other courses of similar reputation the greens fees are a steal—$91 in high season, with twilight rates from just $55. Power carts are an additional $31. The course, which opened in 1939, was designed by Stanley Thompson, the same architect commissioned to design famous courses in Banff and Jasper National Parks.

ACCOMMODATIONS AND CAMPING

Accommodations are spread along the Ingonish coastline, but demand is high in July and August, so book well ahead. Also note the given open dates, as very few places are open year-round.

$50-100
Sea Breeze Cottages and Motel (8 km north of the east park gate, 902/285-2879 or 888/743-4443; mid-Apr.–mid-Dec.) overlooks the ocean and boasts a playground that children will love. Accommodation options include basic motel rooms ($84 s or d) or cottages ($98–140 s or d).

$100-150
Open year-round, **Ingonish Chalets** (36784 Cabot Tr., Ingonish Beach, 902/285-2008 or

Highland Links is one of Canada's finest golf courses.

© ANDREW HEMPSTEAD

888/505-0552, www.ingonishchalets.com) has access to the beach and hiking trails. Nine two-bedroom log chalets go for $150 s or d, while five motel-style rooms cost $110. The rooms are furnished in a very woodsy way, with pine paneling extending from the handcrafted furniture to the wall linings. These units also come with basic cooking facilities—microwave, kettle, and so on.

It would be difficult to claim boredom at **Glenghorm Beach Resort** (Ingonish, 902/285-2049 or 800/565-5660, www.glenghormbeachresort.com; May–Oct.; $115–400 s or d), a sprawling complex that extends from the Cabot Trail to a long narrow arc of sand. Things to do include walking along the beach, relaxing around the outdoor pool, renting kayaks and paddling through quiet offshore waters, or working out in the fitness room. There are also lawn games, tennis, volleyball, and bike rentals. At the end of the day, you can relax with a glass of wine in one of the shoreline Adirondack chairs or try a Nova Scotian brew at the resort pub. Accommodation options are motel rooms, older-style cottages (some right by the ocean), and my favorite rooms in all of Cape Breton Island—casual but stylish kitchen-equipped suites with private balconies.

$150-200

The Cabot Trail has its devoted fans, and so does the **Keltic Lodge** (902/285-2880 or 800/565-0444, www.kelticlodge.ca; mid-May–mid-Oct.; from $180 s or d), on Middle Head Peninsula. The access lane from the Cabot Trail meanders through thick stands of white birches and finishes at the lodge. The long low wood-sided lodge—painted bright white and topped with a bright red roof—is as picturesque as a lord's manor in the Highlands of Scotland. The main lodge has 32 rustic rooms off a comfortable lobby, furnished with overstuffed chairs and sofas arranged before a massive stone fireplace. Another 40 rooms are in the adjacent newer White Birch Inn. In addition, nine cottages with suite-style layouts (nice

© ANDREW HEMPSTEAD

Keltic Lodge

for families) are scattered across the grounds. Well-marked hiking trails meander through the adjacent national park woodlands and ribbon the coastal peninsula. An outdoor pool (a bit chilly), tennis courts, and a spa facility are also available.

Affiliated with one of the region's finest restaurants, **Seascape Coastal Retreat** (36083 Cabot Tr., Ingonish, 902/285-3003 or 866/385-3003, www.seascapecoastalretreat.com; May–mid-Oct.; $229–249 s or d) is suited to couples looking for a quiet getaway in romantic surroundings. Within the walls of this very private resort are 10 wooden cottages, each air-conditioned and with a private deck overlooking the ocean and a separate bedroom. Bathrobes, jetted tubs, and TV/VCR combos add to the appeal. Outside, paths lead through landscaped gardens to an herb garden and courtyard where guests gather in the evening. Rates include a full breakfast and seafood snacks delivered to your door upon arrival.

FOOD

When the sun is shining, there is no better place in all of Nova Scotia to enjoy fresh seafood than the (**Muddy Rudder** (38438 Cabot Tr., 902/285-2280; June–Sept. daily 11 A.M.–8 P.M.), a quirky outdoor eatery south of Ingonish Beach. Place your order at the window—crab, clams, lobster, mussels, and more—and the owner simply plunks your order in a big pot of boiling water that balances on a propane burner out front. Most tables are spread out on a grassed area beside the river, while a couple are under a shelter. Expect to pay about $15 for a full crab with a side of coleslaw and a buttered roll.

Occupying a weathered wooden building on the high headland at Neil's Harbour is the (**Chowder House** (902/336-2463; May–Sept. daily 11 A.M.–8 P.M.). Order at the inside window and wait for your number to be called. Then tuck into creamy clam chowder ($4), fish-and-chips ($8), a lobster burger ($10), or a full crab ($17). Dollar for dollar, you're doing well if you find better value than the food at the always-busy Chowder House.

(**Seascapes Restaurant** (36083 Cabot Tr., Ingonish, 902/285-3003; May–mid-Oct. daily 6–9 P.M.) is a smart stylish dining room overlooking the ocean. Instead of a menu, a blackboard describes nightly choices, which are dependent on the seafood available. Mains range $18–25.

Keltic Lodge

The Keltic Lodge (Middle Head Peninsula, 902/285-2880) is home to two very different restaurants. Along the access road is the **Atlantic Restaurant** (mid-May–mid-Oct. daily 11 A.M.–9 P.M.), a big family-style restaurant with seafood for all tastes and budgets. Beer-battered fish-and-chips is $11, grilled salmon is $20, and most mains except the lobster are less than $25. An excellent add-on is the salad bar ($9). The row of tables along the east side have stunning ocean views. The smart-casual **Purple Thistle Dining Room** (late May–mid-Oct. daily 7–10 A.M. and 6–9 P.M.) has one of Nova Scotia's finest reputations,

especially in seafood. Meals are five courses (about $45) rather than à la carte, with an emphasis on lobster in varied creations and other seafood. If you're tooling along Cabot Trail and hope to stop here for dinner, reservations are very wise.

SOUTH FROM INGONISH

South of Ingonish Beach, the Cabot Trail descends hairpin turns. Stop at 366-meter-high **Cape Smokey** for a picnic or hiking along the cliff top, which has wonderful views. The steep and twisting road finishes in a coastal glide with views of the offshore Bird Islands. Lying off the northwest side of the cape at the mouth of St. Ann's Bay, these two islands are the nesting site of a multitude of seabird species.

ST. ANN'S

During the 1850s, about 900 of St. Ann's residents, dissatisfied with Cape Breton, sailed away to Australia and eventually settled in New Zealand, where their descendants today make up a good part of the Scottish population. Despite this loss of nearly half its population, St. Ann's, 80 kilometers south of Ingonish and 30 kilometers north of Baddeck, is today the center of Cape Breton's Gaelic culture.

(Gaelic College of Celtic Arts and Crafts

The only institution of its kind in North America, the Gaelic College (51779 Cabot Tr., 902/295-3411) was established in 1938. Programs include highland dancing, fiddling, piping, Gaelic language, weaving, and other subjects. The summer session attracts Gaelophiles from around the world. The **Great Hall of the Clans** (July–Aug. daily 9 A.M.–5 P.M.), on the campus, examines the course of Scottish culture and history, including the migrations that brought Highlanders to Cape Breton. Activities include weaving and instrument-making demonstrations, as well as music and dance performances (July–Aug. Mon.–Fri.). The campus gift shop sells a predictable collection of kilts and tartans.

◖ Celtic Colours International Festival

This popular festival (902/562-6700 or 877/285-2321, www.celtic-colours.com) takes place the second full week of October. It celebrates Cape Breton's Gaelic heritage through concerts held at venues around the island, but the Gaelic College of Celtic Arts and Crafts is a focal point, especially for its nightly Festival Club, where musicians get together for an unofficial jam after performing elsewhere. The festival proper features six or seven concerts nightly, usually in small town halls, with visitors enjoying the brilliant colors of fall as they travel from venue to venue.

The Northeast

SYDNEY

Cape Breton Island's only city is Sydney (pop. 24,000), set around a large harbor on the island's northeast corner. In the early 1800s, it was it was the capital of the colony of Cape Breton, and then at the turn of the 20th century the Sydney area boomed, ranking as one of Canada's major steel production centers.

Sights

Historic buildings constructed of stone quarried at nearby Louisbourg dot the streets north of downtown. One of these, the 1830 **St. Patrick's Church Museum** (87 Esplanade; June–Aug. daily 9:30 A.M.–5:30 P.M.; donation), is Cape Breton's oldest Roman Catholic sanctuary. **Cossit House** (75 Charlotte St., 902/539-7973; June to mid-Oct. Mon.–Sat. 9:30 A.M.–5:30 P.M., Sun. 1–5:30 P.M.; adult $2, senior and child $1) is almost as old as Sydney itself. The 1787 manse has been restored to its original condition.

© ANDREW HEMPSTEAD

St. Patrick's Church dates to 1830.

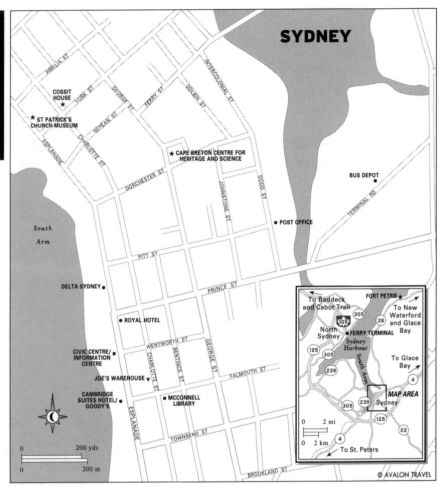

The **Cape Breton Centre for Heritage and Science** (225 George St., 902/539-1572; June–Sept. Mon.–Fri. 9 A.M.–5 P.M., the rest of the year Tues.–Fri. 10 A.M.–4 P.M.; free) offers displays on the social and natural history of eastern Cape Breton, art exhibits, and films.

Accommodations

Motel rooms in Sydney are generally more expensive than they should be. Therefore, use the websites to search out package rates or wait until the last minute and start calling around for deals.

Comfort Inn Sydney (368 Kings Rd., 902/562-0200, www.choicehotels.ca; $120–140 s or d) overlooks the waterfront two kilometers south of downtown. The midsize rooms have contemporary style and modern necessities such as high-speed Internet access.

My pick in Sydney is the modern **Cambridge Suites Hotel** (380 Esplanade, 902/562-6500 or 800/565-9466, www.cambridgesuitessydney

.com), which comprises 150 spacious self-contained units, each with a kitchen and high-speed Internet access. On the roof level are a pool, sauna, exercise room, and sundeck. Summer rates are from $160 s or d, discounted to about $130 the rest of the year.

Right downtown, **Delta Sydney** (300 Esplanade, 902/562-7500 or 800/565-1001, www.deltahotels.com; $200 s or d) is a well-designed comfortable high-rise with more than 150 rooms, a restaurant with water views, an indoor pool and waterslide, a whirlpool, a sauna, an exercise room, and a gift shop. The rack rates of $200 are too high, but the $140 I was quoted for a water-view room in early June seemed about right.

Food

€ **Goody's** (Cambridge Suites Hotel, 380 Esplanade, 902/562-6500; daily for breakfast, lunch, and dinner) stands out as the best place in town for a healthy, well-priced meal in pleasant surroundings. The continental breakfast is $8 (free for hotel guests) while later in the day lunches such as Thai chicken salad are less than $12. In the evening, tasty temptations include salmon stuffed with shrimp and scallops ($25).

Away from the hotel dining scene, **Joe's Warehouse** (424 Charlotte St., 902/539-6686; lunch and dinner daily) is a converted Canadian Tire warehouse. It's spacious enough to accommodate locals on a casual splurge, who come for the specialty prime rib, New York strip steak, and surprisingly good cheesecake.

Information and Services

Sydney Visitor Information Centre is in the waterfront Civic Centre (320 Esplanade, 902/539-9876; late May–mid-Oct. Mon.–Fri. 8:30 A.M.–5 P.M.). Another source of information is the website of Destination Cape Breton (www.cbisland.com).

To get onto the Internet, head for **McConnell Library** (50 Falmouth St., 902/562-3161; Tues.–Fri. 10 A.M.–9 P.M., Sat. 10 A.M.–5:30 P.M.) and tell the staff you're visiting from

out of town. If there's an available terminal, it's yours.

Cape Breton Regional Hospital is at 1482 George Street (902/567-8000). For the **RCMP** call 564-7171, or 911 in emergencies.

Major banks are represented along Charlotte Street. The main **post office** is at 75 Dodd Street.

Getting There and Around

It's just more than 400 kilometers between Halifax and Sydney—easily driven in under five hours. The main reason to fly in would be the ease of getting to Cape Breton Highlands National Park, a 90-minute drive northeast of town. Sydney Airport is 14 kilometers northeast of the city center. A taxi to town costs $18, or rent a car through Avis, Budget, Hertz, and National, all of which have rentals desks at the airport. Sydney is served by **Air Canada** (902/539-7501 or 888/247-2262) with direct flights from Halifax.

The **Acadian Lines** depot (99 Terminal Rd., 902/564-5533) is open daily 6:30 A.M.–1 A.M. and has luggage-storage lockers. Scheduled passenger buses run daily from Sydney to Halifax via North Sydney and Baddeck.

HIGHWAY 28 TO GLACE BAY

From Sydney, the New Waterford Highway (Highway 28) spurs north off Prince Street and follows the eastern side of Sydney Harbour for 26 kilometers to the industrial town of New Waterford. Along the way is **Fort Petrie** (3479 Hwy. 28, 902/862-8367; May–Nov. 10 A.M.–6 P.M.; free), one of seven such forts constructed to protect local coal and steel production facilities from attack during World War II. Not much remains, but an interpretive display tells the story of the fort, and views of the harbor make the stop worthwhile.

Glace Bay

At Glace Bay, 21 kilometers northeast of Sydney, **Cape Breton Miners' Museum** (42 Birkley St., 902/849-4522; June–Aug. daily 10 A.M.–6 P.M., the rest of the year weekdays

9 A.M.–4 P.M.; adult $10, child $5) is the main attraction for visitors. Retired miners guide you on an underground tour of a real mine, the Ocean Deeps Colliery, to show the rough working conditions under which workers manually extracted coal. Above the mine is an exhibit gallery where the highlight is a simulated, multimedia trip into the workings of a modern mine, using laser-disc projection and other special effects. On selected Tuesday evenings through summer (usually at 8 P.M.), the Men of the Deeps, a local singing group composed of miners dressed in their coveralls, give concerts at the museum. Also in the main building is Miners' Village Restaurant (mid-Apr.–Oct. daily noon–8 P.M.), where the food is both tasty and well priced.

LOUISBOURG

This small fishing town (pop. 1,200), 32 kilometers southeast of Sydney along Highway 22 (take Exit 8 from Highway 125), is famous for its historic links to France and for the reconstruction of an entire walled town. Louisbourg may be well off the main Baddeck–Cape Breton Highlands National Park itinerary of many visitors, but it gets a steady flow of visitors through summer and has limited accommodations, so plan accordingly.

(Fortress of Louisbourg National Historic Site

Fortress of Louisbourg National Historic Site (902/733-2280; July–Aug. daily 9 A.M.–5:30 P.M., May–June and Sept.–mid-Oct. daily 9:30 A.M.–5 P.M.; adult $17.60, senior $15, child $8.80) is a fantastic re-creation of the original French fort. Parks Canada has reconstructed 50 of the original 80 buildings, right down to the last window, nail, and shingle, based on historical records.

Louisbourg reveals itself slowly. The seaport covers 10 hectares, and you can spend the better part of a day exploring. From the Visitor Reception Centre, it's a brief bus ride across fields and marsh to the back of the fortress. The reconstructed fortress and town open a window on New France; they are designed to reflect Louisbourg on a spring day in 1744, the year preceding England's first attack, when the seaport hummed with activity. The houses, fortifications, ramparts, and other structures—as authentically 18th-century French as anything you will find in France—were conceived as a statement of grandeur and power in the New World. The fancy houses lining cobbled lanes belonged to the elite, who ate sumptuous meals on fine china and drank the finest French wines. The simpler houses are the rustic cottages of the working class. Guides and animators—portraying soldiers, merchants, workers, and craftspeople—are on hand to answer questions and demonstrate military exercises, blacksmithing, lace making, and other skills. The historical feel flows through to three dining rooms. Hungry visitors can feast on a slice of heavy bread and a chunk of cheese at the **King's Bakery;** at **Hotel de la Marine** servers dish up simple fare in big wooden bowls; while over in **Grandchamps Inn** the "wealthy" can dine on exquisite European cuisine served up on the finest china.

The site is open and fully staffed June to mid-October. In May and through the last two weeks of October, access is by guided tour only (departs daily 10 A.M. and 2 P.M.). There are no services during these periods, and so admission is reduced to adult $6.25, senior $5.25, child $3.25. The grounds are closed the rest of the year.

Be prepared for walking, and bring a sweater or jacket in case of breezy or wet weather. Louisbourg's reconstructed buildings stretch from the bus stop to the harbor. Remaining ruins lying beyond the re-creation are marked by trails. You can wander on your own or join a tour—usually 10 A.M. and 2 P.M. for English tours and 1 P.M. for the French-language tour.

Accommodations and Camping

Accommodations in Louisbourg are limited, so it's wise to make reservations.

Overlooking the fort and harbor is **Stacey House** (7438 Main St., 902/733-2317 or 888/924-2242; June–mid-Oct.; $65–95 s or d).

It offers four rooms, two with private baths, and an antique-filled parlor within walking distance of town. Rates include a cooked breakfast.

With a similar outlook as Stacey House, but in the commercial core of Louisbourg, **Fortress View Suites** (7513 Main St., 902/733-3131 or 877/733-3131, www.fortressview.ca; May–Oct.; $80–90 s or d) comprises five guest rooms, each with an en suite bathroom and television but no phone.

Perfectly situated on a high headland with sweeping views of the fortress, **(Point of View Suites** (15 Commercial St., 902/733-2080 or 888/374-8439, www.louisbourgpointofview.com; mid-May–Oct.) is Louisbourg's finest accommodation. The sun-filled suites ($125 s or d) and much larger apartments ($199 s or d) look as if they are straight out of a glossy architectural magazine with their crisp color schemes, hardwood floors, and sliding doors that open to balconies with ocean views. At the edge of the property is a private beach, and each evening guests are invited to a lobster supper in the "beach house."

CAMPGROUNDS

Louisbourg RV Park (24 Harbourfront Cres., 902/733-3631 or 866/733-3631; June–mid-Oct.; $18–26) enjoys a downtown waterfront setting. Amenities include showers, 30-amp hookups, and modem connections.

Affiliated with Louisbourg's most upscale accommodation, **Point of View RV Park** (15 Commercial St., 902/733-2080 or 888/374-8439, www.louisbourgpointofview.com; mid-May–Oct.; $24) is an RV-only facility right on the ocean. Guests have use of showers and a laundry while breakfast is served in an on-site café, and nightly lobster dinners mean you don't need to worry about cooking.

The wilderness camping nearest to Louisbourg is at **Mira River Provincial Park** (mid-June–early Sept.), 17 kilometers before town off Highway 22. The park has showers, fire pits and firewood sales, and canoe rentals. Sites scattered through the forest or along the river are all $24 per night.

Food

Wander Louisbourg's main street and you'll find numerous dining choices. My favorite is **(Grubstake Restaurant** (7499 Main St., 902/733-2308; daily noon–8:30 P.M.), which has been open since the 1970s but offers an up-to-date menu of seafood such as linguine topped with shrimp, scallops, haddock, and lobster in a cream sauce ($22). If you want to take a break from seafood, this is the place to do so—the pork slow-baked in barbecue sauce ($19) just melts in your mouth.

The food at **Fortress View Restaurant** (7513 Main St., 902/733-3131 or 877/733-3131, www.fortressview.ca; mid-May–mid-Oct. 7 A.M.–9 P.M.) is a little less adventurous than the Grubstake but is still excellent. Breakfasts such as French toast with a side of bacon and bottomless coffee are just $6, poached or grilled fish dishes are $16, lobster dinner is about $25, and all children's meals are less than $5. Affiliated with the Fortress View is the adjacent **CJ's Café and Bakery** (7511 Main St., 902/733-2253), which bakes European-style breads and a tempting array of muffins and pastries.

BACKGROUND

The Land

Nova Scotia is predominantly rocky and thinly covered with soil, making it less conducive to farmland than to forests. Consequently, thick woodlands blanket 80 percent of the province. The Atlantic coast is rugged, edged with granite, and flanked with sandy beaches, salt marshes, and bogs. The Fundy Coast, from Yarmouth to Cape Split, is rimmed by basalt bedrock mixed with tidal flats. Along this coast, Annapolis Valley, famed for its fruit orchards, is a geological oddity; scoured out by glaciers at the end of the last ice age, the valley is sheltered by mountains north and south, creating a hothouse of warmth and humidity.

Along the Northumberland Strait seacoast, rolling terrain with fertile farmlands rises to picturesque high hills and plateaus in Pictou and Antigonish counties.

Cape Breton Island is joined to mainland Nova Scotia by the 1.4-kilometer Canso Causeway. Cape Breton's smaller, eastern section consists of lowlands and rolling hills, with deeply indented Sydney Harbour on its northern coast. The western part of the island rises gradually from sea level to soaring headlands and highlands culminating at Cape Breton Highlands National Park near the northern tip. Much of the island's center

© ANDREW HEMPSTEAD

is taken up by the expansive saltwater Bras d'Or Lakes.

Known as the Graveyard of the Atlantic, the province's shores and treacherous shoals are littered with scores of shipwrecks.

In the Beginning

Nova Scotia was under a shallow sea until 500 million years ago. Then pressurized sand and clay oozed to the surface, where it cooled and hardened to create the first landscape of sandstone, quartzite, and slate. Molten granite later emerged the same way, heaved, and broke apart. You can see these primordial extrusions at Peggy's Cove near Halifax, where the coast is strewn with oddly placed mammoth boulders.

The earth's surface heaved and shuddered, and the land contours and seacoasts were formed. Between 405 million and 190 million years ago, the turbulent earth devoured its own creations; evidence is visible at Joggins on the upper Fundy's Chignecto Bay, where upright trees were enfolded into cliff edges. Archaeologists date these fossils at 280 million to 345 million years old.

Glaciation

Glaciation and eons of erosion, however, have ground down the once-mammoth summits such as 532-meter **White Hill,** in Cape Breton Highlands National Park, which is Nova Scotia's highest point. One of the reasons for this was glacial ice, uncountable trillions of tons of it, formed in the last four ice ages. Glaciers up to an estimated three kilometers (two miles) thick weighed down on the elastic bedrock as recently as 14,000 years ago, submerging the coasts and counteracting the inexorable thrust of tectonic uplift.

The last ice sheet retreated and took what remained of prehistory with it. The ice had scoured the earth's surface as it raked back and forth, and this too can be seen at Peggy's Cove, where the ancient scratches are etched in the granite boulders.

As the ice sheet moved, it bulldozed glacial debris into drumlins, large islands of fine soil piled up in places on the predominantly rocky land. The best known of these drumlins is the steep hill upon which the Halifax Citadel sits, but to see drumlins without the manmade distractions, plan to visit Kejimkujik National Park.

Water

More than any other province, Nova Scotia is defined by water—it is nearly completely surrounded by ocean. The 7,400-kilometer-long coastline is a study in contrasts. While the Atlantic Ocean laps the entire east coast, the planet's mightiest tides surge through the Bay of Fundy, the unexpectedly warm Northumberland Strait creates a broad blue parenthesis dividing Prince Edward Island from Nova Scotia, and the wild and wooly Cabot Strait separates Nova Scotia's Cape Breton Island and the island of Newfoundland.

CLIMATE

Nova Scotia's climate comprises distinct seasons, with mild winters and cool summers. Mainland Nova Scotia's climate differs noticeably from Cape Breton's, where more extreme weather patterns occur. Average precipitation amounts to 130 centimeters, falling mainly as rain during autumn and as snow in winter. Frost-free periods vary from 120 days on Cape Breton to 145 days in the sheltered Annapolis Valley.

Spring high temperatures range from −2.5°C (27.5°F) to 9°C (48°F), although the days begin to warm up toward the end of March. **Summer** weather varies. Daytime temperatures average up to 30°C (86°F). Nights are usually cool at around 12°C (54°F) but can dip to 5°C (41°F) in late summer. Inland areas are generally five degrees warmer. The coasts often bask in morning fog, which is later dispersed by sea breezes and the warming sun. Late in the season, most hurricanes, having spent their force farther south, limp through the region, bringing to the northwestern Atlantic short spells of rain and wind. On occasion, the province is hit by much harder storms, such as in September 2003, when Hurricane Juan touched land in Halifax with winds gusting up to 185 kilometers per hour.

In **autumn,** the evenings start to cool, but warm days continue until the end of September at up to 18°C (64°F). The days are cool to frosty October through mid-November. **Winter** lasts from late November through early March, with high temperatures averaging –10°C (14°F) to 4°C (39°F).

Environment Canada (www.weatheroffice.ec.gc.ca) has updated weather forecasts for towns across the province.

Water Temperatures

The ocean water off Nova Scotia is far from bathtub hot, but water temperatures in some areas can be pleasantly warm. Conditions vary on the four seas and in each region. The warmest seas during August are found around Cape Breton's northern tip and along the Northumberland Strait—in both places temperatures reach 18°C (64°F). The Atlantic is a cool 10–15°C (50–59°F) at Mahone Bay and warms a bit as you head up the coast to the northeast; hence the popularity of surfing at Martinique and Lawrencetown beaches. Generally, Cape Breton's coastal waters range 14–17°C (57–63°F). The Bay of Fundy is always cool to cold, although it becomes bearable where low tide leaves shallow pools that warm up.

ENVIRONMENTAL ISSUES

Humans have been exploiting Nova Scotia's abundant natural resources for thousands of years. Indigenous people hunting and fishing obviously had little effect on ecological integrity, but the arrival of Europeans to local waters, who came especially to harvest cod as early as the 1500s, did. Today, the state of local fisheries, most notably the collapse of cod stocks, is the most important environmental issue facing the province. The beginning of the end was the arrival of "factory ships" in the 1960s, which could harvest up to 200 tons of cod per hour. By the late 1980s the cod stock had been mostly obliterated, and by the early 1990s a moratorium was put in place until the fishery had recovered. Unfortunately, what was not fully understood at that time was that overfishing was only a part of the problem. Cod are a groundfish, and the factory ships had been bottom trawling—scooping up the cod in nets with an opening up to one kilometer wide that dragged along the sea floor and decimated the very ecosystem that was a breeding ground for the fish. It is widely thought that the cod stock will never fully recover, although it is currently in better shape than in the waters off Newfoundland.

Contacts

An excellent website for learning more about the state of the ocean is www.seachoice.org. For information on general environmental issues in Nova Scotia, contact the following organizations: **Canadian Parks and Wilderness Society Nova Scotia** (www.cpawsns.org), **Greenpeace** (www.greenpeace.ca), **Ecology Action Centre** (www.ecologyaction.ca), and **Nova Scotia Environmental Network** (www.vws.org).

Flora and Fauna

To a great extent, it was the land's natural resources—and the potential riches they represented—that attracted Europeans to Canada over the centuries. Since time immemorial, mammals, fish, and varied plant species had, of course, fed and clothed the indigenous peoples of Nova Scotia, who harvested only enough to sustain themselves. But the very abundance of the wildlife seemed to fuel the rapacity of the newcomers, driving them to a sort of madness of consumption—and hastening the exploration and settlement of the newfound continent. Luckily for today's visitor, much remains, in sometimes astonishing abundance and variety, thanks to each species' own unique genius for survival, to blind luck, to the shifting vagaries of public tastes, and even to the occasional glimmer of human enlightenment.

FLORA

The receding glaciers of the last ice age scoured the land and left lifeless mud and rubble in their wake. Overall, the climate then was considerably cooler than it is today, and the first life-forms to recolonize in the shadow of the glaciers were hardy mosses, lichens, and other cold-tolerant plants. Junipers and other shrubs later took root, and afterward came coniferous trees—hardy fast-growing spruce and fir—that could thrive here despite the harsh climate and relatively brief growing season. In the boggy interior sprouted moisture-loving willows and tamaracks. As the climate warmed and the soil grew richer, broadleaf deciduous trees arrived. Today 80 percent of Nova Scotia is thickly blanketed by typical Acadian forest of mixed hardwoods and conifers. Common trees include hemlock, spruce, balsam fir, yellow and paper birches, cedar, maple, ash, and oak. In autumn the brilliant hues of the changing leaves are one of the province's most cherished attractions.

Large tracts are set aside in the province at Kejimkujik and Cape Breton Highlands National Parks, which protect areas of unique plant habitat. In the Cape Breton Highlands, for example, stands of 300-year-old maples (believed to be the oldest in the country) have survived, and unusual wild orchid species thrive there as well. In the highlands' highest elevations, the stunted taiga and alpine-arctic plant communities have been included in an international biological preserve. Bogs in the national parks nourish insectivorous pitcher plants, more orchids, and other specially adapted species.

Along the Atlantic Coast

Along the Atlantic coast, familiar plants—spruces, hardy cinnamon ferns, northern juniper—take on a stunted, gnarled look from contending with the unmitigated elements. It can take endurance and adaptation to survive here amid often harsh conditions. Trees and bushes lie cropped close to the ground or lean permanently swept back by the wind as if with a giant hairbrush. Taylor Head Provincial Park, along the Marine Drive, is a good place to view this phenomenon. Living on or near the beach requires specialization too. Maram grass, also called American beach grass, is abundant all along the Atlantic coast. Its extensive root systems help to stabilize the sand dunes on which it grows. Beach pea, seaside goldenrod, dusty miller, and sea rocket are a few of the other plants that can manage on the less-than-fertile soils just above the high-tide line. Lower down grow cord grass and glasswort, whose systems can tolerate regular soakings of salt water.

Wildflowers

Common wildflowers throughout Nova Scotia—easily seen along roadsides in summertime—include lupine, Queen Anne's lace, yarrow, pearly everlasting, and a variety of daisies. Everywhere, the showy spikes of purple loosestrife, a pretty but aggressive and unwelcome pest, flourishes. Bayberry bushes and wild roses bloom in the northeast corner of Nova Scotia during June. The bayberry bush grows clusters of dimpled fruits close along woody stems and releases a pleasant spicy aroma popular in potpourris and Christmas candles. The provincial flower is the trailing arbutus (mayflower), which blooms in early spring in woodlands and barrens.

The yellow beach heather colors the Northumberland Strait dunes and sandy plains, and the rhodora (miniature rhododendron) brightens coastal marshes. Another dune resident, the beach plum, grows snowy-white to pinkish flowers in June, which produce fruit welcomed by birds, beasts, and man in late summer and early fall.

LAND MAMMALS

Nova Scotia is home to 70 different mammals. Some, such as beavers, are common. Others, such as the lynx, are endangered, while the presence of cougars is unproven, and species such as woodland caribou have disappeared completely. But it's not all bad news—wildlife-viewing opportunities present themselves throughout the province.

Moose

The giant of the deer family is the moose, an awkward-looking mammal that appears to have been designed by a cartoonist. It has the largest antlers of any animal in the world, stands up to 1.8 meters (six feet) at the shoulder, and weighs up to 500 kilograms (1,100 pounds). Its body is dark brown, and it has a prominent nose, long spindly legs, small eyes, big ears, and an odd flap of skin called a bell dangling beneath its chin. Apart from all that, it's good-looking. Each spring the bull begins to grow palm-shaped antlers that by August will be fully grown. Moose are solitary animals preferring marshy areas and weedy lakes, but they are known to wander to higher elevations searching out open spaces in summer. They forage in and around ponds on willows, aspen, birch, grasses, and all aquatic vegetation. Although they may appear docile, moose will attack humans if they feel threatened.

While Nova Scotia's moose population has fluctuated greatly since the arrival of Europeans, it is today mostly stable. The densest populations find a home in Cape Breton Highlands National Park as well as in and around Kejimkujik National Park.

White-Tailed Deer

Populations of deer are not particularly high in Nova Scotia; they were nonexistent by the late 1800s but came back in the ensuing years. The color of the white-tailed deer varies with the season, but it is generally light brown in summer, turning dirty gray in winter. The white-tailed deer's tail is dark on top, but when the animal runs, it holds its tail erect, revealing an all-white underside. White-tails frequent thickets along the rivers and lakes of interior forests.

WAS THAT A COUGAR?

Probably not. Cougars (called mountain lions or pumas elsewhere in North America) may still be common on Canada's west coast, but in Nova Scotia their presence is a bit of a mystery.

These large members of the cat family can grow to more than two meters in length and weigh up to 90 kilograms. Elsewhere in Canada, their fur varies in color from light brown to a reddish-tinged gray, but one thing many local sightings have in common is reports of much darker fur. They are incredibly agile creatures. They can spring forward more than eight meters from a standstill, leap four meters into the air, and safely jump from a height of 20 meters (66 feet).

Once widespread through the province, they were hunted to supposed extinction by 1900. Today, there are a few sightings every year, many in the remote backcountry of the Marine Drive. Because they are solitary animals, cunning and cautious, sightings are generally fleeting.

Black Bears

Black bears are the only bears present in Nova Scotia. But black bears are not always black (they can be brown), causing them to be called brown bears when in fact they are not. Black bears are widespread through the province but are not particularly common, numbering about 3,000 of Canada's total estimate of 360,000. Their weight varies considerably, but males average 150 kilograms (330 pounds) and females 100 kilograms (220 pounds). Their diet is omnivorous, consisting primarily of grasses and berries but supplemented by small mammals. They are not true hibernators, but in winter they can sleep for up to a month at a time before changing position. During this time, their heart rate drops to 10 beats per minute, their body temperature drops, and they lose up to 30 percent of their body weight. Females reach reproductive maturity after five years; cubs, usually two, are born in late winter while the mother is still asleep.

Lynx

The elusive lynx is an endangered species in Nova Scotia and is present only within the remote interior of Cape Breton Highlands National Park. Easily identifiable by its pointy black ear tufts and an oversize tabby-cat appearance, the animal has broad padded paws that distribute its weight, allowing it to float on the surface of snow. It weighs up to 10 kilograms (22 pounds) but appears much larger because of its coat of long thick fur. The lynx is a solitary creature that prefers the cover of forest, feeding mostly at night on small mammals.

Beavers

One of the animal kingdom's most industrious mammals is the beaver. Growing to a length of 50 centimeters (20 inches) and tipping the scales at around 20 kilograms (44 pounds), it has a flat rudder-like tail and webbed back feet that enable it to swim at speeds up to 10 kilometers per hour (six miles per hour). Once hunted for their fur, beavers can be found in flat forested areas throughout the province. They build their dam walls and lodges of twigs, branches, sticks of felled trees, and mud. They eat the bark and smaller twigs of deciduous plants and store branches underwater near the lodge as a winter food supply.

SEA LIFE

Although the province is just 560 kilometers from north to south, Nova Scotia's coastline is 7,400 kilometers long. The surrounding fertile seas nurture an astonishing abundance and variety of sea creatures, from tiny uncounted single-celled organisms up through the convoluted links of the food chain to the earth's largest beings—the great whales.

Tidal Zones

Along the shores, the same conditions that provide for rich and diverse plant zones—rocky indented coasts, dramatic tidal variations—also create ideal habitats for varied animal communities in the tidal zone. Between the highest and lowest tides, the Maritime shore is divided into six zones, each determined by the amount of time it is exposed to air. The black zone, just above the highest high-water mark, gets its name from the dark band of primitive blue-green algae that grows here. The next zone is called the periwinkle zone, for the small marine snails that proliferate there. Able to survive prolonged exposure to air, the periwinkles can leave the water to graze on the algae. The barnacle zone, encrusted with the tenacious crustaceans, while also exposed several hours daily during low tides, receives the brutal pounding of breaking waves. Next is the rockweed zone—home to mussels, limpets, and hermit crabs (which commandeer the shells of dead periwinkles)—and the comparatively placid Irish moss zone, which shelters and feeds sea urchins, starfish, sea anemones, crabs, and myriad other animals familiar to anyone who has peered into the miniature world of a tide pool. Last is the laminarian zone, where lobsters, sponges, and fishes thrive in the forests of kelp growing in the deep, churning water.

Fish

Beyond the tidal life zones lie the waters of the continental shelf, and then the open sea. Flowing south from the Arctic, cold oxygen-laden currents also carry loads of silica, ground out of the continental granite by the glaciers and poured into the sea by coastal rivers. Oxygen and silica together create an ideal environment for the growth of diatoms, the microscopic one-celled plants that form the bedrock of the ocean's food chain. In the sunlight of long summer days in these northern latitudes, the numbers of diatoms increase exponentially. They are the food source for shrimp and herring, which in turn support larger fish, such as mackerel, Atlantic salmon, and tuna.

The northeastern Atlantic fisheries have been the economic engine driving exploration and development of these coasts for centuries. In days past, codfish were said to carpet the sea floor of the shallow Grand Banks, and the men who caught them—first with lines from small dories, then with nets, and finally from great trawlers that scour the sea—have hauled in untold millions of tons of not only cod but also flounder, salmon, pollack, haddock, anchovies, and dozens of other species. But the fish are in serious trouble and so too, inexorably, are the people and communities whose lives have revolved around them.

Whales

The whales that frequent Nova Scotia arrive from the Caribbean between June and mid-July and remain through October. Watching the whales cavort is one of summer's great visitor delights; whale-watching boats leave from Brier Island on the Bay of Fundy and Cape Breton's Chéticamp. The Fundy is especially rich in whales, and the fast incoming tides bring in the mammoth mammals in pursuit of herring schools. Among the 20 species that summer offshore, the most frequently sighted are minkes, pilots, fins, orcas, and humpbacks. The Atlantic right whale is a treasured August visitor.

Seals

Gray and harbor seals inhabit Nova Scotian waters at various times of the year. Whale-watching tours often include a stop at an offshore seal colony, although you may also spot one unexpectedly, such as while dining at a waterfront restaurant in Halifax or in the ocean far below while walking the trail to Cape Chignecto. Harp seals, Arctic dwellers that fatten themselves on fish off the Labrador and Greenland coasts, are occasionally sighted around Cape Breton Island.

BIRDS

About 280 bird species have been reported in Nova Scotia. The province is best known for its bald eagles; about 250 pairs nest here, the second-largest population on North America's east coast after Florida. The season for eagle-watching is July and August. Some of the prime viewing areas are the Lake Ainslie and St. Ann's Bay coastlines; the village of Iona, where Bras d'Or Lakes meets St. Andrews Channel on Cape Breton Island; and the St. George's Bay coastline. Ospreys nest on McNabs Island in Halifax Harbour. Other raptors may be seen at Brier Island on the Bay of Fundy.

As Nova Scotia lies on the Atlantic flyway, many migratory species can be spotted, including common and arctic terns, kittiwakes, great and double-crested cormorants, Leach's storm petrels, Atlantic puffins, guillemots, and various gulls, ducks, and geese.

Bird-Watching

The **Nova Scotia Bird Society** (www.nsbs .chebucto.org) can put you onto prime birding sites and answer even the most esoteric questions about the province's many and varied species. Its website has bird lists, a schedule of field trips, and links to local contacts. Bird-watchers visiting Mahone Bay on the South Shore should make a point of visiting **For the Birds Nature Shop** (647 Main St., 902/624-0784, www.forthebirdsnature-shop.ca).

History

THE EARLIEST INHABITANTS

The earliest evidence of human habitation in Nova Scotia dates from about 8600 B.C. and is found at the present site of Debert, northwest of Truro. Here, at one of the northernmost Paleo-Indian sites in North America, archaeologists have uncovered a wealth of artifacts, including telltale Clovis-like spear tips. The people who once set up camp here were descendents of *Homo sapiens* who migrated from northeast Asia across a land bridge spanning the Bering Strait starting 15,000 years ago. At the time, the northern latitudes of North America were covered by an ice cap, forcing these people to travel south down the west coast before fanning out across the ice-free southern latitudes. As the ice cap receded northward, the people drifted north also, perhaps only a few kilometers in an entire generation, and began crossing the 49th parallel about 12,000 years ago.

Mi'Kmaq

Culturally and linguistically related to Algonquian people, the largest language group in Canada, the Mi'Kmaq made a home throughout present-day Nova Scotia as well as northern New Brunswick and as far west as Québec. They were coastal dwellers who fished with spears and hook and line while also collecting shellfish from the shoreline. Hunting was of lesser importance for food but held a great degree of status among other members of the group. Canoes with sails were built for summer travel, while in winter toboggans (*toboggan* originates from the Mi'Kmaq word *topaghan*) and snowshoes were essential.

Like other aboriginal peoples across North America, the Mi'Kmaq practiced a kind of spiritual animism, deeply tied to the land. The trees, animals, and landforms were respected and blessed. Before food could be consumed or a tree felled, for example, it was appreciated for its life-sustaining sacrifice. Mythology also played an important part in spiritual life,

along with rituals, shamanism, and potlatch ceremonies.

The name Mi'Kmaq (also Micmac) is thought to have derived from the word *nikmaq*, meaning "my kin-friends," which early French settlers used as a greeting for the tribe.

ACADIA

Nova Scotia's tie to Europe began in 1497, when the explorer John Cabot sighted Cape Breton Island and claimed it for England. A few decades later, explorer Jacques Cartier also claimed much of the same coastline. For France, the region was a choice piece of property, a potential New France in the New World. On the other hand, England's colonial aspirations centered farther south, where colonization had begun at Virginia and Massachusetts. England didn't *need* what is now Nova Scotia, though the region offered much with its rich fisheries, but it was a place to confront the expansion of the French, England's most contentious enemy in Europe.

Colonization

England's claim notwithstanding, France eyed the area for colonization and dispatched explorer Samuel de Champlain to the region in 1604. After a tough winter on an island on the St. Croix River (which today forms the New Brunswick–Maine border), the encampment moved across the Bay of Fundy, where the fortified Port-Royal was established near what is now Annapolis Royal. The French named the region—encompassing what is now Nova Scotia, New Brunswick, Prince Edward Island—Acadia (Peaceful Land). Not to be outdone, England's James I named the same region Nova Scotia (New Scotland) and granted it to Sir William Alexander in 1621.

After a 1632 peace treaty forced England to surrender Nova Scotia to the French, Acadian settlements quickly spread beyond the Port-Royal area to the Fundy and Minas Basin coastlines. The merchant Nicholas Denys,

ACADIAN DEPORTATION

After the signing of the Treaty of Utrecht in 1713, England had demanded but not enforced an oath of allegiance from the Acadians who lived under its jurisdiction. By the 1750s, however, the British decided to demand loyalty. Those who refused to sign the oath of allegiance were rounded up and deported, and their villages and farmlands were burned. The Acadians being deported were herded onto ships bound for the English colonies on the Eastern Seaboard or any place that would accept them. Some ships docked in England, others in France, and others in France's colonies in the Caribbean. As the ports wearied of the human cargo, many of them refused the vessels entry, and the ships returned to the high seas to search for other ports willing to accept the Acadians. In one of the period's few favorable events, the Spanish government offered the refugees free land in Louisiana, and many settled there in 1784, where they became known as Cajuns. Many Acadians fought the British in guerrilla warfare or fled to the hinterlands of Cape Breton Island, Prince Edward Island, New Brunswick, and Québec.

Exact deportation numbers are unknown. Historians speculate that 10,000 French inhabitants lived in Acadia in 1755; by the time the deportation had run its course in 1816, only 25 percent of them remained. The poet Longfellow distilled the tragedy in his *Evangeline*, a fictional story of two lovers divided by the events.

---

whose name is entwined with France's early exploration, established a fortified settlement on Cape Breton Island at St. Peters and also at Guysborough in 1653. So many Acadians settled at Grand-Pré that it became the largest settlement and hub of villages along the Fundy Coast. Other settlements were established across Acadia on Cape Breton Island, the Cobequid Bay and Cape Chignecto coastlines, and in what is now New Brunswick. The villagers cultivated grains and forage crops on wetlands reclaimed by dikes and planted the region's first orchards.

Through Acadian expansion, bitter military confrontations continued. The two powers had different strategies: France first built settlements, then used its military to defend them. England, boasting a superior military savvy, fought its battles first, then used settlements to stabilize areas. As it turned out, England had the edge, and it was on this advantage that Nova Scotia's history frequently turned during the following century and a half.

Treaty of Utrecht

Hostilities between England and France in the New World mirrored political events in Europe. Fighting ebbed and flowed across the region as the powers jockeyed for control on the European continent. Queen Anne's War (1701–1713), the War of Austrian Succession (1745–1748), and the Seven Years' War (1756–1763) were all fought in Europe, but corresponding battles between the English and French took place in North America as well (where they were known collectively as the French and Indian Wars).

The Treaty of Utrecht in 1713 settled Queen Anne's War in Europe. Under the terms of the treaty, England fell heir to all of French Acadia (though the borders were vague), which became an English colony. Nova Scotia (New Scotland) rose on the ashes of New France and the fallen Port-Royal; the British took the fort in 1710, renamed it Fort Anne, and renamed the settlement Annapolis Royal. The town was designated the colony's first capital, remaining as such until Halifax was established and became the capital in 1749.

ONGOING CONFLICT

The French military regrouped after the fall of Port-Royal. It fled from the region and began to build the Fortress of Louisbourg on Cape

© ANDREW HEMPSTEAD

Port-Royal National Historic Site protects the first permanent European settlement north of Florida.

Breton Island in 1719. Once again, the French envisioned the fortification as a New Paris and France's major naval base, port city, and trading center in North America.

The British quickly responded. A fort at Grassy Island on Chedabucto Bay was their first effort, a site close enough to the Fortress of Louisbourg to watch the arrivals and departures of the French fleets. By 1745, Louisbourg represented a formidable threat to England, so the Brits seized the fortress and deported the inhabitants. But no sooner had they changed the flag than the French were moving back in again. The War of Austrian Succession in Europe ended with the Treaty of Aix-la-Chapelle in 1748, which, among other things, returned Louisbourg to France.

Full-Fledged War

In 1749 a British convoy sailed into Halifax Harbour, established England's military hub in the North Atlantic in the capacious harbor, and named Halifax the capital of Nova Scotia. Seven years later, the Seven Years' War broke out in Europe, and once more both powers geared for confrontation across the Atlantic Ocean. In 1758 the British again seized the Fortress of Louisbourg and toppled Port la Joye, renaming it Fort Amherst. In the ultimate act of revenge, the British troops returned to Louisbourg in 1760 and demolished the fortress stone by stone so it would never rise again against England.

Fort Edward, on the Fundy Coast, went up in the midst of an Acadian area and guarded the overland route from Halifax. Fort Lawrence on the Chignecto Isthmus, between Nova Scotia and New Brunswick, was built to defend the route to the mainland.

BRITISH SETTLEMENT

After the Acadian deportation, the British began peopling the territory with pro-Crown settlers. Lunenburg began with 2,000 German, Swiss, and French "foreign Protestants." In 1760 England resettled the prime Fundy Coast once farmed by the Acadians with 12 shiploads of farmers from its colonies farther south. The Crown officially regained the region, including Cape Breton Island, with the Peace of Paris in 1763. After the American Revolution, 25,000 British Loyalists poured into Nova Scotia.

SCOTTISH HERITAGE

Nova Scotia's Scottish heritage originated with a shipload of immigrants who arrived at Pictou in 1773, followed by hundreds of settlers to New Glasgow in the 1780s, and the Arisaig area in the next decade.

It was during the early 1800s, however, that the region's decidedly Scottish complexion was firmly established. England and France were engaged in the Napoleonic War, and the French had blocked British ports. England desperately needed food and began the Highland Clearances—poor tenant farmers in Scotland were turned off their land, their homes were burned, and the farmlands were converted to sheep and cattle pastures. The Clearances continued for almost two decades. Thousands of Scots died of starvation and disease, while

CABLE TO CANSO

© ANDREW HEMPSTEAD

On the outskirts of tiny Canso, at the northeastern end of the Marine Drive, is **Hazel Hill Cable Station** (pictured), an imposing but crumbling brick building that has important ties to the history of communications. The first cable link between Europe and North America came ashore in Newfoundland, and the company that established the link was given landing rights for 50 years. With problems providing a reliable link between Newfoundland and New York, the Commercial Cable Company laid its own cable, which came ashore at Canso and then continued south to Boston and New York. Completed in 1884, the Hazel Hill Cable Station was a state-of-the-art facility, helping transmit messages from one side of the Atlantic to the other in less than one minute. The distress signal from the sinking *Titanic* and news of the 1929 stock market crash were transmitted through the station before the final message was sent in 1962.

thousands more took the Crown up on its offer of free land in Nova Scotia. They left their beloved Highlands forever and re-created their old home in a new land. Intense emotional ties remain to this day, and the Scots' heritage is kept alive with festivals commemorating their history and culture.

NOVA SCOTIA TAKES SHAPE

In the late 18th century, Nova Scotia was defined as a distinct colony. Cape Breton Island, for a while a separate colony, was reannexed to Nova Scotia in 1820. Fortunes were founded on trade. Halifax's Samuel Cunard started a shipping empire based on steamship service to England in 1839. During the Great Age of Sail, shipbuilding seaports thrived. In 1878 Yarmouth ranked as Canada's second-largest port. Coal mining began in 1872 at Springhill, near Amherst, where the 1,220-meter shaft was Canada's deepest.

Confederation

In 1864, Nova Scotia sent five delegates across to neighboring Prince Edward Island for a landmark event in Canada's history. The "Fathers

Nova Scotia is filled with historic sites, including the town of Lunenburg, which is protected as a UNESCO World Heritage Site.

of the Confederation"—from Nova Scotia as well as New Brunswick, Prince Edward Island, Ontario, and Québec—met at Province House in Charlottetown to discuss the potential joint dominion that followed. England gave the union its blessing and signed the British North America Act (now known as the Constitution Act). Confederation was not popular with all Nova Scotians, but it offered economic inducements, including the rail connections to central Canada that Nova Scotia wanted. Finally, the Dominion of Canada was born on July 1, 1867, as a confederation of Québec, Ontario, New Brunswick, and Nova Scotia united under a parliamentary government, with the other provinces of today joining between 1870 and 1949 (neighboring Newfoundland and Labrador was last to join).

Economy and Government

ECONOMY

Traditionally, Nova Scotia's economy revolved around resource-based industries such as fishing, forestry, and mining. Although communities established around fishing and farming areas continue to thrive, the economy today is a lot more diverse. In addition to all the stalwarts discussed below, other growing sectors include information technology, the medical field (Nova Scotia is a world leader in multiorgan transplants), and the film industry.

In 2008, Nova Scotia's gross domestic product (GDP) was a little more than $30 billion, with ocean industries generating the largest segment ($2.6 billion). Second most important to the economy is manufacturing ($1.8 billion). Among the largest of 2,000 manufacturers in Nova Scotia are Michelin Tire, Volvo, Crossley Karastan Carpet, and Pratt and Whitney. Governments are usually better at spending money than earning it, but they are officially listed as having contributed $1.7 billion to the provincial economy.

Ocean Industries

Fishing, the traditional stalwart of the Nova Scotia economy, has decreased greatly in importance dollar-wise in the last two decades. Poor resource management and overfishing have destroyed its once-bounteous supplies. Cod stocks especially have declined greatly, and quotas have been put in place in an effort to protect and rebuild existing stocks. Even so, fisheries and fish-processing still remain an important contributor to Nova Scotia's gross domestic product, and cod, haddock, herring, and lobster are caught inshore and off the Atlantic's Scotian Shelf. The province is the world's largest lobster exporter.

The government has put a positive spin on the decline of the fishing industry by claiming that the "ocean industries" sector is growing, and it may be, but only because other industry is being added to the fishing equation, including aquaculture, boatbuilding, offshore gas and oil drilling, ocean-related tourism, sea-based government services, and transportation. Regardless of how you approach the issue, the ocean is extremely important to the Nova Scotian economy, generating $2.6 billion dollars annually.

Tourism

Tourism ranks as the third most important component of the provincial economic pie, generating $1.6 billion annually. It is also the fastest-growing sector of the economy, having doubled in worth during the last decade. Most visitors (38 percent) are from the neighboring provinces, while the rest of Canada contributes 30 percent, and the United States adds almost 25 percent. Of the 1.6 million people who arrive annually, more than three-quarters are returning visitors.

Agriculture and Forestry

Although just 8 percent of Nova Scotia's land is arable, agriculture contributes heavily to the economy, producing fruits (including

© ANDREW HEMPSTEAD

Salt from a mine at Pugwash is loaded onto a tanker for export.

Annapolis Valley apples), dairy products, poultry, hogs, and the world's largest share of blueberries.

Although fishing gets all the attention, forestry has historically been an important component of the provincial economic pie. In the 1800s, local lumber was used in shipbuilding but today the pulp and paper industries use the great majority of harvested wood. About 37,000 square kilometers of Nova Scotia is deemed to be productive forest, and most of it is owned by private companies. Nova Scotia also exports 1.7 million Christmas trees each year.

Military

Nova Scotia is the region's federal civil service and military center. Halifax has served as a naval center since its founding in 1749 as headquarters for the Royal Navy. The city is now Maritime Command headquarters for the Canadian Armed Forces. Other in-province military installations are at Shearwater, Cornwallis, and Greenwood; training stations are at Barrington, Mill Cove, Shelburne, and Sydney.

Mining

Offshore deposits of oil and gas below the Scotian Shelf near Sable Island, 250 kilometers from the mainland, have been drilled since the early 1990s. It is estimated that two billion barrels of oil and up to 40 trillion cubic feet of natural gas remain. Important salt deposits are mined along the Northumberland Strait, including at Pugwash. Nova Scotia is the leading Canadian supplier of gypsum, which is exported to the United States. Historically, coal was the most important mineral product, with mines on Cape Breton Island supplying coal to power stations and to produce iron and steel. The last of these mines closed in 2001, creating an economic catastrophe for Cape Bretoners.

GOVERNMENT

Canada is a constitutional monarchy. The federation of 10 provinces and three territories operates under a parliamentary democracy in which power is shared between the federal government, based in Ottawa, and the provincial governments. Canada's three nonprovincial territories, Nunavut, Yukon, and the Northwest Territories, exercise delegated—rather than constitutionally guaranteed—authority. The power to make, enforce, and interpret laws rests in the legislative, executive, and judicial branches of government respectively.

The Federal Government

Under Canada's constitutional monarchy, the formal head of state is the queen of England, who appoints a governor-general to represent her for a five-year term. The governor-general stays out of party politics and performs largely ceremonial duties such as opening and closing parliamentary sessions, signing and approving state documents on the queen's behalf, and appointing a temporary replacement if the prime ministry is vacated without warning. The head of government is the prime minister, who is the leader of the majority party or party coalition in the House of Commons.

The country's legislative branch, the Parliament, comprises two houses. The House of Commons, with 295 members, is apportioned by provincial population and elected by plurality from the country's districts. The Senate comprises 104 members appointed by the governor-general (formerly for a life term, though retirement is now mandatory at age 75) on the advice of the prime minister. Legislation must be passed by both houses and signed by the governor-general to become law.

National elections are held whenever the majority party is voted down in the House of Commons or every five years, whichever comes first. Historically, it has been unusual for a government to last its full term.

Provincial and Local Governments

Whereas the federal government has authority over defense, criminal law, trade, banking, and other affairs of national interest, Canada's 10 provincial governments bear responsibility for civil services, health, education, natural resources, and local government. As in the other provinces, Nova Scotia's Legislative Assembly consists of a one-house legislative body with members elected every four years. The nominal head of the provincial government is the lieutenant governor, appointed by the governor-general of Canada. Executive power, however, rests with the cabinet, headed by a premier, the leader of the majority party.

As elsewhere, local government in Nova Scotia has always been top-heavy with bureaucracy, and so in the 1990s the number of incorporated towns was trimmed by creating regional municipalities. One of these was Cape Breton Regional Municipality, formed by amalgamating six incorporated towns and one existing county. The main population base lives in Halifax Regional Municipality, which was created through the amalgamation of the cities of Halifax and Dartmouth and the town of Bedford.

People and Culture

While the rugged topography of Nova Scotia has tended to separate people and isolate them in scattered settlements, centuries of some-times turbulent history have bound the Nova Scotians together: the mutual grief of the early wars, the Acadian deportation, immigration upheavals, and the abiding hardships common to resource-based economies.

DEMOGRAPHY

Nova Scotia's population is 920,000. It is the seventh-most populous province and is home to 3.2 percent of Canada's total population (32 million). The population density is 18 people per square kilometer. Distribution is closely divided between urban and rural, with a full third of Nova Scotians concentrated in and around Halifax.

Four of five Nova Scotians trace their lineage to the British Isles. Forty-nine original Scottish families, from Archibald to Yuill, are still on the rolls of the Scottish Societies Association of Nova Scotia, which does genealogical surveys.

After the American Revolution, 25,000 United Empire Loyalists poured into Nova Scotia. Several thousand African Americans arrived during the War of 1812, followed by Irish immigrants from 1815 to 1850. Recent worldwide immigration has added more than 50 other ethnic groups (including Poles, Ukrainians, Germans, Swiss, Africans, and Lebanese) to the province's cultural milieu, making it the most cosmopolitan in the region. About 8,000 black people live in Nova Scotia today, many of them descendants of immigrants from colonial America.

Mi'Kmaq

For thousands of years before the arrival of Europeans, the Mi'Kmaq people had lived off the land's abundant natural resources. As the Mi'Kmaq were forced to sign treaties, they gave up traditional land and settled on reserves (known as reservations in the United States). They were no longer free, they no longer hunted or fought, their medicine men could do nothing to stop the spread of the white man's diseases, and they slowly lost their pride. The first Indian Act, drafted in 1876, attempted to prepare natives for "European" society, but it only ended up isolating them from the rest of society.

Today, a total of 45 reserves and bands create affiliation for 6,000 Mi'Kmaq. The total number of aboriginal people in Nova Scotia is quoted at 26,000; many of the remaining 20,000 live off reserves but on traditional lands.

Various names are used to describe aboriginal Canadians, and all can be correct in context. The government still uses the term "Indian," regardless of its links to Christopher Columbus and the misconception he had landed in India. "Native" is generally considered acceptable only when used in conjunction with "people," "communities," or "leaders." "Indigenous" or "aboriginal" can have insulting connotations when used in certain contexts. The Mi'Kmaq themselves most often refer to themselves and others by none of the above, preferring to use band names.

Métis

The progeny of native people and Caucasians, the Métis (named for an old French word meaning "mixed") form a diverse and complex group throughout Canada. They date from the time of earliest European contact; in Nova Scotia, unions between European fishermen and Mi'Kmaq women—sometimes casual, sometimes formal—produced Métis offspring by the early 1600s. In the 17th century, the French government encouraged this mixing, seeing it as conducive to converting the native people to Christianity and to more speedily increasing the population of New France. Samuel de Champlain said, "Our young men will marry your daughters, and we shall be one people." That policy had changed by the 1700s, however, and France then *discouraged* mixed unions, in part because of the increased availability of white women in North America.

Today, Métis culture in Nova Scotia remains strongest along the Fundy Coast.

LANGUAGE AND RELIGION

Although Canada is constitutionally bilingual, English is the language of choice for most of the country and for the majority of Nova Scotians. (French is the mother tongue of about 22 percent of Canadians, while the figure in Québec is 88 percent.) The Official Languages Acts of 1969 and 1988 established French and English as equal official languages and designated rights for minority-language speakers throughout the country. Still, there has been no shortage of acrimony between francophone Québec and the rest of the country over the issue of language (as well as broader cultural distinctions), which has led to constitutional crisis and nearly to the secession of Québec from the confederation.

English is spoken by 94 percent of Nova Scotians, while 6 percent are bilingual. French has gained appeal as a second language, and one in four primary schoolchildren in Halifax is enrolled in French immersion classes.

Francophones are a small minority in Nova Scotia (4 percent). The French spoken here is not a patois; it's closely tied to the language that was brought to the continent by the original settlers from France. Visitors who have studied standard Parisian French may have a little trouble with the accent, syntax, and vocabulary here (the differences are not unlike those between American and British English).

Canada, Eh!

Canadian English is subtly different from American English, not only in pronunciation but also in lexicon. For instance, Canadians may say "serviette," "depot," and "chesterfield" when Americans would say "napkin," "station," and "couch." Spelling is a bit different as well, as Canadians have kept many British spellings—for example, *colour, kilometre, centre, cheque.* "Eh?" is a common lilt derived from British and Gaelic in which each sentence ends on a high note, as though a question had been asked. At the same time, Canadian English has been profoundly influenced by its neighbor to the south. Nevertheless, you'll find that language variations pose no serious threat to communication.

Religion

Although the domination of organized religions over the lives of Canadians has waned substantially since the 1960s, church affiliation in Nova Scotia is higher than elsewhere in the country.

Nova Scotia's cultural diversity is reflected in religion. Protestants and Roman Catholics make up 58 and 37 percent of the mainland population respectively, while on Cape Breton Catholics are in the majority. Anglicans account for almost 16 percent on the mainland and 10 percent on Cape Breton. Other denominations include the United Church of Canada and the Baptist and Presbyterian churches, as well as small populations of Jews, Buddhists, and Hindus, living mainly in Halifax.

THE ARTS

The Canada Council gives grants to theaters, dance troupes, orchestras, and arts councils to promote and keep the arts alive. The provincial tourism office (902/425-5781 or 800/565-0000, www.novascotia.com) can tell you what's going on, or you can check out the local paper. See each travel chapter for specific listings detailing nightlife, theater, dance, and music options.

Halifax attracts concerts and major events to the Halifax Metro Centre. Farther up the hillside, the Neptune Theatre hosts year-round repertory theater, as does Dalhousie University's Rebecca Cohn Auditorium, which doubles as the home of the Symphony of Nova Scotia. Dozens of nightclubs and other venues around the capital city showcase established and up-and-coming local bands, such as Sloan, which are earning the province, and especially Halifax, a reputation as an influential breeding ground for pop, rock, and alternative music.

Cape Breton is renowned for its contributions to folk music. Not surprisingly, Scottish and Irish fiddle tunes form much of the source material, but Cape Breton musicians have taken that extremely rich foundation and made something with a uniquely Maritime flavor: frisky jigs and reels for dancing, as well as ballads, often centering on the theme of fishing and the ubiquitous sea. In addition to its Celtic-themed folk musicians, Cape Breton Island is also home to Rita MacNeil, whose rich and emotional songs are a source of inspiration worldwide.

Museums

With an ethnic heritage as varied as Nova Scotia's, it's no wonder that its museums are among the country's best. Some museums are moving tributes to the people, such as Grand Pré National Historic Site, while others, such as Fortress of Louisbourg National Historic Site, re-create early Anglo years with authentic buildings and demonstrations.

On a smaller scale, county and town museums document regional historic, cultural, and economic subjects. Municipal or privately operated museums in towns and villages put the emphasis on local history or specialties.

DANCING THE JIG

Through the first half of the 18th century, life in the northeast and Highlands of Scotland was becoming more and more difficult. Not only was there discontent over the union with England, the Scots were facing ever-decreasing resources, the dismantling of clans, and the confiscation of property. After the defeat of Bonnie Prince Charlie in 1745, thousands of these Gaelic speakers migrated to the New World, with many of them settling in Nova Scotia. They brought with them their farming skills, their language, and their music. Centuries later, these Celtic traditions remain a strong part of life in Nova Scotia.

Music is the best-known part of the Celtic culture, especially fiddle music, which creates the perfect rhythm for step dancing. While this style of music is all but forgotten in Scotland, it thrives in Nova Scotia. Many cherished songs describing life on the land have been passed down through the generations, while a new wave of lively tunes (known as jigs and reels) creates a spirited mix of music heard throughout the region and beyond.

Cape Breton-born **Natalie MacMaster** has the highest profile of Nova Scotia's fiddlers. Her energetic performances, in which she steps the dances while playing, bring crowds around the world to their feet. Born and raised on the west coast of Cape Breton Island, five siblings comprise **The Rankins,** who infuse a variety of musical styles into their music. The fiddle, mandolin, and percussion instruments keep the traditional vibe going, while the songs vary from country to folk. The fiddle is central to the music performed by **Ashley MacIssac,** but his shows are anything but traditional. Described by some as "grunge fiddle," his music crosses from Celtic to garage rock and heavy metal – he's a unique nonconformist who performs in sold-out shows across North America. In addition to the big names, bands such as **Beolach** and the **Irish Descendants** are worth watching for, while bands churning out lively foot-stomping, beer-drinking tunes can be heard in pubs throughout the province.

ESSENTIALS

Getting There

Visitors to Nova Scotia have the option of arriving by road, rail, ferry, or air. The main gateway city for flights from North America and Europe is the capital, Halifax. Ferries cross to Yarmouth from Maine and to Digby from New Brunswick, while the main rail line enters the region from New Brunswick and terminates at Halifax.

Unless otherwise noted, telephone numbers given in this section are the local (North American) contacts.

AIR

Most long-haul international and domestic flights into eastern Canada set down at Toronto, Ottawa, or Montréal, with connecting or ongoing flights to Halifax.

Air Canada

Air Canada (888/247-2262, www.aircanada.ca or http://aircanada.com in the United States) is one of the world's largest airlines, serving five continents. The company has one of the world's easiest-to-understand fare systems, with five fare levels and multiple ways of searching for online flights and fares. It offers direct flights to Halifax from Fredericton, Saint John, Moncton, St. John's, Montréal, Ottawa, Toronto, Calgary, Boston, Detroit, and New York City. All other flights from

North America are routed through Toronto or Montréal, with connections made in Halifax to Sydney. From Europe, Air Canada flies from London to Halifax. From the South Pacific, Air Canada operates flights via Honolulu from Sydney and in alliance with Air New Zealand from Auckland and other South Pacific islands to Honolulu, where passengers change to an Air Canada plane for the flight to Vancouver and onward connections to the east coast. Asian cities served by direct Air Canada flights include Beijing, Hong Kong, Nagoya, Osaka, Seoul, Shanghai, Taipei, and Tokyo. All terminate in Vancouver. Air Canada's flights originating in the South American cities of Buenos Aires, Santiago, and Sao Paulo are routed through Toronto.

WestJet

Canada's second-largest airline, WestJet (403/250-5839 or 888/937-8538, www.westjet .com), is a low-cost carrier that operates along the same lines as Southwest. Based in Calgary, its flights extend as far east as St. John's, with flights routed through Toronto to Halifax.

AIR TAXES

The Canadian government collects a variety of "departure taxes" on all flights originating from Canada. These taxes are generally not in the advertised fare, but they will all be included in the ticket purchase price. First up is the **Air Travellers Security Charge**, $5-10 each way for flights within North America and $25 round-trip for international flights. **NAV Canada** also dips its hand in your pocket, collecting $9-20 per flight for maintaining the country's navigational systems. Additionally, passengers departing Halifax International Airport must pay an **Airport Improvement Fee** of $10, while those departing Sydney pay $25 (the second highest in Canada). Additionally, if your flight transits through Toronto, you pay an $8 improvement fee for that airport.

U.S. Airlines

Air Canada offers the most flights into Nova Scotia from the United States, but Halifax is also served by **American Eagle** (800/433-7300, www.aa.com), from New York City; **Continental** (800/231-0856, www.continental .com), from Newark; and **Northwest** (800/225-2525, www.nwa.com), from Detroit.

RAIL

Amtrak (800/872-8725, www.amtrak.com) has service from New York City to Toronto (via Buffalo), and from New York City to Montréal.

VIA Rail

Once you're in Canada, rail travel is handled by VIA Rail (416/366-8411 or 888/842-7245, www.viarail.ca). Best known for the transcontinental rail route, the spectacular journey from Vancouver to Toronto through the Rockies and central Canada's farmlands, VIA Rail has replicated the transcontinental route's deluxe trappings and service with its Easterly class aboard the *Ocean.* The *Ocean* departs Montréal, follows the St. Lawrence River's southern shore to northern New Brunswick, cuts across the province to Moncton, speeds into Nova Scotia via Amherst and Truro, and finishes at Halifax. The trip takes 21 hours. The train has a variety of economy classes (called Comfort), but it is the Easterly class that gets all the attention. These luxuriously restored vintage carriages include a domed car with three small salons (one of which is a replica of the transcontinental's mural lounge), a dining car with art deco trappings, and a more informal car designed for lighter dining. Rates range from $140 each way in Comfort class to $520 in Easterly class, the latter including sleeping-car accommodations and all meals.

Passes

If you're planning on extensive rail travel within Canada, the least expensive way to travel is on a **Canrailpass,** which allows unlimited travel anywhere on the VIA Rail system for 12 days within any given 30-day period. During high

CUTTING FLIGHT COSTS

Ticket structuring for air travel is so complex that finding the best deal requires some time and patience (or a good travel agent). In the first place, to get an idea of what you will be paying, call the airlines or check their websites and compare fares. **Air Canada** (www.aircanada.com) has a streamlined fare structure that makes it easy to find the fare that serves your needs and budget. Also look in the travel sections of major newspapers – particularly in weekend editions – where budget fares and package deals are frequently advertised. While the Internet has changed the way many people shop for tickets, having a travel agent that you are comfortable in dealing with – who takes the time to call around, does some research to get you the best fare, and helps you take advantage of any available special offers or promotional deals – is an invaluable asset in starting your travels off on the right foot.

Within Canada, **Travel Cuts** (866/246-9762, www.travelcuts.com) and **Flight Centre** (888/967-5302, www.flightcentre.ca), both with offices in all major cities, including Halifax, consistently offer the lowest airfares available, with the latter guaranteeing the lowest. Flight Centre offers a similar guarantee from its U.S. offices (866/967-5351, www.flightcentre.us), as well as those in the United Kingdom (tel. 0870/499-0040, www.flightcentre.co.uk), Australia (tel. 13/31-33, www.flightcentre.com.au), and New Zealand (tel. 0800/24-35-44, www.flightcentre.co.nz). In London, **Trailfinders** (215 Kensington High St., Kensington, tel. 0845/058-5858, www.trailfinders.com) always has good deals to Canada and other North American destinations. Reservations can be made directly through airline or travel agency websites, or use the services of an Internet-only company such as **Travelocity** (www.travelocity.com) or **Expedia** (www.expedia.com).

When you have found the best fare, open a **frequent flyer** membership with the airline – **Air Canada** (www.aeroplan.com) has a very popular reward program that makes rewards easily obtainable.

---

season (June 1–October 15) the pass is adult $879, senior (older than 60) and child $791, with extra days (up to three are allowed) $75 and $68 respectively. The rest of the year, the pass costs adult $549, senior and child $494, with extra days $47 and $42 respectively. VIA Rail has cooperated with Amtrak (800/872-7245) to offer a North American Rail Pass, with all the same seasonal dates and discounts as the Canrailpass, and similarly priced passes.

On regular fares, discounts of 25–40 percent apply to travel in all classes October–June. Those older than 60 and younger than 25 receive a 10 percent discount that can be combined with other seasonal fares. Check for advance-purchase restrictions on all discount tickets.

The VIA Rail website (www.viarail.ca) provides route, schedule, and fare information, takes reservations, and offers links to towns and sights en route. Or pick up a train schedule at any VIA Rail station.

BUS

North America's main bus line, **Greyhound** (800/231-2222, www.greyhound.ca or www.greyhound.com), doesn't provide service to Nova Scotia. Instead, you will need to get yourself to a gateway city such as Montréal, Toronto, or Bangor (Maine) and connect with **Acadian Lines** (902/454-9321 or 800/567-5151, www.acadianbus.com), which provides service from these three cities to locations throughout Nova Scotia.

Passes

Acadian Lines honors all Greyhound passes. Greyhound's **Discovery Pass** comes in many forms. The Canada Discovery Pass is sold in periods of seven days ($329), 15 days ($483), 30 days ($607), and 60 days ($750) and allows unlimited travel throughout the country, as well as on select rail routes and from U.S. gateway cities south of the 49th parallel. Passes can be bought 14 or more

Arriving in Nova Scotia by ferry is an enjoyable way to start your travels.

© ANDREW HEMPSTEAD

days in advance online, seven or more days in advance from any Canadian bus depot, or up to the day of departure from U.S. depots.

FERRY

From the United States, and even from Toronto, the most direct driving route to Halifax includes a ferry trip. One ferry service operating mid-May to mid-October and one year-round service save the drive around the Bay of Fundy.

From Maine

North America's fastest vehicular ferry, *The Cat* (902/742-6800 or 888/249-7245, www.catferry.com) crosses to Yarmouth from Portland (Maine) and Bar Harbor (Maine) in 5.5 and three hours respectively. It runs three or four times weekly from each port June to mid-October. From Portland, peak-season one-way fares (July–August) are adult US$99, senior US$79, child US$55, vehicle under 6.6 feet US$164. From Bar Harbor, fares are adult US$69, senior US$58, child US$48, vehicle under 6.6 feet US$115.

From New Brunswick

Bay Ferries (902/245-2116 or 888/249-7245, www.acadianferry.com) handles the busy Bay of Fundy crossing between Saint John (New Brunswick) and Digby (a three-hour drive from Halifax), a shortcut that saves drivers a few hours of driving time. Operating once or twice daily year-round, one-way high-season fares are adult $40, senior $25, child $24, vehicle $80 plus a $20 fuel surcharge. Reservations are essential through summer.

CAR
Principal Routes into Nova Scotia

The majority of visitors drive to Nova Scotia. From the United States, Highway 9 heads east from Bangor, Maine, and enters New Brunswick—Atlantic Canada's principal land gateway—at St. Stephen. From this point, the options are to continue north via Moncton to Nova Scotia, or to jump aboard the ferry at Saint John. The TransCanada Highway from central Canada is more roundabout, following the St. Lawrence River through Québec, and then passing through northern New Brunswick to enter Nova Scotia at Amherst.

Getting Around

Driving, whether it be your own vehicle or a rental car, is by far the best way to get around Nova Scotia. This section talks about driving in Canada as well as the public transportation options.

AIR

While Halifax International Airport, 35 kilometers from Halifax, serves as Atlantic Canada's principal air hub, there is a just a single intraprovincial flight within Nova Scotia—the daily **Air Canada** (888/247-2262, www.aircanada.com) link between Halifax and Sydney.

BUS

Getting around Nova Scotia by bus is made possible by **Acadian Lines** (902/454-9321 or 800/567-5151, www.acadianbus.com), which links all major cities and towns as well as many minor ones. It operates seven days a week year-round. Although Acadian Lines has no travel passes, those issued by Greyhound are accepted.

Halifax has an extensive public transportation system that revolves around scheduled bus service. If you have a day on your hands and no other plans, consider an early-morning bus to an unexplored area, and a late-afternoon or early-evening return to the city. Few outsiders do it, but mixing among the locals on a bus circuit is a terrific way to explore the capital.

DRIVING IN CANADA

United States and international driver's licenses are valid in Canada. All highway signs give distances in kilometers and speeds in kilometers per hour. Unless otherwise posted, the maximum speed limit on the highways is 100 kilometers per hour (62 miles per hour).

Use of safety belts is mandatory, and motorcyclists must wear helmets. Infants and toddlers weighing up to nine kilograms (20 pounds) must be strapped into an appropriate children's car seat. Use of a child car seat for larger children weighing 9–18 kilograms (20–40 pounds) is required. Before venturing north of the 49th parallel, U.S. residents should ask their vehicle insurance company for a Canadian Non-resident Inter-provincial Motor Vehicle Liability Insurance Card. You may also be asked to prove vehicle ownership, so carry your vehicle registration form.

If you're a member in good standing of an automobile association, take your membership card—the Canadian AA provides members of related associations full services, including free maps, itineraries, excellent tour books, road- and weather-condition information, accommodations reservations, travel agency services, and emergency road services. For more information contact the **Canadian Automobile Association** (613/247-0117, www.caa.ca).

Note: **Drinking and driving** (with a blood-alcohol level of 0.08 percent or higher) in Nova Scotia can get you imprisoned for up to five years on a first offense and will cost you your license for at least 12 months.

Highways and Byways

Long distances notwithstanding, the province has a superb system of roads, classified by numbers. For example, the TransCanada (Highway 104) enters at Amherst, zips east across the mainland, and finishes at North Sydney. The highway is one of the new 100-series roads designed for rapid transit. Similar highways connect major towns in the central region and rim the heavily traveled southwest region's seacoast along the Fundy.

The highways numbered 1–99 often parallel the 100-series expressways and connect major cities and towns. Roads numbered 200–399 are paved, rambling, two-lane routes that take visitors to all the interesting out-of-the-way places. These roads often work as diversionary routes off major sightseeing highways such as Highway 316, which departs the Marine

© ANDREW HEMPSTEAD

The Cabot Trail, on Cape Breton Island, is one of the world's most scenic drives.

Drive's Highway 7 and meanders through Canso and Guysborough on its way to the Canso Strait. The Cabot Trail around western Cape Breton is the exception. It is unnumbered and ranks as a special scenic highway.

Car Rental

All major car-rental companies have outlets at Halifax International Airport, in downtown Halifax, and in major towns across the province. Try to book well in advance, especially in summer. Expect to pay from $50 a day and $250 a week for a small economy car with unlimited kilometers.

Major rental companies with outlets in Halifax include:

- **Avis** (800/331-1084, www.avis.ca)
- **Budget** (800/268-8900, www.budget.ca)
- **Discount** (800/263-2355, www.discountcar.com)
- **Enterprise** (800/261-7331, www.enterprise.com)
- **Hertz** (800/654-3131, www.hertz.ca)
- **National** (800/227-7368, www.nationalcar.com)
- **Rent-a-Wreck** (800/327-0116, www.rentawreck.ca)
- **Thrifty** (800/847-4389, www.thrifty.com)

RV and Camper Rental

You might want to consider renting a campervan or other recreational vehicle for your trip. With one of these apartments-on-wheels, you won't need to worry about finding accommodations each night. Even the smallest units aren't cheap, but they can be a good deal for longer-term travel or for families or two couples traveling together. The smallest vans, capable of sleeping two people, start at $175 per day with 100 free kilometers (62 miles) per day. Standard extra charges include insurance, a preparation fee (usually around $60 per rental), a linen/cutlery charge (around $60 per person per trip), and taxes. Major agencies with rental outlets in Halifax include **Cruise Canada** (800/671-8042, www.cruisecanada.com) and **Canadream** (800/461-7368, www.canadream.com). Both of these companies also have rental outlets across the country.

Visas and Officialdom

ENTRY FOR U.S. CITIZENS

Citizens and permanent residents of the United States are required to carry a passport for both entry to Canada and for reentry to the United States. At press time, the U.S. government was developing alternatives to the traditional passport. For further information, see the website http://travel.state.gov/travel. For current entry requirements to Canada, check the Citizenship and Immigration Canada website (www.cic.gc.ca).

ENTRY FOR OTHER FOREIGN VISITORS

All other foreign visitors must have a valid passport and may need a visa or visitors permit, depending on their country of residence and the vagaries of international politics. At present, visas are not required for citizens of the United States, the British Commonwealth, or Western Europe. The standard entry permit is for six months, and you may be asked to show onward tickets or proof of sufficient funds to last you through your intended stay. Extensions are available from the **Citizenship and Immigration Canada** office in Halifax. This department's website (www.cic.gc.ca) is the best source of the latest entry requirements.

ENTRY BY PRIVATE AIRCRAFT OR BOAT

If you're going to be entering Canada by private plane or boat, contact the **Canada Border Services Agency** (204/983-3500 or 800/461-9799, www.cbsa.gc.ca) in advance for a list of official ports of entry and their hours of operation.

CLEARING CUSTOMS

Visitors are allowed to bring in personal items that will be used during a visit, such as cameras, fishing tackle, and equipment for camping, golf, tennis, scuba diving, and so on. You can also bring the following into Canada duty-free: reasonable quantities of clothes and personal effects, 50 cigars and 200 cigarettes, 200 grams of tobacco, 1.14 liters of spirits or wine, food for personal use, and gas (normal tank capacity). Pets from the United States can generally be brought into Canada, with certain caveats. Dogs and cats must be more than three months old and have a rabies certificate showing date of vaccination. Birds can be brought in only if they have not been mixing with other birds, and parrots need an export permit because they're on the endangered species list.

Handguns, automatic and semiautomatic weapons, and sawn-off rifles and shotguns are not allowed into Canada. Visitors with firearms must declare them at the border; restricted weapons will be held by customs and can be picked up on exit from the country. Those not declared will be seized and charges may be brought. It is illegal to possess any firearm in a national park unless it is dismantled or carried in an enclosed case. Up to 5,000 rounds of ammunition may be imported but should be declared on entry.

On reentering the United States, if you've been in Canada more than 48 hours, you can bring back up to US$400 worth of household and personal items, excluding alcohol and tobacco, duty-free. If you've been in Canada less than 48 hours, you may bring in only up to US$200 worth of such items duty-free.

For further information on all customs regulations contact **Canada Border Services Agency** (204/983-3500 or 800/461-9799, www.cbsa.gc.ca).

Recreation

In Nova Scotia's great outdoors, just about every form of recreation is feasible and first-rate: bicycling, hiking, scuba diving, canoeing, sea kayaking, sailing, sailboarding, rockhounding, bird-watching, surfing, fishing, golfing, and downhill skiing—you name it. Many outfitters around the province rent bikes, boats, and other equipment and can equip you for wilderness expeditions and all sorts of other activities.

PARKS

The province's national and provincial parks come in a wide range of personalities and offer an equally eclectic array of activities and facilities, from searching for gemstones at Blomidon Provincial Park to lounging in luxury at Cape Breton Highlands' Keltic Lodge resort.

National Parks

Nova Scotia has two of Canada's 43 national parks. Nova Scotians dote on **Kejimkujik National Park** (kedgie-muh-KOO-jick), which combines interesting ice-age topography with an interior network of lakes ideal for canoeing. But it is **Cape Breton Highlands National Park** that ranks as a showstopper among all of Canada's national parks. It's more than twice as large as Kejimkujik, and whereas that park can be uncrowded even in summer, the Highlands park attracts hordes of visitors for its ocean scenery, abundant wildlife, and network of hiking trails.

Permits are required for entry into all Canadian national parks. These are sold at park gates, at all park information centers, and at campground fee stations. Day passes (under $10 per person) are the best deal for short visits, but if you're planning to visit both Nova Scotia parks, as well as those in other provinces, consider an annual **National Parks of Canada Pass,** good for entry into all of Canada's national parks for one year from the date of purchase. The cost is adult $67.70, senior $57.90,

child $33.30 up to a maximum of $136.40 per vehicle. The **Discovery Package** pass (adult $84.40, senior $72.60, child $42.20 to a maximum of $165.80 per vehicle) is a good choice for history buffs. It allows unlimited entry into both national parks and national historic sites for a full year from purchase. For more information on park passes, check the Parks Canada website (www.pc.gc.ca).

Provincial Parks

The **Department of Natural Resources** (902/662-3030, www.novascotiaparks.ca) manages a system of 122 parks within Nova Scotia. Of these, 98 are scenic day-use parks

A PHOTOGRAPHER'S DREAM

Nova Scotia has incredible light for photography. The sky turns from a Wedgwood color to sapphire blue – a beautiful background for seacoast photographs. Rise at dawn to take advantage of the first rays of sunlight hitting picturesque east coast villages such as popular **Peggy's Cove** (home to the "world's most photographed lighthouse") and **Fisherman's Cove,** both within an hour's drive of Halifax, as well as delightful seaside gems such as **Blue Rocks,** beyond Lunenburg. The town of Lunenburg itself attracts photographers for its harborfront panorama of colorful buildings (best in the late afternoon).

While photography is simplest when the weather is favorable – and that's more often than not – don't pass up a morning basking in thick mist, as bright sun illuminates the sky behind the thick clouds. The fog breaks apart gradually, and when it does, the sun radiates like a spotlight, illuminating the sparkling dampness that clings briefly to the landscape.

(called "picnic parks") with picnic facilities and often hiking trails and beaches for clam digging and swimming. Picnic parks are open mid-May to mid-October and often boast sensational views; Blomidon Provincial Park, for example, north of Wolfville, provides access to a hiking trail atop towering red cliffs that jut into the Bay of Fundy and overlook the foaming sea. In addition, some of Nova Scotia's best beach scenes are found at the day-use parks; some have lifeguards, but otherwise facilities are limited. The best of the beaches are **Risser's Beach** near Lunenburg and **Clam Harbour** northeast of Halifax, which often has sand-sculpture contests. Naturalists go for **Martinique Beach** near Musquodoboit Harbour because of its dunes, salt marshes, and the nearby bird sanctuary; and **Taylors Head** near Spry Bay, which has boardwalk-laced dunes, a beach, and peninsula hiking trails. A good number of provincial parks have campgrounds and summer interpretive programs. Camping fees are $18, with many campgrounds having flush toilets and showers but no hookups. Most campgrounds are open mid-May to mid-October.

HIKING AND WALKING

Hiking is one of the most popular activities in Nova Scotia. Not only are there hundreds of trails to explore, it's free and anyone can do it. The hiking season spans spring to fall. Coastal areas are generally free of pesky insects, but insect repellent is wise inland May–September. As national and provincial parks protect the most spectacular scenery, it'll be no surprise that this is where you find the best hiking. One standout is **Cape Breton Highlands National Park** on Cape Breton Island. Here you can find anything from short interpretive trails along raised boardwalks to strenuous slogs that end at high ocean lookouts. Nova Scotia's provincial parks generally lack long trails, but short walks often lead to local natural landmarks. Brochures on these walking trails are widely available at information centers, or check the Department of Natural Resources website (www.novascotiaparks.ca).

Among the best of many books on the subject is *Hiking Trails of Nova Scotia* by Michael Haynes (Goose Lane Editions, 2002). Also check out www.novatrails.com and www.trails.gov.ns.ca.

FISHING

Neighboring New Brunswick and Newfoundland and Labrador get most of the attention by anglers, but Nova Scotia has a wide range of fishing experiences and a diverse number of species.

Salmon

Just one species of salmon is native to the tidal waters of Nova Scotia—the Atlantic salmon. It is anadromous, spending its time in both freshwater and salt water. They spend up to three years in local rivers before undergoing massive internal changes that allow them to survive in salt water. They then spend between two and three years in the open water, traveling as far as Greenland. After reaching maturity, they begin the epic journey back to their birthplace, to the exact patch of gravel on the same river from where they emerged. It is the returning salmon that are most sought after by anglers, with Cape Breton Island's Margaree River the focus for serious anglers. Atlantic salmon grow to 36 kilograms (79 pounds), although their landlocked relatives rarely exceed 10 kilograms (22 pounds).

Deep-Sea Fishing

Deep-sea fishing's star attraction is the giant bluefin tuna; its season runs September–November. In 1979, a bluefin weighing a record 679 kilograms (1,497 pounds) was caught off St. Georges Bay. The bay ranks as the top tuna area, while the Fundy coast off Yarmouth from Cape St. Mary to Wedgeport is another prime fishing area. Expect to pay $160–300 per person per day for a tuna charter. In addition to tuna, other deep-sea catches include pollack, mackerel, striped bass, sea trout, and bottom dwellers such as haddock, cod, and halibut.

Freshwater Fish

Speckled trout (also known as brook trout) are widespread throughout the region and are fun to catch and tasty to eat. They tend to gravitate to cooler water, such as spring-fed streams, and can be caught on spinners or flies. A 3.4-kilogram (7.5-pound) specimen, one of the largest ever caught, is on display in Halifax's Museum of Natural History (the record is one that weighed in at 4.1 kilograms, which was reeled in from Porters Lake, east of Halifax). Introduced in the late 1800s, **rainbow trout** are in lakes and rivers across Nova Scotia. Sherbrooke Lake and Dollar Lake, both near Halifax, have healthy populations of **lake trout. Brown trout** are found in some streams and larger lakes.

Long and lean, **striped bass** inhabit rivers and estuaries throughout the region. There is a definite art to catching the species—it is estimated it takes an average of 40–50 hours of fishing to catch one. **Smallmouth bass** are a popular sport fish introduced to the waterways of southwestern Nova Scotia. They live in clear, calm water, usually with a gravelly bottom. Common throughout North America, **whitefish** are easily caught in most rivers and lakes, although they rarely exceed 15 centimeters (6 inches) in length. **Atlantic whitefish** (also called Acadian whitefish) are endemic to southwestern Nova Scotia. As they are a protected species, angling for them is prohibited, so carry an identification chart if fishing these waters. **Yellow perch** (also known as lake perch) are identified by wide vertical stripes. Most often caught in shallow rivers and lakes throughout Nova Scotia, they are great fun for children to reel in.

Around 1.7 million fingerlings from two hatcheries are released at 400 easily accessible lakes and rivers across the province each year. Most are speckled trout because they are easy to raise and adapt to varying conditions; other stocking fish are rainbow and brown trout. You can catch them on artificial flies, small spinners, or spoons.

Fishing Licenses and Regulations

Before casting a line, make yourself aware of provincial regulations. The recreational fishery is managed by the **Department of Fisheries and Aquaculture** (902/485-5056, www.gov.ns.ca/natr). A freshwater license for nonresidents costs 12.46 for one day, $31.74 for seven days, or $57.45 per year. Residents pay $24.13 for an annual license. No license is required for ocean fishing.

Fishing in national parks requires a separate license, which is available from park offices and some sport shops—$8 for a seven-day license, $25 for an annual license.

CYCLING AND MOUNTAIN BIKING

Reasonably good roads and gorgeous scenery make Nova Scotia excellent road-biking territory, while mountain biking has caught on among the adventurous as a way to explore more remote areas of the region. Except on main arteries, particularly the TransCanada Highway, car traffic is generally light. Cyclists, nonetheless, should remain vigilant: Narrow lanes and shoulders are common, and in some areas, drivers may be unaccustomed to sharing the road with bicycles. The premier bike-touring route is the **Cabot Trail** through Cape Breton Highlands National Park.

Many shops rent decent- to good-quality road and mountain bikes. But if you plan to do some serious riding, you'll probably want to bring your own; most airlines will let you bring a bike for little or no extra charge. An outstanding information resource is **Bicycle Nova Scotia** (902/425-5454, www.bicycle.ns.ca), which handles cycling information and publishes *Nova Scotia by Bicycle,* detailing 4,000 kilometers of roads along 20 detailed routes. Also contact **Atlantic Canada Cycling** (902/423-2453, www.atlanticcanadacycling.com), which publishes extensive information on cycling routes (including descriptions and ratings of highways and byways throughout the province), tours, races, clubs, and equipment.

Guided Tours

Halifax-based **Freewheeling Adventures** (902/857-3600 or 800/672-0775, www.freewheeling.ca) leads agreeable arrangements of guided trips in small groups, each accompanied by a support van to carry the luggage and, if necessary, the weary biker. Owners Cathy and Philip Guest plan everything—snacks, picnics, and meals at restaurants en route, and overnight stays at country inns. Expect to pay around $200–300 per person per day for an all-inclusive tour. The trips pass through some of Nova Scotia's prettiest countryside, including the South Shore, the Annapolis Valley, and the Cabot Trail.

GOLFING

Nova Scotia has 85 golf courses and a season that extends from mid-April to late October.

Greens fees are generally very reasonable, with rates at less than $20 at some municipal courses. Where you really see a difference in fees is at better courses such as **Chester Golf Club,** a mature seaside layout kept in pristine condition, where the high-season rate is just $50. The best-known course in the province, and considered one of the world's finest, is **Cape Breton Highland Links,** which costs just $90 per round. A limited number of resort-style courses have been developed in the last decade, with the most upscale being **Fox Harb'r Golf Resort and Spa,** along Northumberland Strait, where greens fees are over $200.

The provincial governing body is the **Nova Scotia Golf Association** (902/468-8844, www.nsga.ns.ca), which provides a listing of all courses with contact numbers and fees. The website www.golfingns.com holds similar information while **Golf Nova Scotia** (800/565-0000, www.golfnovascotia.com) promotes a selection of the province's better courses.

© ANDREW HEMPSTEAD

Chester Golf Club enjoys a waterfront location.

Ingonish Beach attracts sun-worshippers throughout the warmer months.

WATER SPORTS

This ocean-bound province has no shortage of beaches, and most waterside provincial parks have a supervised **swimming** area. The warmest beaches are found along the Northumberland Strait. The Bay of Fundy and Atlantic shores tend to be much cooler, although conditions vary considerably throughout the region.

With so much water surrounding and flowing through the province, **boating** opportunities are nearly infinite. Sailing is popular in the Bay of Fundy, in spacious Halifax and Sydney harbors, and in protected inland areas such as Bras d'Or Lakes.

Canoeing and Kayaking

Canoeing is a traditional form of transportation that remains extremely popular throughout Nova Scotia. You can rent canoes at many of the more popular lakes, including those protected by Kejimkujik National Park. If you bring your own, you can slip into any body of water whenever you please, taking in the scenery and viewing wildlife from water level.

Coastal kayaking is another adventure, especially around picturesque South Shore fishing villages, along the remote coast near Tangier, and along Cape Breton Island's Atlantic coast. Expect to pay around $100 per person for a full day of kayaking. The tour cost always includes kayak and wetsuit rental, and usually also lunch.

Tidal-Bore Rafting

Instead of white-water rafting, Nova Scotia is known for wild and wooly trips on the tidal bore created by the world's highest tides in the Bay of Fundy. **Tidal Bore Rafting Park** (902/758-4032, www.tidalboreraftingpark.com) offers trips for varying levels of adrenaline rushes in motorized Zodiacs, riding the bore as it rushes upriver before blasting back across its face. Trips last two or four hours and cost about $60 and $80 per person respectively. This company is based a one-hour drive north of Halifax.

Whale-Watching

Today's lucrative whaling industry is based not on butchering but on simply bringing curious onlookers to observe the wonderful animals up close. Prime whale-watching areas are the Bay of Fundy (commercial operators are based along Digby Neck and on Brier Island) and off the west coast of Cape Breton Island. Minke, pilot, finback, orca, and humpback whales are the most populous species, and Atlantic right whales are spotted during a short window of time (August) in the Bay of Fundy.

Surfing

Nova Scotia is home to a small but dedicated population of surfers who hit the waves of the province's east coast year-round. **Lawrencetown Beach,** less than an hour's drive north of Halifax, is the best-known spot, with beach breaks along the long stretch of sand and a right-hander breaking off the rocky point. Other surf spots are scattered along the province's east coast. Water temperatures rarely rise above 16°C (61°F), meaning a 4/3 mm or 3/2 mm wetsuit is necessary, even in midsummer.

Boards and wetsuits can be rented in Halifax at **DaCane Surf Shop** (5239 Blowers St., 902/431-7873, www.hurricanesurf.com), along the South Shore in Port Joli at **Rossignol Surf Shop** (White Point Beach Lodge, 902/683-2140, www.surfnovascotia.com), and at a small concession at Lawrencetown Beach itself. Locals will be more than happy to tell you the cleanest, most consistent waves roll through in winter, but with air temperatures that drop to −20°C (−4°F) and water temperatures hovering around 0°C (32°F), only the keenest surfers take to the water.

WINTER SPORTS

Winter is definitely low season for travel to Nova Scotia. Outdoor recreation is severely limited by the weather, although snow-related sports are popular with the locals. In addition to downhill skiing and boarding, skating on

© ANDREW HEMPSTEAD

Surfers gravitate to Lawrencetown Beach for some of Canada's finest waves.

frozen ponds is a hit, while locals cheer for minor-league ice-hockey teams scattered throughout the region.

Skiing and Snowboarding

The three alpine resorts of Nova Scotia may lack the vertical rise of their western counterparts, but snowfall is high and outsiders will be greeted with open arms wherever they choose to ski or board. Day passes top out at $40, and each resort has day lodge facilities and rentals. Vertical rises range from 180 to 300 meters (590–980 feet), and the season generally runs from Christmas to late March. Closest to Halifax is **Ski Martock,** south of the Annapolis Valley; **Wentworth** is near the New Brunswick border; and **Ski Cape Smokey,** with sweeping ocean views, sits at the north end of Cape Breton Island.

Cross-Country Skiing

The province's two national parks stay open year-round. In winter, hiking routes are transformed by snow into excellent cross-country ski trails, many of which are groomed by local ski clubs that charge a nominal fee for their use. **Ski Tuonela,** on Cape Breton Island (902/929-2144, www.skituonela.com), is one of North America's only lift-served telemark hills. In addition to a rope tow, the resort has 20 kilometers of groomed trails, a day lodge, and overnight accommodations.

Organizations with handy websites loaded with information and links to ski clubs are **Canada Trails** (www.canadatrails.ca) and **Cross Country Canada** (www.cccski.com).

SPECTATOR SPORTS

Windsor, Nova Scotia, claims its place in history as the birthplace of ice hockey (known simply as "hockey" in Canada). Although the region is home to no National Hockey League (NHL) teams, the exploits of the Toronto Maple Leafs, Montréal Canadiens, and other NHL franchises are passionately followed here. You can also see lively play from the Québec Major Junior Hockey League's Halifax Mooseheads, as well as high-quality college and amateur teams in cities and towns throughout the region. The season runs October–March; check with local tourist-information offices for game schedules and ticket information.

Accommodations and Food

Nova Scotia has all the chain hotels you know, as well as a range of accommodations that showcase the region—historic bed-and-breakfasts, grand resorts, waterfront cottage complexes, and rustic campgrounds. This section will give you a taste of the choices and some hints on reserving a room. (Throughout the travel chapters of this book, I detail my favorites in all price ranges.)

To make reservations at any of the chain properties, simply phone their toll-free reservation centers or book online using their websites. Another option is a province-sponsored free reservation system, which is online at www.novascotia.com.

HOTELS, MOTELS, AND RESORTS

International, Canadian, and regional lodging chains are represented in Nova Scotia. At the more expensive properties, expect all the requisite amenities and services—swimming pools, air-conditioning, high-speed Internet access, room service, toiletries, restaurants, and bars. This type of accommodation can be found in central locations in Halifax, Sydney, and major tourist areas. Rates at four- or five-star hotels start at $150 s or d in high season. Prices for a basic motel room in a small town start at $50 s, $60 d, rising to $100 for a room in a chain hotel within walking distance of a major city's downtown core.

GETTING A GOOD DEAL ON ACCOMMODATIONS

Rates quoted through this guidebook are for a standard double room in the high season (usually July and August, but sometimes as early as June and as late as September). Almost all accommodations are less expensive outside of these busy months, with some discounting their rates by up to 50 percent. You'll enjoy the biggest seasonal discounts at properties that rely on summer tourists, such as those in Lunenburg or along the Northumberland Strait. The same applies in Halifax on weekends – many of the big downtown hotels rely on business and convention travelers to fill the bulk of their rooms; when the end of the week rolls around, the hotels are left with rooms to fill at discounted rates Friday, Saturday, and Sunday nights.

While you have no influence on the seasonal and weekday/weekend pricing differences detailed above, *how* you reserve a room *can* make a difference in how much you pay. First and foremost, when it comes to searching out actual rates, the Internet is an invaluable tool. All hotel websites listed in *Moon Nova Scotia* show rates, and many have online reservation forms. Use these websites to search out specials, many of which are available only on the Internet. Don't be afraid to negotiate during slower times. Even if the desk clerk has no control over rates, there's no harm in asking for a bigger room or one with a better view. Just look for a VACANCY sign hanging out front.

Most hotels offer auto association members an automatic 10 percent discount, and whereas senior discounts apply only to those older than 60 or 65 on public transportation and at attractions, most hotels offer discounts to those age 50 and older, with chains such as Best Western also allowing senior travelers a late checkout. "Corporate Rates" are a lot more flexible than in years past; some hotels require nothing more than the flash of a business card for a 10-20 percent discount.

When it comes to frequent-flyer programs, you really do need to be a frequent flyer to achieve free flights, but the various loyalty programs offered by hotels often provide benefits simply for signing up.

The chains you know are represented in Nova Scotia, as well as the following you may not be familiar with.

Best Western

OK, I assume you have heard of the world's largest motel chain, but the website www.bestwesternatlantic.com is helpful in providing direct links to local properties.

Choice Hotels Canada

Choice Hotels (800/424-6423, www.choicehotels.ca) owns 275 properties across the country. It operates seven brands, including Sleep, with smallish but clean, comfortable, and inexpensive rooms; Comfort, where guests enjoy a light breakfast and newspaper with a no-frills room; Quality, a notch up in quality with a restaurant and lounge; and Econo Lodge, older properties that have been renovated to Choice's standard and often have a pool and restaurant.

Delta Hotels and Resorts

This Canadian-owned company (416/874-2000 or 877/814-7706, www.deltahotels.com) is a class operation; expect 40-plus fine hotels with splendid facilities in notable settings. Locations include Halifax and Sydney. Check the Delta website for package deals offered year-round.

Maritime Inns and Resorts

With package deals and locations in Pictou, Antigonish, Port Hawkesbury, and the Cape Breton resort town of Baddeck, these properties (902/752-5644 or 877/768-3969, www.maritimeinns.com) are popular with holidaying locals. Generally, packages include meals and activities such as golfing for about $100 per person per day.

Signature Resorts

Nova Scotia's provincial government owns

three stunning resorts. They appeal to the carriage trade—travelers who like the understated ambience of a resort lodge with a tony rustic setting and furnishings, gourmet dining, a remote location with manicured grounds, and the genteel sports of golf or fly-fishing. Provincial resorts in Nova Scotia are the Pines Resort at Digby; the Keltic Lodge at Ingonish Beach, Cape Breton; and Liscombe Lodge at Liscomb Mills. The website www.signatureresorts.com has links to all three.

BED-AND-BREAKFASTS
Nova Scotia is blessed with hundreds of bed-and-breakfasts. Concentrations are in Halifax, Mahone Bay, Lunenburg, the Annapolis Valley, and Baddeck. Styles run the gamut from historic mansions to rustic farmhouses, and as a result, amenities can also vary greatly. Regardless, guests can expect hearty home cooking, a peaceful atmosphere, personal service, knowledgeable hosts, and conversation with like-minded travelers. They are usually private residences, with hosts who live on-site and up to eight guest rooms. As the name suggests, breakfast is included in quoted rates; ask before booking whether it is a cooked or continental breakfast. Rates fluctuate enormously—from $50 s, $60 d for a spare room in an otherwise regular family home to $200 in a grandly restored Victorian mansion.

Finding and Reserving a Room
My favorite bed-and-breakfasts are recommended throughout the travel chapters of this book. You can also use the provincial accommodation guide, *Doers' and Dreamers' Guide,* and local information centers to find out about individual properties. **Select Atlantic Inns** (www.selectinns.ca) is an organization of mid-to top-end bed-and-breakfasts, with online reservations and lots of information on specific properties. The **Canadian Bed and Breakfast Guide** (www.canadianbandbguide.ca) is a regularly updated database, although listings aren't recommendations as such. Finally, **Bed and Breakfast Online** (www.bbcanada.com) doesn't take bookings, but links are provided

The Maple Inn, at Parrsboro, is just one of hundreds of historic homes that provide visitors with overnight accommodations.

and an ingenious search engine helps you find the accommodation that best fits your needs.

Before reserving a room, it is important to ask a number of questions of your hosts. The two obvious ones are whether or not you'll have your own bathroom and how payment can be made (many establishments don't accept debit cards or all credit cards).

BACKPACKER ACCOMMODATIONS
As accommodation prices are reasonable throughout Nova Scotia, there is less of a need to find a dorm bed than in other parts of North America. Privately operated backpacker lodges are limited (those at Mahone Bay and Brier Island are both excellent) and **Hostelling International** operates four hostels around the province.

Hostelling International
The curfews and chores are long gone in this worldwide nonprofit organization of 4,200

hostels in 60 countries. Hostelling International Canada has hostels in Nova Scotia at Halifax, South Milford (near Kejimkujik National Park), and Wentworth. For a dorm bed, members of Hostelling International pay $15–25 per night, nonmembers pay $17–30. Generally, you need to provide your own sleeping bag or linen, but most hostels supply extra bedding (if needed) at no charge. Accommodations are in dormitories (2–10 beds), although single and double rooms are often available for an additional charge. All also offer a communal kitchen, lounge area, and laundry facilities, while some have Internet access, bike rentals, and organized tours.

You don't *have* to be a member to stay in an affiliated hostel of Hostelling International, but membership pays for itself after only a few nights of discounted lodging. Aside from discounted rates, benefits of membership vary from country to country but often include discounted air, rail, and bus travel; discounts on car rental; and discounts on some attractions and commercial activities. For Canadians, the membership charge is $35 annually, or $175 for a Friend (lifetime) Membership. For more information contact HI–Canada (604/684-7111, www.hihostels.ca). Joining the Hostelling International affiliate of your home country entitles you to reciprocal rights in Canada, as well as around the world; click through the links at (www.hihostels.com) to your country of choice.

CAMPING

Camping out is a popular summer activity across Nova Scotia, and you'll find campgrounds in both national parks, many provincial parks, on the outskirts of cities and towns, and in most resort areas. Facilities at park campgrounds vary considerably, but most commercial operations have showers and water, electricity, and sewer hookups.

National parks provide some of the nicest surroundings for camping. All sites have picnic tables, fire grates, toilets, and fresh drinking water, although only some provide showers. Prices range $18–38, depending on

Corney Brook Campground, Cape Breton Highlands National Park

facilities and services. A percentage of sites can be reserved through the **Parks Canada Campground Reservation Service** (877/737-3783, www.pccamping.ca). Backcountry camping in a national park costs $8 per person per night.

Whenever possible, reservations for campsites—especially at the national parks and most popular provincial parks—should be made at least six weeks in advance. Most provincial parks, however, do not accept reservations, but instead assign sites on a first-come, first-served basis. At those parks, it's best to arrive before noon to assure yourself a spot. Most provincial parks are open mid-May to mid-October. Most privately owned campsites accept reservations, which are more likely to be held if you send a small deposit.

FOOD AND DRINK

Thankfully, the Nova Scotian cuisine promoted today is very different from what locals traditionally dined on. In what was a difficult environment, generations past were happy eating salt pork, salt cod, hardtack (a type of vegetable), and vegetables that were boiled longer than necessary. Locals shun hot spices and go lightly on other condiments. While country-style cooking embodies the essence of provincial style in the smaller towns and seaports, dining in Halifax and towns such as Wolfville offers sophisticated fare from continental to nouvelle cuisine.

If you travel on your stomach, look for the Taste of Nova Scotia emblem affixed to restaurants' front windows or doors. The emblem is awarded to dining places judged noteworthy by the province; a booklet of the same name costs $1 and is available from tourist information centers.

Highlights

Regardless of cooking styles, seafood, red meat, and produce abound. Local lamb originates in Pictou County. Fruits and vegetables are fresh and are often picked from backyard inn and restaurant gardens. Local delicacies include wild chanterelle mushrooms, smoked mackerel pâté, and seafood from lobster to locally caught Digby scallops and Solomon Gundy (pickled herring). Preserves are generally homemade. Soups vary from lobster chowder thickened with whipped cream to pea soup brimming with corned-beef chunks.

Salmon is often cooked on a board plank before an open fire, as the Mi'Kmaq historically prepared it. Desserts know no limit and vary from trifles rich with raspberry jam and sherry, to cheesecakes concocted of local cheese and cream, to molded flans embellished with fruit toppings.

Acadian

While Anglo cuisine features red meats, Acadian fare is based on seafood. Common Acadian-style dishes include seafood chowder, shellfish (shrimp and crab), and fish (especially mackerel, herring, and cod). For variety, Acadian menus might offer chicken *fricot* (chicken stew), *poutine râpé* (boiled or deep-fried pork and grated raw potatoes, rolled into

a ball and dipped in corn or maple syrup or molasses), and rappie pie (filled with a mixture of clams or chicken with grated potatoes as translucent as pearls). Desserts include sugar pie, apple dumplings, or cinnamon buns. Acadian cooking may be terribly hard on the waistline, but it's delicious. The best places to sample Acadian cuisine are along La Côte Acadienne (Fundy Coast) and in Chéticamp (Cape Breton Island).

Drinks

All the popular Canadian and American beers are available at bars and liquor stores, but you should be drinking the Halifax-brewed **Keith's** if you want to look like a local. Halifax also has a number of microbreweries.

Nova Scotia has five wineries and 120 hectares of commercially harvested grapes. Local wines are prominently displayed on wine lists throughout the province, especially those from Jost Vineyards, along the Northumberland Strait. Most grapes are French hybrids, but the

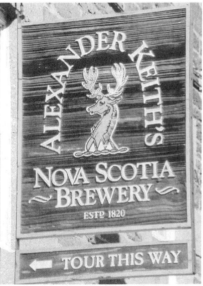

Nova Scotians have been enjoying beer from Alexander Keith's Brewery for almost 200 years.

© ANDREW HEMPSTEAD

TWO TRADITIONAL ACADIAN RECIPES

RAPPIE PIE

This traditional recipe is unique for the texture of the potato filling, and one succulent bite will make you a convert. (For best results, read the recipe all the way through before starting.)

    5-6 lbs. chicken
    6 large onions
    2 tsp. salt (or 2 tbsp. salted onions)
    1 tsp. pepper
    1 pail (10 lbs.) of big potatoes

1. Cut chicken in pieces, place in large pot, and cover with water. Bring to a boil. Add three large chopped onions, salt, and pepper. (While chicken is cooking, continue with the following steps.) When chicken is cooked, remove it from the pot, remove meat from bones, and break pieces into desired size. Keep broth simmering to be used later.

2. Chop the remaining onions and sauté in butter or margarine until tender but not brown. Set aside to be used later.

3. Peel, rinse, and grate potatoes in a large bowl. Take note of how much grated potato you have, because later you will use this same large bowl to scald the potatoes after they are squeezed, and you should have the same amount of potato mixture then as you have grated potatoes now.

4. Squeeze potatoes (about two cups at a time) in a fine cotton bag or cloth until quite dry. Place the squeezed potatoes in a second bowl as you go, and transfer them back into the large bowl when done. Add the sautéed onions.

5. Scald the squeezed potatoes by adding the boiling chicken broth gradually and stirring constantly. Remember, you must end up with the same amount of scalded-potato mixture in this bowl as you had grated potatoes before. If you do not have enough broth, add boiling water. When you're through scalding, the mixture should be slightly thicker and darker. Add salt and pepper to taste.

6. Grease 17-by-12-inch pan and dust with flour. Spread half of the potato mixture in the pan. Spread chicken meat evenly over this. Cover with other half of potato mixture. Bake at 400°F for 2.5 hours. It should come out brown, crusty, and delicious! The more often you make it, the better it gets.

CHICKEN FRICOT

A cross between a soup and a stew, this dish is especially appreciated on a cold winter evening.

    2 lbs. chicken (meat cut in small pieces)
    2 large onions, diced
    2 tsp. salted onions (or 1 tsp. salt)
    ½ tsp. pepper
    8 medium-size potatoes, diced and rinsed
    2 medium-size potatoes, grated

In a soup pot put chicken pieces, diced onions, salted onions, and pepper. Add 12 cups of water and bring to a boil. Cook for 30 minutes on medium heat. Add diced potatoes and continue to boil until cooked. To thicken *fricot*, lower heat to simmer and add grated potatoes. Cook a few minutes more. Serve hot in bowls.

Courtesy of Imelda Chiasson, lifetime resident of Nova Scotia, from the village of Concession, La Côte Acadienne.

---

local specialty is **ice wine,** made by a process in which the grapes aren't harvested until *after* the first frost; the frost splits the skins and the fermentation process begins with the grapes still on the vine. These concentrated juices create a supersweet wine. Ice wine is generally marketed in a distinctively narrow 375-milliliter bottle and promoted as a dessert wine.

The legal drinking age in Nova Scotia is 19, the same as all other Canadian provinces except Québec, Manitoba, and Alberta (where it is 18).

Tips for Travelers

EMPLOYMENT AND STUDY

International visitors wishing to work or study in Canada must obtain authorization *before* entering the country. Authorization to work will only be granted if no qualified Canadians are available for the work in question. Applications for work and study are available from all Canadian embassies and must be submitted with a nonrefundable processing fee. The Canadian government has a reciprocal agreement with Australia for a limited number of **holiday work visas** to be issued each year. Australian citizens aged 30 and younger are eligible; contact your nearest Canadian embassy or consulate. For general information on immigrating to Canada check the **Citizenship and Immigration Canada** website (www.cic.gc.ca).

VISITORS WITH DISABILITIES

A lack of mobility should not deter you from traveling to Nova Scotia, but you should definitely do some research before leaving home.

If you haven't traveled extensively, start by doing some research at the website of the **Access-Able Travel Source** (www.access-able.com), where you will find databases of specialist travel agencies and lodgings in Canada that cater to travelers with disabilities. **Flying Wheels Travel** (507/451-5005 or 877/451-5006, www.flyingwheelstravel.com) caters solely to the needs of travelers with disabilities. The **Society for Accessible Travel and Hospitality** (212/447-7284, www.sath.org) supplies information on tour operators, vehicle rentals, specific destinations, and companion services. For frequent travelers, the membership fee (US$45 per year) is well worthwhile. *Emerging Horizons* (www.emerginghorizons.com) is a U.S. quarterly magazine dedicated to travelers with special needs.

Access to Travel (www.accesstotravel.gc.ca) is an initiative of the Canadian government that includes information on travel within and between Canadian cities. For vision-impaired visitors, **CNIB** (www.cnib.ca) offers a wide range of services from its Halifax office (902/453-1480 or 800/563-2642). Finally, the **Canadian Paraplegic Association** (www.canparaplegic.org) is another good source of information; the provincial head office is in Halifax (902/423-1277).

FAMILY TRAVEL

Regardless of whether you're traveling with toddlers or teens, you will come upon

---

NATIONAL HOLIDAYS

New Year's Day	January 1
Good Friday	late March–mid-April
Easter Monday	late March–mid-April
Victoria Day	third or fourth Monday in May
Canada Day	July 1
Labour Day	first Monday in September
Thanksgiving Day	second Monday in October
Remembrance Day	November 11
Christmas Day	December 25
Boxing Day	December 26

WHAT TO TAKE

You'll find little use for a suit and tie in Nova Scotia. Instead, pack for the outdoors. At the top of your must-bring list should be walking or **hiking boots.** Even in summer you should be geared up for a variety of weather conditions, especially at the change of seasons or if you'll be spending time along the coast. Do this by preparing to **dress in layers,** including at least one pair of fleece pants and a heavy long-sleeved top. For breezy coastal sightseeing, a sweater or windbreaker, hat, sunscreen, and comfortable shoes with rubber soles will come in handy. For dining out, **casual dress** is accepted at all but the most upscale restaurants.

Electrical appliances from the United States work in Canada, but those from other parts of the world will require a **current converter** (transformer) to bring the voltage down. Many travel-size shavers, hairdryers, and irons have built-in converters.

happily accommodate children, but always try to reserve your room and let the reservations desk know the ages of your brood. Often, children stay free in major hotels, and in the case of some major chains—such as Holiday Inn—eat free also. Generally, bed-and-breakfasts aren't suitable for children and in some cases don't accept kids at all. Ask ahead.

When it comes to traveling with children, let them help you plan the trip, looking at websites and reading up on Nova Scotia together. To make your vacation more enjoyable if you'll be spending a lot of time on the road, rent a minivan (all major rental agencies have a supply). Don't forget to bring along favorite toys and games from home—whatever you think will keep your kids entertained when the joys of sightseeing wear off.

The provincial tourism website (www.novascotia.com) has a section devoted to children's activities. Another handy source of online information is **Traveling Internationally with Your Kids** (www.travelwithyourkids.com).

decisions affecting everything from where you stay to your choice of activities. Luckily for you, Nova Scotia is very family-friendly, with a variety of indoor and outdoor attractions aimed specifically at the younger generation, such as Shubenacadie Wildlife Park, north of Halifax, and Upper Clements Parks, near Annapolis Royal. The Annapolis Valley is also home to a number of campgrounds where the emphasis is on keeping the kids busy rather than being simply somewhere to stay the night. The best of these in this region are South Mountain Park and Look-Off Family Camping.

Admission prices for children are included throughout the travel chapters of this book. As a general rule, these reduced prices are for 6–16-year-olds. For two adults and two-plus children, always ask about family tickets. Children younger than six nearly always get in free. Most hotels and motels will

TRACING FAMILY ROOTS

If you are interested in tracing family ties, the place to start is with **Nova Scotia Archives and Records Management** (6016 University Ave., Halifax, 902/424-6060, www.gov.ns.ca/nsarm). It is open to the public Monday-Friday 8:30 A.M.-4:30 P.M. and on Saturday (with limited services) 9 A.M.-5 P.M. It's possible to take advantage of the department's resources without visiting in person. Its website is an excellent starting point – helpful for everyone from those searching out long-lost relatives to professional genealogists.

Ancestries originating on Cape Breton can be traced at the **Beaton Institute** (Cape Breton University, Glace Bay, 902/563-1329, http://beaton.uccb. ns.ca).

Health and Safety

Nova Scotia is a healthy place. To visit, you don't need to get any vaccinations or booster shots. And when you arrive you can drink the water from the faucet and eat the food without worry.

If you need an ambulance, call 911 or the number listed on the inside front cover of local telephone directories. Halifax and most of the large towns have local hospitals (look in the travel chapters of this book for locations and telephone numbers).

INSURANCE AND PRESCRIPTIONS

Intraprovincial agreements cover the medical costs of Canadians traveling across the nation. As a rule, the usual health-insurance plans from other countries do not include medical-care costs incurred while traveling; ask your insurance company or agent if supplemental health coverage is available, and if it is not, arrange for coverage with an independent carrier before departure. Hospital charges vary from place to place but can be as much as $3,000 a day, and some facilities impose a surcharge for nonresidents. Some Canadian companies offer coverage specifically aimed at visitors.

If you're on medication, bring adequate supplies with you, and get a prescription from your doctor to cover the time you will be away. You may not be able to get a prescription filled at Canadian pharmacies without visiting a Canadian doctor, so don't wait till you've almost run out. If you wear glasses or contact lenses, ask your optometrist for a spare prescription in case you break or lose your lenses, and stock up on your usual cleaning supplies.

SEXUALLY TRANSMITTED DISEASES

AIDS and other venereal and needle-communicated diseases are as much of a concern here as anywhere in the world today. Take exactly the same precautions you would at home—use condoms, and don't share needles.

GIARDIA

Giardiasis, also known as beaver fever, is a real concern for those who drink water from backcountry water sources. It's caused by an intestinal parasite, *Giardia lamblia,* that lives in lakes, rivers, and streams. Once ingested, its effects, although not instantaneous, can be dramatic; severe diarrhea, cramps, and nausea are the most common. Preventive measures should always be taken and include boiling all water for at least 10 minutes, treating all water with iodine, or filtering all water using a filter with a small-enough pore size to block the *Giardia* cysts.

WINTER TRAVEL

Travel through Nova Scotia during winter should not be undertaken lightly. Before setting out in a vehicle, check antifreeze levels, and always carry a spare tire and blankets or sleeping bags.

Frostbite can occur in a matter of seconds if the temperature falls below freezing and if the wind is blowing. Layer your clothing for the best insulation against the cold, and don't forget gloves and, most important, a warm hat, which can offer the best protection against heat loss. Frostbite occurs in varying degrees. Most often it leaves a numbing, bruised sensation and the skin turns white. Exposed areas of skin such as the nose and ears are most susceptible, particularly when cold temperatures are accompanied by high winds.

Hypothermia occurs when the body fails to produce heat as fast as it loses it. Cold weather combined with hunger, fatigue, and dampness creates a recipe for disaster. Symptoms are not always apparent to the victim. The early signs are numbness, shivering, slurring of words, dizzy spells, and, in extreme cases, violent behavior, unconsciousness, and even death. The best treatment is to get the patient out of the cold, replace wet clothing with dry, slowly give hot liquids and sugary foods, and place the victim in a sleeping bag. Prevention is a better strategy; dress for cold in layers, including a waterproof outer layer, and wear a warm wool cap or other headgear.

CRIME

Nova Scotia enjoys one of the country's lowest crime rates. Violent crimes are infrequent; the most common crime is petty theft. If you must leave valuable items in your car unattended, keep them out of sight, preferably locked in the vehicle's trunk. Women have few difficulties traveling alone throughout the region.

Remember that Halifax is an international port with seamy (albeit interesting) bars and taverns at or near the working area of the waterfront; keep your wits about you here, especially late at night. Better yet, leave these night scenes to the sailors and others who frequent the areas.

Both possession and sale of illicit drugs are considered serious crimes and are punishable with jail time and/or severe fines. Furthermore, Canadians consider drinking while driving equally serious; the penalty on the first conviction is jail and/or a heavy fine. A conviction here or in your home country can even be grounds for exclusion from Canada.

Royal Canadian Mounted Police (RCMP)

Despite the romantic image of the staid red-jacketed officer on horseback, Mounties (as they are most often called) nowadays favor the squad car as their mount of choice and a less colorful uniform. They are as ubiquitous a symbol of the country as the maple leaf and are similar to the highway patrol or state police in the United States. They operate throughout all the country's provinces and territories (except Ontario and Québec), complementing the work of local police.

Information and Services

MONEY

Unless noted otherwise, prices quoted in this book are in Canadian currency.

Canadian currency is based on dollars and cents, with 100 cents equal to one dollar. Coins come in denominations of one, five, 10, and 25 cents, and one and two dollars. The 11-sided, gold-colored, one-dollar coin is known as a "loonie" for the bird featured on it. The unique two-dollar coin is silver with a gold-colored insert. The most common notes are $5, $10, $20, and $50. A $100 bill does exist but is uncommon.

The safest way to carry money is in the form of travelers checks from a reputable and well-known U.S. company such as American Express, Visa, or Bank of America; those are also the easiest checks to cash. Cash only the amount you need when you need it. Banks offer the best exchange rates, but other foreign-currency exchange outlets are available. It's also a good idea to start off with a couple of

CURRENCY EXCHANGE

For the best exchange rate, take your foreign currency to a bank. Current exchange rates (into CDN$) for major currencies are:

US$1	=	$1.05
AUS$1	=	$0.92
€1	=	$1.55
HK$10	=	$1.38
NZ$1	=	$0.76
UK£1	=	$2.00
¥100	=	$0.98

On the Internet, check current exchange rates at www.xe.com/ucc.

travelers checks in Canadian dollars so you're never caught without *some* money if you don't make it to a bank on time.

Visa and MasterCard credit and debit cards are also readily accepted throughout Nova Scotia. By using these cards you eliminate the necessity of thinking about the exchange rate—the transaction and rate of exchange on the day of the transaction will automatically be reflected in the bill from your credit-card company. On the downside, you'll always get a better exchange rate when dealing directly with a bank.

Costs
The cost of living in Nova Scotia is similar to that in the surrounding provinces but lower than elsewhere in the country. By planning carefully, having a tent, or traveling in the shoulder seasons, it is possible to get by on about $100 per person per day or less. If you will be staying in hotels or motels, accommodations will be your biggest expense. Gasoline is sold in liters (3.78 liters equals one U.S. gallon) and is generally $1.30–1.50 a liter for regular unleaded.

Tipping charges are not usually added to your bill. You are expected to add a tip of 15 percent to the total amount for waiters and waitresses, barbers and hairdressers, taxi drivers, and other such service providers. Bellhops, doormen, and porters generally receive $1 per item of baggage.

Harmonized Sales Tax (HST)
In the spring of 1997, the Harmonized Sales Tax, a tax levied on most goods and services, supplanted the "goods and services" and provincial sales taxes. Originally pegged at 15 percent, the GST portion has since been reduced by two percent, making the HST 13 percent. All residents must pay the tax, as must visitors.

SHOPPING
Export Details
Americans can bring $400 worth of duty-free goods back into the United States after a 48-hour stay in Canada; $25 is the duty-free limit after stays of less than 48 hours. Gifts sent by mail and worth a total of $50 or less are duty-free also.

If you are interested in shopping for exotic wares, such as whalebone carvings or bearskin rugs, beware of customs regulations prohibiting the export of these types of items; hundreds of animals and their by-products are on the Convention on International Trade in Endangered Species of Wild Fauna and Flora list, which is online at www.cites.org. For a list of imports banned in your home country, contact your nearest customs office before departure.

Business Hours
Shopping hours are generally Monday–Saturday 9 A.M.–6 P.M. Late shopping in most areas is available until 9 P.M. on Thursday and Friday, and supermarkets open 24 hours have begun to appear in a few towns. Generally, banks are open Monday–Wednesday 10 A.M.–4 P.M. and Thursday–Friday 10 A.M.–5 P.M. A few banks may open on Saturday, but all are closed on Sunday. Nova Scotia is the only Canadian province that disallows Sunday shopping, although exceptions are made for essential services such as gas stations and in "tourist areas" such as the Halifax waterfront.

MAPS AND INFORMATION
Maps
Driving maps such as those published by **MapArt** (www.mapart.com) and **Rand McNally** (www.randmcnally.com) are available at bookstores, gas stations, and even some grocery stores across the province. In Halifax, **Maps and Ducks** (Historic Properties, 1869 Upper Water St., 902/422-7106) and **Trail Shop** (6210 Quinpool Rd., 902/423-8736) are specialty map stores. The most detailed atlas to the province is the *Nova Scotia Atlas,* produced by Formac Publishing.

Nautical maps are handled by the **Canada Hydrographic Service,** a division of Fisheries and Oceans Canada, but it doesn't sell directly to the public. To request a map catalog and

HEADING FARTHER AFIELD?

- **Tourism New Brunswick** (800/561-0123, www.tourismnewbrunswick.ca)

- **Prince Edward Island Tourism** (902/368-4444 or 800/463-4734, www.gov.pe.ca/visitorsguide)

- **Tourisme Québec** (514/873-2015 or 877/266-5687, www.bonjourquebec.com)

- **Newfoundland and Labrador Tourism** (709/729-2830 or 800/563-6353, www.newfoundlandlabrador.com)

- **Maine Office of Tourism** (888/624-6345, www.visitmaine.com)

a list of dealers, call 613/995-4413 or check www.charts.gc.ca. This department also distributes *Sailing Directions,* a composite of general navigational information, port facility descriptions, and sailing conditions (in English or French) for Nova Scotia and the Gulf of St. Lawrence.

Tourism Information

Begin planning your trip by contacting the government tourist office: **Tourism Nova Scotia** (902/425-5781 or 800/565-0000, www.novascotia.com). Its literature and a provincial map can be downloaded from the website or ordered by phone. This organization also operates **Provincial Visitor Centres** at major gateways, including one at Halifax International Airport (902/873-1223; year-round daily 9 A.M.–9 P.M.) and another along the downtown waterfront (1655 Lower Water St., 902/424-4248; year-round daily 8:30 A.M.–6 P.M.). Other locations are Yarmouth (mid-May–mid-Oct.), Digby (May–mid-Oct.), Amherst (year-round), and Pictou (May–mid-Dec.). Other locations are Portland and Bar Harbour, Maine, at the departure point for ferries to Yarmouth.

Every town of any size in Nova Scotia has a locally operated **Visitor Information Centre** (hours vary, but most are open mid-May–mid-Oct.).

COMMUNICATIONS
Postal Services

Canada Post (www.canadapost.ca) issues postage stamps that must be used on all mail posted in Canada. First-class letters and postcards sent within Canada are $0.52, to the United States $0.96, to foreign destinations $1.60. Prices increase along with the weight of the mailing. You can buy stamps at post offices (closed weekends), some hotel lobbies, airports, many retail outlets, and some newsstands.

Phone

The country code for Canada is 1, the same as the United States, and the area code for all of Nova Scotia is **902**. This prefix must be dialed for all long-distance calls. Toll-free numbers have the 800, 888, 877, or 866 prefix, and

Some information centers, such as this one ensconced in a tidal plant at Annapolis Royal, are attractions within themselves.

may be good for Nova Scotia, the Maritimes, Canada, North America, or, in the case of major hotel chains and car rental companies, will work worldwide.

To make an international call from Canada, dial the prefix 011 before the country code or dial 0 for operator assistance.

Public phones accept 5-, 10-, and 25-cent coins; local calls are $0.35 and most long-distance calls cost at least $2.50 for the first minute. The least expensive way to make long-distance calls from a public phone is with a **phone card.** These are available from convenience stores, newsstands, and gas stations.

Internet Access

If your Internet provider doesn't allow you to access your email away from your home computer, open an email account with **Hotmail** (www.hotmail.com) or **Yahoo** (www.yahoo.com). Although there are restrictions on the size and number of emails you can store and junk mail can be a problem, these services are handy and best of all, free.

Free public Internet access is available throughout Nova Scotia through the **Community Access Program (CAP).** To find out addresses and hours of the 400-odd locations across the province, call 866/569-8428 or go to http://cap.ic.gc.ca.

All major hotels and many bed-and-breakfasts have high-speed or Wi-Fi access from guest rooms. Those that don't—usually mid- and lower-priced properties—often have an Internet booth in the lobby. You'll also find Internet booths in many cafés. Aside from a lack of privacy, the downside to these public

access points is the lack of a mouse at most terminals—instead you must move around the screen using a touch pad.

WEIGHTS AND MEASURES

Canada uses the metric system, with temperature measured in degrees Celsius, liquid measurements in liters, solid weights in kilograms and metric tons, land areas in hectares, and distances in kilometers, meters, and centimeters. This newfangled system hasn't completely taken hold everywhere, and many Nova Scotians still think in terms of the imperial system; expect to hear a lobster described in pounds, local distances given in miles, and the temperature expressed in Fahrenheit degrees.

The electrical voltage is 120 volts. The standard electrical plug configuration is the same as that used in the United States—two flat blades, often with a round third pin for grounding.

Time Zones

Even though Nova Scotia was home to Sir Sandford Fleming, the man who devised time zones, the province didn't receive any special favors. It is on **Atlantic standard time (AST),** the same as New Brunswick and Prince Edward Island. **Newfoundland standard time (NST),** 30 minutes ahead of Atlantic standard time, is used on the island of Newfoundland and the southeastern Labrador communities on the Strait of Belle Isle; the rest of Labrador is on AST.

Atlantic standard time is one hour ahead of eastern standard time and four hours ahead of Pacific standard time.

RESOURCES

Suggested Reading

NATURAL HISTORY

Dawson, Joan. *The Mapmaker's Eye: Nova Scotia Through Early Maps.* Halifax: Nova Scotia Museum, 1988. Nova Scotia evolved through the centuries, as did the art of mapping. This illustrated book is a cartographer's dream.

Grescoe, Taras. *Bottomfeeder.* Toronto: Harper .Collins, 2008. An insight into the fisheries industry made more readable by the author's firsthand accounts of visits to the world's most important fisheries, including Nova Scotia.

Griffin, Diane. *Atlantic Wild Flowers.* Toronto: Oxford University Press, 1984. A glorious combination of text by Griffin and photography by Wayne Barrett and Anne MacKay—a must for every naturalist who revels in wildflowers.

Hare, F. K., and M. K. Thomas. *Climate Canada.* Toronto: John Wiley & Sons, 1974. One of the most extensive works on Canada's climate ever written. Includes a chapter on how the climate is changing.

Lee, Albert (photographer) and Alexa Thompson. *Destination Nova Scotia.* Halifax: Nimbus Publishing, 2000. Stunning photography and lyrical descriptions of the landscape are combined in this coffee-table book.

Lyell, Charles. *Geological Observations on the U.S., Canada, and Nova Scotia.* New York: Arno Press, 1978. During an early 1840s visit, Lyell thought enough of Nova Scotia's unusual landscape and geology to give it equal space among the nations in this insightful account.

MacAskill, Wallace R. *MacAskill Seascapes and Sailing Ships.* Halifax: Nimbus Publishing. Cape Breton's famed photographer captures the misty moods of fishermen, schooners, seaports, and seacoasts.

Natural History of Nova Scotia. Halifax: Departments of Education and Lands and Forests, two volumes. Everything on land or beneath the nearby seas is comprehensively detailed here with illustrations.

Saunders, Gary. *Discover Nova Scotia: The Ultimate Nature Guide.* Halifax: Nimbus Publishing, 2001. Perfect for a daypack, this handy guide includes maps, trail descriptions, and the natural wonders of Nova Scotia's parks.

Thurston, Harry. *Tidal Life: A Natural History of the Bay of Fundy.* Halifax: Nimbus Publishing, 1998. The lavishly illustrated contents describe natural habitats formed by the Fundy.

Towers, Julie, and Anne Camozzi. *Discover Nova Scotia: Wildlife Viewing Sites.* Halifax: Nimbus Publishing, 1999. Another of Nimbus's popular "Discover Nova Scotia" titles, this one gives detailed directions to more than 100 sites.

Tufts, Robbie. *Birds of Nova Scotia*. Halifax: Nimbus Publishing, 2007. The authoritative guide since 1961. The most recent edition includes color plates, detailed illustrations, a provincial map, and all the descriptive information bird-watchers will need to find and identify species across the province.

Wagg, Len (photographer). *Nova Scotia Landmarks*. Halifax: Formac Publishing, 2004. Filled with stunning aerial photography, this coffee-table book pinpoints natural highlights across the province. A great souvenir.

HUMAN HISTORY

Boileau, John. *Half Hearted Enemies*. Halifax: Formac Publishing, 2005. Examines the intriguing story of how Nova Scotia and New England continued to trade through the War of 1812.

Brasseaux, Carl A. *The Founding of New Acadia*. New Orleans: Louisiana State University Press, 1997. A little academic, but this book will make interesting reading for anyone from the South who wants to learn about the links between Cajuns and the Acadians of Nova Scotia.

Bruce, Harry. *An Illustrated History of Nova Scotia*. Halifax: Nimbus Publishing, 1998. Primarily aimed at the younger set, this book is highly readable and well worth a look, even for adults.

Campey, Lucille H. *After the Hector: The Scottish Pioneers of Nova Scotia and Cape Breton 1733–1852*. Edinburgh: Birlinn Publishing, 2005. An account of those who arrived in Pictou aboard the *Hector* and how their Scottish Highlands heritage helped them adapt and thrive in the New World.

Candow, James E. *Industry and Society in Nova Scotia*. Toronto: Fernwood Books, 2001. The history of industry and the way it has shaped the people of Nova Scotia today. One section is devoted to the phenomenal growth and importance of tourism.

Crowell, Clement W. *Novascotiaman*. Halifax: Nova Scotia Museum, 1979. A sea captain's correspondence forms the basis for a retelling of the story of Nova Scotia's Great Age of Sail.

Daigle, Jean, ed. *Acadians of the Maritimes*. Moncton, New Brunswick: Chaire d'Études Acadiennes, Université de Moncton, 1995. The history of the Acadians in Atlantic Canada is a tangled tale of upheaval and survival, cultural clashes and passions. Daigle's collection of Acadian literature is among the best on the bookshelves.

Faragher, John Mack. *A Great and Noble Scheme: The Tragic Story of the Expulsion of the French Acadians from Their American Homeland*. New York: W. W. Norton, 2005. In this hefty 560-page book, Faragher describes the evolution of Acadia, the horrors of the deportation, and the resulting pockets of Acadian culture that thrive to this day.

Finnan, Mark. *Oak Island Secrets*. Halifax: Formac Publishing, 2002. One of many books devoted to the world's longest treasure hunt, this one does a noble job of unraveling the story, although the Freemasonry connections are pushed a little strongly for my liking.

Lawrence, Ian. *Historic Annapolis Royal*. Halifax: Nimbus Publishing, 2002. Filled with historic photographs, this book details the history of the oldest town north of St. Augustine, Florida.

Ledger, Don. *Swissair Down*. Halifax: Nimbus Publishing, 2000. The story of the September 1998 crash of a Swissair jetliner off the village of Peggy's Cove from a pilot's point of view.

Lyell, Charles. *Travels in North America in the Years 1841–2*. New York: Arno Press, 1978. The author included Nova Scotia in his 19th-century travel observations.

Nunn, Bruce. *History with a Twist*. Halifax: Nimbus Publishing, 2002. Light yet interesting reading that covers a few dozen tales from Nova Scotia's past. And if you're looking for more, there's *More History with a Twist* by the same author, as well as a third volume released in 2008.

Oickle, Vernon. *Busted: Nova Scotia's War on Drugs.* Halifax: Nimbus Publishing, 1997. Stories of local lawmen and their struggle to curb the trade of illicit drugs along Nova Scotia's remote coastline.

Parker, Mike. *Guides of the North Woods.* Halifax: Nimbus Publishing, 2005. If you enjoy history and hunting or fishing, you'll enjoy sitting around a campfire reading tales of Nova Scotia's outdoorsmen from the last century.

Paul, Daniel N. *We Were Not the Savages.* Toronto: Fernwood Books, 2000. A fascinating look at the unhappy relationship between the Mi'Kmaq and Europeans.

Sanderberg, Anders, and Peter Clancy. *Against the Grain: Foresters and Politics in Nova Scotia.* Vancouver: University of British Columbia Press, 2000. A detailed look at the province's forestry practices and the viability of the industry in this millennium.

Vacon, Shirley Irene. *Giants of Nova Scotia: The Lives of Anna Swan and Angus McAskill.* East Lawrencetown, Nova Scotia: Pottersfield Press, 2008. The remarkable story of two Nova Scotians who toured the world as the "world's tallest couple" in the 1800s.

CULTURE AND CRAFTS

Carter, Pauline. *The Great Nova Scotia Cookbook.* Halifax: Nimbus Publishing, 2001. In-depth look at local cuisine, including many traditional dishes incorporating modern trends in cooking.

Field, Richard Henning. *Spirit of Nova Scotia: Traditional Decorative Folk Art 1780–1930.* Toronto: Dundurn Press, 1985. The Nova Scotians' historic use of textiles, sculpture, paintings, and decorated utilitarian objects is

expertly explained by subject and splendidly illustrated with photographs.

Harper, Marjory. *Myth, Migration and the Making of Memory: Scotia and Nova Scotia.* Halifax: John Donald Publishers, 2000. Explores Nova Scotia's Scottish heritage and the importance of the province's links to Scotland through the years.

Metcalfe, Robin. *Studio Rally.* Halifax: Goose Lane Editions, 2001. A coffee-table book highlighting 52 Nova Scotian artists and their work.

Parsons, Catriona. *Gaidhlig Troimh Chomhradh (Gaelic Through Conversation).* South Gut St. Ann's, Nova Scotia: Gaelic College of Celtic Arts and Crafts. The college's mission is to keep the language alive, and it does so with this text and accompanying cassette tapes as well as a number of other books and varied literature.

Penney, Allen. *Houses of Nova Scotia: An Illustrated Guide to Architectural Style Recognition.* Halifax: Nova Scotia Museum and Formac Publishing, 1989. Penney, a professor of architecture, sums up provincial architectural styles and explains how to identify styles by dates, similarities, and differences.

Pilsworth, Graham. *Nova Scotia Drink-o-pedia.* Halifax: Nimbus Publishing, 2008. Local author Pilsworth takes a detailed yet humorous look into the culture of drinking in Nova Scotia, from the days of rum-running to the success of Alexander Keith's brewery.

RECREATION GUIDES AND GUIDEBOOKS

Canoe Routes of Nova Scotia. Halifax: Canoe Nova Scotia and Camping Association of Nova Scotia, 1983. A description of canoe routes for novice to expert paddlers.

Doers and Dreamers Guide. Free annual publication from Tourism Nova Scotia. Lists accommodations, campgrounds, and some attractions. Order online at www.novascotia.com or by calling 902/425-5781 or 800/565-0000.

Dunlop, Dale, and Alison Scott. *Exploring Nova Scotia.* Halifax: Formac Publishing, 2003. Golf, cycling, rockhounding, and more—it's all covered in this well-researched book.

Friends of McNabs Island Society. *Discover McNabs Island.* Halifax: Friends of McNabs Island Society, 1997. This island in Halifax Harbour has become a provincial park since this book was published, but it is an essential reference guide and well worth buying even if you're just visiting for the day.

Haynes, Michael. *Hiking Trails of Nova Scotia.* Fredericton, New Brunswick: Goose Lane Editions, 2002. The eighth edition of this comprehensive yet compact guide details about 50 trails throughout the province. Each description, up to five pages long, is accompanied by a map.

Hempstead, Andrew. *Moon Atlantic Canada.* Berkeley, California: Avalon Travel, 2009. For those traveling beyond Nova Scotia.

Lawley, David. *A Nature and Hiking Guide to Cape Breton's Cabot Trail.* Halifax: Nimbus Publishing, 1994. The first half of this 200-page book covers all major trails along the Cabot Trail. The second half delves into the region's natural history, complete with descriptions of all flora and fauna.

Saunders, Gary L. *Discover Nova Scotia.* Halifax: Nimbus Publishing, 2001. Divides the province by highway, with each of 17 sections broken into paragraphs of worthwhile stops. Unfortunately, notes on distances are few and far between, but otherwise it's an excellent investment for those interested in the province's natural history.

Townsend, Chris. *The Backpacker's Handbook.* Camden, Maine: Ragged Mountain Press, 1998. Although some of the specifics on gear recommendations need updating, this is the best book for reading up on your backcountry and hiking skills.

MAGAZINES, MAPS, AND ATLASES

Canadian Geographic. Ottawa: Royal Canadian Geographical Society (www.cangeo.ca). Bimonthly publication pertaining to Canada's natural and human histories and resources.

Explore. Toronto. Bimonthly publication of adventure travel throughout Canada (www.explore-mag.com).

Hamilton, William B. *Place Names of Atlantic Canada.* Toronto: University of Toronto, 1996. Although no book is devoted to the toponymy of Nova Scotia, this tome includes definitions of all the province's most unusual and interesting place-names.

Lifestyle Nova Scotia. Halifax. Quarterly magazine that promotes modern living—architecture, fashion, food, and more (www.lifestylenovascotia.com).

MapArt. Driving maps for all of Canada, a Halifax-Dartmouth street atlas, and folded maps of Atlantic Canada and Nova Scotia (www.mapart.com).

Nature Canada. Ottawa. Quarterly magazine of the Canadian Nature Federation (www.cnf.ca).

Nova Scotia Atlas. Halifax: Formac Publishing, 2006. This comprehensive atlas breaks the province down into 90 topographical-style maps, including geographical features and all public roads. The back matter includes an index of 14,500 place-names and a short description of all provincial and national parks.

Rand McNally. Products include the *Atlantic Canada Road Atlas* and *Halifax and Nova Scotia Communities StreetFinder,* as well as folded maps of Nova Scotia, Halifax, and Cape Breton Island (www.randmcnally.com).

Internet Resources

TRAVEL PLANNING

Canadian Tourism Commission
www.canadatourism.com

Official tourism website for all of Canada.

Destination Halifax
www.destinationhalifax.com

In addition to all the usual travel information, use this website to order free literature, learn about current festivals and events, and read up on Halifax trivia.

Nova Scotia Department of Tourism, Culture, and Heritage
www.novascotia.com

The first place to go when planning your trip to Nova Scotia. This site includes a distance calculator, order forms for brochures, and detailed events calendars.

PARKS

Department of Natural Resources and Parks
www.novascotiaparks.ca

This department manages Nova Scotia's provincial park system. The website details seasons, fees, and has a handy search tool to make help finding parks easy.

Parks Canada
www.pc.gc.ca

Official website of the agency that manages Canada's national parks and national historic sites, of which two and 16 respectively are located in Nova Scotia.

Parks Canada Campground Reservation Service
www.pccamping.ca

Use this website to make reservations for campsites in Kejimkujik and Cape Breton Highlands National Parks.

GOVERNMENT

Citizenship and Immigration Canada
www.cic.gc.ca

Check this government website for anything related to entry into Canada.

Environment Canada
www.weatheroffice.gc.ca

Five-day forecasts from across Canada, including over 50 locations in Nova Scotia. Includes weather archives such as seasonal trends, hurricane history, and sea ice movement.

Government of Canada
www.gc.ca

The official website of the Canadian government.

Halifax Regional Municipality
www.halifax.ca

Official website of the Halifax Regional Municipality. Has links to transit schedules as well as information on visiting the city for business and local government issues.

Nova Scotia Museum
www.museum.gov.ns.ca

A network of 27 museums and 200 historic sites managed by the Nova Scotia Department of Tourism, Culture, and Heritage. This website includes details on each site, as well as passes for those planning on extensive touring.

ACCOMMODATIONS

Bed and Breakfast Online
www.bbcanada.com

Easy-to-use tools for finding and reserving bed-and-breakfasts that suit your budget and interests.

Check-In Nova Scotia
www.checkinnovascotia.com

Online accommodations reservation system operated by the Nova Scotia government.

Hostelling International–Canada
www.hihostels.ca

Canadian arm of the worldwide organization.

Select Atlantic Inns
www.selectinns.ca

A loosely affiliated group of mid- to top-end bed-and-breakfasts use this online presence to promote their properties and take bookings.

Signature Resorts
www.signatureresorts.com

Upscale lodging chain owned and operated by the Government of Nova Scotia. Locations include Digby, Liscomb Mills, and Ingonish Beach.

TRANSPORTATION

Acadian
www.acadianbus.com

Where Greyhound buses terminate, Acadian takes over, with inexpensive service throughout Nova Scotia.

Air Canada
www.aircanada.ca

Canada's national airline.

Halifax International Airport
www.flyhalifax.com

The official airport website is www.hiaa.ca (with information on airport services), but the airport authority also maintains this site. It includes images of departure and arrival boards, tools to help reach Halifax using the most direct flights, and virtual flight maps that show the location of all incoming and outgoing flights.

VIA Rail
www.viarail.ca

Passenger rail service across Canada, including Montreal to Halifax.

WestJet
www.westjet.com

Before booking with Air Canada, check out this airline for flights into Halifax from throughout Canada.

CONSERVATION

Canadian Parks and Wilderness Society Nova Scotia
www.cpawsns.org

Particularly active local chapter of a nonprofit organization that is instrumental in highlighting conservation issues throughout Canada.

Ducks Unlimited Canada
www.ducks.ca

Respected organization responsible for the protection of over 30,000 hectares of wetland throughout Nova Scotia.

Nova Scotia Nature Trust
www.nsnt.ca

Provincial nonprofit organization that has been instrumental in land protection through the purchase and donation of land.

Sable Island Green Horse Society
www.greenhorsesociety.com

A group of individuals interested in Sable Island and its unique environmental issues.

OTHER INTERNET RESOURCES

Cape Breton Music
www.cbmusic.com

Cape Breton Island is a hotbed of Celtic music, and this site profiles the artists you know (Natalie MacMaster, the Rankins, and more), with up and coming talent.

Dill's Atlantic Giant
www.howarddill.com

Dill, the world's preeminent super-sized pumpkin grower, sells his record-breaking seeds through this website. He also gives growing tips and uploads photos of his massive vegetables.

Nimbus Publishing
www.nimbus.ns.ca

While all the best books on Nova Scotia are detailed under *Suggested Reading,* check the website of this prolific Nova Scotia publisher for the latest titles.

Pugwash Conferences on Science and World Affairs
www.pugwash.org

This is the official website of a Nobel Prize–winning peace movement that had its beginnings in Pugwash, Nova Scotia.

Titanic–The Unsinkable Ship and Halifax
http://titanic.gov.ns.ca

Maintained by the Government of Nova Scotia, this website includes everything from full passenger lists to local links as obscure as a plaque in the Halifax YCMA that commemorates the sinking with the wrong date.

Index

List of Maps

www.moon.com

DESTINATIONS | ACTIVITIES | BLOGS | MAPS | BOOKS

MOON.COM is ready to help plan your next trip! Filled with fresh trip ideas and strategies, author interviews, informative travel blogs, a detailed map library, and descriptions of all the Moon guidebooks, Moon.com is all you need to get out and explore the world—or even places in your own backyard. While at Moon.com, sign up for our monthly e-newsletter for updates on new releases, travel tips, and expert advice from our on-the-go Moon authors. As always, when you travel with Moon, expect an experience that is uncommon and truly unique.

MOON IS ON FACEBOOK—BECOME A FAN!
JOIN THE MOON PHOTO GROUP ON FLICKR

MAP SYMBOLS

≋≋≋ Expressway	◖ Highlight	✕ Airfield	⅃ Golf Course	
⋯⋯ Primary Road	○ City/Town	✈ Airport	ⓟ Parking Area	
≋≋≋ Secondary Road	◉ State Capital	▲ Mountain	◬ Archaeological Site	
▪▪▪▪ Unpaved Road	⊛ National Capital	✚ Unique Natural Feature	▮ Church	
‑ ‑ ‑ ‑ Trail	★ Point of Interest			
⋯⋯⋯ Ferry	• Accommodation	🀣 Waterfall	▤ Gas Station	
⋯⋯⋯ Railroad	▾ Restaurant/Bar	▲ Park	⬭ Glacier	
≋≋≋ Pedestrian Walkway	▪ Other Location	▯ Trailhead	▨ Mangrove	
▥▥▥ Stairs	⋀ Campground	⤨ Skiing Area	▨ Reef	
			▦ Swamp	

CONVERSION TABLES

°C = (°F – 32) / 1.8
°F = (°C x 1.8) + 32
1 inch = 2.54 centimeters (cm)
1 foot = 0.304 meters (m)
1 yard = 0.914 meters
1 mile = 1.6093 kilometers (km)
1 km = 0.6214 miles
1 fathom = 1.8288 m
1 chain = 20.1168 m
1 furlong = 201.168 m
1 acre = 0.4047 hectares
1 sq km = 100 hectares
1 sq mile = 2.59 square km
1 ounce = 28.35 grams
1 pound = 0.4536 kilograms
1 short ton = 0.90718 metric ton
1 short ton = 2,000 pounds
1 long ton = 1.016 metric tons
1 long ton = 2,240 pounds
1 metric ton = 1,000 kilograms
1 quart = 0.94635 liters
1 US gallon = 3.7854 liters
1 Imperial gallon = 4.5459 liters
1 nautical mile = 1.852 km

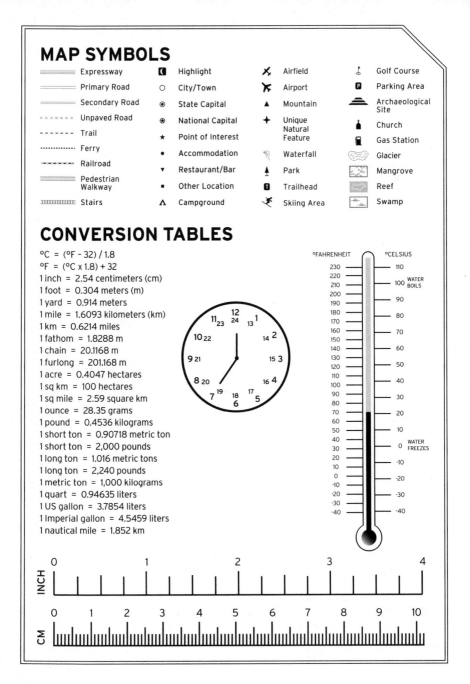

MOON NOVA SCOTIA
Avalon Travel
a member of the Perseus Books Group
1700 Fourth Street
Berkeley, CA 94710, USA
www.moon.com

Editor: Erin Raber
Series Manager: Kathryn Ettinger
Copy Editor: Christopher Church
Graphics and Production Coordinator:
  Lucie Ericksen
Cover Designer: Nicole Schultz
Map Editor: Albert Angulo
Cartography Director: Mike Morgenfeld
Cartographers: Chris Markiewicz, Kat Bennett
Indexer: Greg Jewett

ISBN-13: 978-1-59880-157-6
ISSN: 1930-1502

Printing History
1st Edition – 2006
2nd Edition – May 2009
5 4 3 2

KEEPING CURRENT

If you have a favorite gem you'd like to see included in the next edition, or see anything
that needs updating, clarification, or correction, please drop us a line. Send your
comments via email to feedback@moon.com, or use the address above.